VIRGIL
AENEID VI

VIRGIL

AENEID VI

Edited by Keith Maclennan

Bristol Classical Press

First published in 2003 by
Bristol Classical Press
an imprint of
Gerald Duckworth & Co. Ltd.
61 Frith Street, London W1D 3JL
Tel: 020 7434 4242
Fax: 020 7434 4420
inquiries@duckworth-publishers.co.uk
www.ducknet.co.uk

A catalogue record for this book is available
from the British Library

ISBN 1 85399 653 X

Cover illustration: 'Strife, that shakes her hissing tresses
and unfolds her snakes'. Engraving by Francis Cleyn,
first published in John Ogilby's translation of the *Aeneid* in
1654 and subsequently reproduced in
John Dryden's translation of 1697.

Printed and bound in Great Britain by
Antony Rowe Ltd

Contents

Preface

It is a very great honour to have been asked by John Betts to compose an edition of *Aeneid* VI, and quite a task to replace Gould and Whiteley's admirably straightforward and complete school version of 1946. As my reading list will show, I have approached the task from the timeless heart of the school classroom, and most of those who use this book as part of their teaching will be able to supplement extensively the scholarship upon which it is based. But I hope it will be of some service to those for whom it is intended, that is anyone who is coming to this text as one of the first passages of unaltered Latin he or she has read.

There cannot be many works of literature which offer more encouragement to go beyond themselves into other works which have inspired them or which they themselves have inspired. Homer, Dante, Milton, Purcell, Berlioz make an impressive assembly. Nor is it, these days, simply a matter of Dead White European Males. Cerberus makes his appearance in Harry Potter, and Philip Pullman has recreated brilliantly Virgil's *loca senta situ* in *The Amber Spyglass*. May his readers come back to Virgil and enjoy seeing how Pullman has reLucretianised the anti-Lucretius of Virgil's Elysian fields!

I have used the Austin / Mynors text, with some changes to the punctuation and the following different readings: 39 *de more*, 255 *lumina*, 495 *vidit*, 630 *ducta*, 900 *litore*. All consonant *u*'s have been changed to *v*, and all accusatives plural in *-is* to *-es*.

I have of course been assisted, cajoled, teased, entertained and extensively corrected by many helpers, among whom I must mention John Betts himself for encouraging me to get started, Judith Affleck and Ben Shaw who checked the first draft thoroughly, put me right in many matters and pointed me in several useful directions, but especially David West and James Morwood, both of whom I have been pestering for eighteen months with a few sensible and masses of outlandish ideas, all of which they have received patiently and with a sense of fun. John Penney has given very good advice on matters of language, and Edward Griffiths has offered an invaluable student's-eye view of the first section of the notes.

Brampton, Carlisle   Keith Maclennan
April 2003

Introduction

1. Historical background

1a. A few dates may create a context:

89 BCE: Rome captured by an invading army – for the first time in 300 years – but the army is a Roman army under Lucius Sulla. Sulla immediately withdraws until –

83: Rome captured again by Sulla after a bloody battle beneath the walls.

70: Virgil born near Mantua in northern Italy.

64: Pompeius Magnus completes the conquest of Asia Minor and Syria and adds them to the Roman Empire.

58-51: Julius Caesar invades and conquers Gaul.

49-8: Civil war again. Pompeius defeated by Julius Caesar.

44: Julius Caesar murdered.

43: Authority in the Roman world divided between Caesar's great-nephew Octavian, Mark Antony and Lepidus – the 'triumvirs'.

39 (*approx*): Virgil's *Eclogues* published.

31: Competition and civil war between the triumvirs come to an end at the Battle of Actium when Octavian defeats Mark Antony and his ally Cleopatra Queen of Egypt.

30: Octavian invades Egypt, which becomes a province of the Roman Empire.

29: Virgil's *Georgics* published.

27: Octavian given the title Augustus.

23: Death of Augustus' nephew Marcellus (*Aeneid* 6.860-86)

19: Virgil dies; the unrevised *Aeneid* is published on Augustus' orders.

These years cover the change in Rome from a 'republican' form of government (competition for power between aristocrats decided by more or less free and open election) to the rule of the emperors. Augustus was the first of the emperors. The name Augustus is a title of honour, conferred in 27 BCE. Before that date we refer to him as 'Octavian', though he referred to himself as 'Caesar'.

1b. It is easy to see from the above that Virgil's whole life was lived in a period of huge expansion of the Roman Empire and terrifying political disturbance. The period as I have given it begins with Sulla's capture of Rome. At the time the Romans were in bitter conflict with many of the other inhabitants of Italy, and Sulla was the leader of an 'aristocratic' Roman political party in even more bitter conflict with a 'popular' party led by Marius. This conflict went on sporadically for years, and developed into the next conflict, between great political and military leaders, Caesar and Pompeius among them, who made their fortunes in imperial conquest and exploited those fortunes in often violent schemes to dominate life in Rome. 'No laws, no sense of right and wrong'[1] said the later historian Tacitus about the period 52-32 BCE. Livy, another historian and a contemporary of Augustus, described the following years as 'modern times, when we can stand neither our own vices nor the cures for them.'[2] An unknown Roman, in a funeral speech for his wife, speaks of the misery of life in these times, as he was a refugee from Italy and she protected herself and their property from corrupt political leaders and gangsters.[3] It is easy to find modern parallels for the insecurity and terror of the period.

1c. In 49, government finally collapsed into the civil war between Julius Caesar and Pompeius Magnus. Within a year Pompeius was defeated and murdered. In 44 Caesar himself was murdered, and there developed a struggle for power between the old aristocracy, Caesar's political associate Mark Antony, Caesar's great-nephew and heir Octavian, and Pompeius' son Sextus. Slowly and with much violence this four-sided (even 'four' is an over-simplification) contest resolved into a struggle between two men, Antony and Octavian, and in 31 this too was settled when Antony was defeated in the naval battle off Actium in Western Greece.

1d. By the time Octavian-Augustus established his own power, the centre of Rome was a ruin, Italy was in chaos, and Roman control was disputed over huge areas of the empire. A new beginning was needed. Augustus was determined to provide it. He would re-establish the rule of law, he would restore the structure of society, he would rebuild religion,[4] he would make Italians no longer conquered subjects of Rome[5] but partners in the imperial enterprise,[6] and he would create an ideology for his reforms in which they were seen not as the makeshift repair of a shattered system but as the realisation of Rome's true identity, long foreseen and planned by the gods.[7]

1e. In the general despair and insecurity, there were many looking for some such faith. Augustus was also surrounded by people well able to put his ideas into practice. All over Italy, a huge building programme began: the Roman Forum was redesigned,[8] roads were re-laid, temples reconstructed,[9] aqueducts and sewers[10] rebuilt. The army was restructured and brought under effective control; a social and political hierarchy was established.[11] At the same time artists[12] and poets[13] were brought into the programme, Virgil among them.

2. Virgil's life and writings

2a. Virgil was born in 70 BCE near Mantua in a part of northern Italy still called 'Gallia' in his day. We can be reasonably confident of this, although very little is known for sure about the details of his life. His family seems to have had no important connections with the aristocracy, but was at least affluent enough to afford him a good education at Cremona and Milan. A brief biography was written by Suetonius in the early second century CE; although this is lost, it is believed that the *Life* which appears under the name of the fourth-century grammarian Aelius Donatus is substantially derived from Suetonius.[14] According to this Virgil came to Rome in the late 50s BCE to begin his career, like many ambitious young Romans, in legal activity. In the event, he spoke in one case only, and it was a flop. This was at the beginning of the 20-year period of social collapse mentioned by Tacitus (see **1b** above). One source[15] suggests that he now left Rome and spent most of the following years living near Naples, studying and practising Epicurean philosophy. But he must have attracted the attention of some important people by his poetry, because in the years following the death of Caesar we find him acknowledging the patronage of the accomplished general and writer Asinius Pollio and others.[16] Shortly afterwards[17] he entered the circle of C. Maecenas, one of Octavian's closest colleagues, an astute politician and an energetic patron of the arts. Virgil subsequently dedicated the *Georgics* to Maecenas.

2b. There is much argument about Virgil's early writings. A collection known as *Appendix Vergiliana* consists of several poems attributed to him. Some of them may be genuine.[18] They range from epigram to mock-epic. His first published collection, the *Eclogues*,[19] is written in a 'pastoral' tradition inherited from Greek predecessors and dealing with life among shepherds in an idealised countryside. But Octavian and his associates were even then developing their ideas of national restoration, and Virgil uses the pastoral context to convey such themes.[20] This becomes clearer still in his next work, the *Georgics*, which he seems to have read to Octavian in 29 BC.[21] This poem is written in a different Greek tradition which we call 'didactic'.[22] Didactic poems are set out as manuals of technical or philosophical instruction. The *Georgics* offer instruction in agriculture. But this is agriculture seen as part of Octavian's plan for the regeneration of Italy by the restoration of rural life, along with the health-giving ideals associated with that life.[23] Finally Virgil set his mind to the grandest and most challenging task an ancient poet could undertake, the composition of an epic poem.

2c. If Virgil finished the Georgics in 29 BCE and began immediately on the *Aeneid*, the author of the *Life* is right in saying that he was working on the poem for 11 years.[24] Even this was not enough. In 19 BCE, he decided to leave Italy and spend three years in retirement, revising the *Aeneid*. But meeting Augustus in Athens, he was persuaded to return to Italy. When he reached Brundisium he was ill, and he died there a few days later on 21 September. It is said that he was so dissatisfied with the *Aeneid* in its unrevised condition that he instructed Varius, a fellow-poet and friend, to burn the manuscript. Varius refused, and the poem was published unrevised.[25]

3. Virgil and his predecessors

3a. In writing the *Aeneid*, Virgil was conscious of the challenge which might be made to him: 'The world already has two unsurpassable epic poems in Homer's *Iliad* and *Odyssey*. Who are you to foist another one on us?' That the challenge was made we know from a poem written by Propertius in about 26 BCE: 'Give place, you authors, Romans and Greeks as well: something greater than the *Iliad* is on its way.'[26] The *Aeneid* acknowledges a debt to Homer in every part – and uses Homer to make something new. For example, in the *Iliad*, we are told about a war. The *Odyssey* follows it, telling of a man's long attempt to reach his home after that war. The *Aeneid* combines an *Odyssey*-half, as Aeneas travels in Books 1-6 from Troy to Italy, and an *Iliad*-half, Books 7-12, in which he fights against Italian resistance to the Trojans. But Homer's order (*Iliad*, then *Odyssey*) is reversed. Homer's stories too become the opposite of themselves. Odysseus travels to a known home; Aeneas travels from his known home to an unknown destination. In the *Iliad* a war is fought which aims at the destruction of a city; in the *Aeneid*, a war is fought which aims at the foundation of a city.[27]

3b. Homer is by no means the only poet whose influence can be traced in Virgil. There were several other epic poems dealing with the Trojan story, all now lost, though the outline of their contents is known. The *Iliu Persis* ('sack of Troy') dealt with the end of the war, which is not covered in the *Iliad*, but is the subject matter of *Aeneid* 2. The *Aethiopis* told of the Amazon queen Penthesilea, who came to the aid of the Trojans and was killed by Achilles. She is represented in the *Aeneid* by Camilla (Book 10). Dido (Books 1-4) is a complex figure influenced not merely by Nausicaa, Calypso and Circe from the *Odyssey*, but also by characters in later epic (Medea in the *Argonautica* of Apollonius Rhodius, a writer of the third century BCE) and tragedy (Euripides' Phaedra in the *Hippolytus* as well as his Medea in the eponymous play). Apart from these and many other Greek writers, Virgil acknowledged a debt to his Roman predecessors, in particular to Ennius (died 169 BCE) author of the epic *Annales* and many tragedies (179-182 & Appendix 1; 842), Catullus (died perhaps 54 BCE, author of a varied collection of love-poems, satirical epigrams, elegiacs and a mini-epic – '*epyllion*'), Lucretius (died 55 BCE), on whom see below **6.iii.g** and Appendix 1, and Cicero, who translated the astronomical didactic poems of Aratus, wrote an epic poem on the subject of his own consulship, and in these and other works made an important contribution to the development of the hexameter metre in Latin.

4. The *Aeneid* as a poem

4a. The *Aeneid* is the foundation-story of Rome. To put it very simply, it accommodates three ideas about that foundation. (i) Roman history or mythology had it that the city was founded in 753 BCE by Romulus, a member of the royal house of the nearby city of Alba Longa. (ii) However, Rome was more than a location in central Italy: it was a great city along with other great cities of the Mediterranean world. That was a world whose dominant civilisation was Greek. Greek mythology created a background for almost every other community in the Mediterranean, and there was a place in Greek mythology for Rome too. Homer's *Iliad* was the single most important reference-point in Greek civilisation, and in the *Iliad* Aeneas has a part as one of the leaders of the Trojans. Of him it is said[28] that he is fated to escape the destruction of Troy and become king over the revived Trojans. Long before Virgil's time, the story of Aeneas had been connected with the foundation of Rome.[29] (iii) Finally,

Virgil was writing as if the history of the city, originating with Aeneas in the legendary past, first built by Romulus at the beginning of recorded time, was moving by the will of the gods toward its re-foundation by Augustus. In making a unity of these three different strands, he was blessed by a remarkable stroke of fortune. Roman aristocratic families made much of stories about their own past. Many years before, Julius Caesar had made political use of the legendary descent of his family from the goddess Venus.[30] Venus was Aeneas' mother; Aeneas' son was Ascanius, also called Iulus. Iulus founded Alba Longa and the line of kings from which Romulus was descended. Thus a line of descent could be traced connecting Venus, Aeneas, Romulus, the family of Julius Caesar and hence Augustus himself.

4b. The *Aeneid* is the story of the first part of this process, from the fall of Troy to the point where Aeneas and his Trojans settle in Italy. But as we read it, we are left in no doubt that the poem takes in the whole history of Rome. In Book 1, Venus is grieving at the misfortunes suffered by Aeneas on his journey. Jupiter consoles her with a prophecy which looks forward, past Aeneas' time, to the reign of Augustus: *imperium sine fine dedi*,[31] 'I have granted them power without end'. In Book 6, Aeneas in the underworld is shown a great line of his descendants stretching as far as Augustus' nephew Marcellus.[32] In Book 8, Aeneas visits the place on the banks of the Tiber where Rome will be built.[33] While Aeneas explores the rustic settlement, Virgil comments on its future splendour. Later in Book 8, Aeneas is given a shield, on which the craftsman-god Vulcan has carved scenes from Roman history to come.[34] In Book 4, the death of Dido Queen of Carthage looks forward to the wars between Rome and Carthage.[35] Throughout the poem there are references to Roman social and religious practices as having their ancestry in Aeneas' time.[36] Aeneas himself is described by the traditional adjective *pius* – 'dutiful'.[37] Aeneas' *pietas* was shown first in rescuing his father from the flames of Troy.[38] The event looks forward to Augustus, who could not save from death his adoptive father Julius Caesar, but based his claim to authority on the *pietas* with which he avenged his murder.

5. Summary of the *Aeneid*

Introductory note: Virgil assumes that we are familiar with the story of the Trojan war: how Paris, son of King Priam of Troy, took Helen from her husband Menelaus king of Sparta; how Menelaus with his elder and mightier brother Agamemnon led an expedition of the greatest Greek leaders to recover Helen; how the siege of Troy lasted ten years and ended only after Achilles, the greatest of the Greeks, had killed Hector, the greatest of the Trojans, and then been killed himself by Paris. The fall of Troy itself is described from Aeneas' own point of view in Book 2.

Scattered through this summary are passages in italics: these give a very few illustrations of Virgil's use of the Homeric epics.

Book 1. The poet introduces the theme: the story of how war and heroism led, in spite of the hostility of Juno, to the foundation of Rome. We first meet Aeneas and the Trojans sailing from Sicily on what ought to be the last leg of their journey to Italy. Juno raises a storm which wrecks some of Aeneas' ships, separates the rest from each other, and drives Aeneas with seven of them to the coast of Africa. *(Odyssey 10: Odysseus is within sight of home when a storm drives him back into the unknown.)* While Aeneas rests here, overcome by despair, his mother Venus protests in heaven to Jupiter that Juno is permitted to interfere with her son's destiny, which is the foundation of Rome. *(Odyssey 5: Odysseus' patron-goddess Athena protests to Zeus that Odysseus is being kept away from home.)* Jupiter responds with a great prophecy looking forward to the triumphs of Aeneas' descendant Augustus. Aeneas is now guided by Venus to Carthage, recently founded by Queen Dido, a refugee from Tyre, and still being built. There he finds that the friends whom he thought wrecked have made their way to Carthage and are being welcomed by Dido. Dido, seeing in him a fellow-exile, offers him and the Trojans partnership in Carthage. She invites them all to a great feast. *(Odyssey 6: Odysseus, shipwrecked on the coast of Phaeacia is found and helped by the princess Nausicaa, who is captivated by him.)* Meanwhile Venus, anxious to prevent any tricks by Juno, ensures Dido's kindness by making her fall in love with Aeneas. In this spirit she asks him to tell the story of the fall of Troy and his journey to Italy.

Book 2. Aeneas tells the story. *(Odyssey 9-12: the story of the nine years of Odysseus' wanderings after he left Troy is told by Odysseus himself to his hosts in Phaeacia.)* 'The Greeks, after ten years of unsuccessful war, pretended to sail home, leaving on the shore a wooden horse filled with their men. We were tricked by the Greek agent Sinon into believing that it was an offering to the goddess Minerva. We brought it into Troy. The priest Laocoon who opposed Sinon was killed by two giant sea-serpents. That night those in the horse opened the city gates to the returning Greeks. Troy was destroyed. King Priam was killed. As all this was happening, I was warned in a dream by the ghost of Hector to escape, taking with me the Penates – the household gods of Troy. At first I ignored this advice, but later was convinced by my mother that it was futile to fight against the gods, and that it was my duty to persuade my reluctant father to join me, my wife and my son in flight. As we crept out of the city, my wife was lost. I ran back to look for her, but saw only her ghost, in which form she told me that I must search in the West for the lands round the river Tiber. My father Anchises and my son Iulus escaped with me.'

Book 3. 'We went first to Thrace and then to Delos. In Delos Apollo's voice told us to seek the land of our ancestral origin. Supposing this to be Crete, we settled there until dreadful events and a vision of the household spirits of Troy, sent by Apollo, persuaded us to seek further, and we set sail for Italy. Driven by a storm we came to the land of the Harpies, monstrous bird-women, who warned us to recognise our destination by the starvation we should be suffering on arriving there. Then we came to Epirus, home of the prophet Helenus, last surviving son of Priam, living now with Hector's widow Andromache on the Adriatic coast of north-western Greece. He told us to travel to Italy by the long route round Sicily, avoiding the straits of Messina and the monsters Scylla and Charybdis. *(Odyssey 12.)* When we reached Drepanum in the west of Sicily my father died. Setting sail from there, we were driven here by a storm.'

Book 4. Dido is now fully in love with Aeneas. Attempts to shake off her passion fail. Juno intervenes again. She accepts Venus' plan for Dido and hopes to extend it so that Aeneas will stay in Carthage and Rome will never be founded. Now Aeneas, captivated by Dido and no longer confident of his own future, joins Dido in the building of Carthage. News of Dido's love reach the African king Iarbas, who had hoped to marry Dido. He complains to Jupiter, who sends Mercury to tell Aeneas to move on to Italy. *(Odyssey 5: Odysseus is captive in the island of the nymph Calypso; Hermes (= Mercury) is sent to tell Calypso to send him away.)* Dido discovers that he is secretly planning to leave, tries unsuccessfully to make him change his mind, disbelieves him when he says he is acting at Jupiter's command, curses him, and on the funeral pyre which she has built stabs herself to death on the day the Trojans depart.

Book 5. The Trojans land in Sicily. They celebrate the anniversary of Anchises' death with games: *(Iliad 23: games in honour of the death of Achilles' friend Patroclus)* a boat-race, running, boxing and archery. The games conclude with an equestrian pageant performed by the Trojan boys. But Juno tricks the Trojan women, who are not among the spectators, into burning all their ships and thus avoiding the inevitable distress of their onward journey to Italy. Aeneas saves all but four ships. He leaves the infirm and unadventurous in Sicily and sets sail for Italy. Before he leaves, Anchises appears in a vision with instructions that Aeneas should go first to Cumae and from there down to the underworld to find him. *(Odyssey 10: Circe tells Odysseus to visit the underworld.)* Venus begs Neptune to grant the ships safe passage. Neptune promises to do so at the cost of one of the company. It is the helmsman Palinurus, who is lulled to sleep and pushed overboard.

Book 6. *(Homeric references in Book 6 are discussed on the Notes; there is also a summary of Odyssey 11 at 6.ii.a.)* Aeneas lands at Cumae by the temple of Apollo. There he visits the Sibyl, who gives him instructions for the journey to the underworld. First he must find a mysterious golden bough in a forest: it is the token which will gain him admission to the world below. Then he must bury one of his men who has just died. He carries out both of these instructions, and sets off with the Sibyl to the gate of the underworld at Lake Avernus. After a night-time sacrifice, the cave-entrance to the underworld opens. Aeneas and the Sibyl walk a dark road down to the River Styx, at whose bank are crowded those awaiting passage, particularly the unburied, who are not permitted to cross. Among these he meets his lost helmsman Palinurus. Charon, the ferryman of the Styx, is persuaded to give Aeneas passage. Over the river, Aeneas sees first those who died in infancy, then suicides, then those who died for love (here he again meets Dido), then a section for brave warriors, including his former colleagues and opponents from the Trojan war, notably his cousin Deiphobus. His way now leads past the walls of Tartarus, the place of punishment, about whose occupants the Sibyl tells him. She names several traditional sinners, who have offended the gods in various ways, and lists a number of more contemporary-sounding crimes which qualify for punishment. Now at last they reach Elysium, where happy souls dwell. They are directed over a hill into a valley where they meet Anchises. Anchises points to a great crowd gathered by a river. They are souls waiting to drink the water of Lethe, the river of forgetfulness, before they are born again. Anchises explains a theology of reincarnation and purification, and then points to the long procession of souls due to be reborn as founders and heroes of the Roman nation, culminating in the emperor Augustus. But the book ends on a note of sadness as Anchises tells of the premature death of Marcellus, Augustus' son-in-law and hoped-for successor. Aeneas and the Sibyl return to the upper world through the Gate of Dreams.

Book 7. The Trojans land at the mouth of the river Tiber. The fulfilment of a prophecy indicates that they have at last reached their goal. They are near the city of King Latinus, whose daughter Lavinia is engaged to the Rutulian prince Turnus. Latinus knows of a prophecy according to which Lavinia should marry not Turnus, but a newly arrived foreigner. Aeneas sends an embassy to Latinus, who welcomes the Trojans and invites Aeneas to marry Lavinia. But hearing this, Juno prompts the Fury Allecto to rouse opposition, first in Latinus' wife Amata, then in Latinus' people as a whole, and finally in Turnus. *(Turnus' rage at the loss of Lavinia recalls Achilles' at the loss of Briseis in Iliad 1.)* She also arranges for Ascanius to kill a pet stag belonging to Latinus' herdsman, which leads to a clash between Aeneas' and Latinus' men. Now a whole host of Italians gathers to oppose the Trojans, and the book ends with a description of the various individuals and contingents of this army. *(Iliad 2: the Catalogue of Achaean and Trojan forces.)*

Book 8. In a dream Aeneas sees the river god Tiber, who instructs him to sail upstream to the city of Pallanteum on the site of future Rome, where he will be offered help. Next day the Trojans reach Pallanteum just as King Evander with his son Pallas and all his people are feasting in honour of Hercules. The Trojans join them, and Evander tells how Hercules, passing through on his way from the farthest west, killed the monster Cacus who lived on the Aventine hill. As Evander takes Aeneas to his house, he points out many of the sites which will be part of Rome. That night, Venus persuades Vulcan to make Aeneas new armour. Next morning, Evander agrees on an alliance with Aeneas, who sets out with Evander's son Pallas on a further mission to secure the support of the Etruscans. On the way, Venus presents Aeneas with his new arms. *(Iliad 18: Achilles is given by his mother Thetis new arms, including a magnificently-decorated shield.)* The book ends with a description of the shield, onto which have been carved and moulded scenes from future Roman history, culminating in the great triumph which Octavian celebrated following his victories at Actium and in Egypt (above, **1a**).

Book 9. Turnus takes advantage of Aeneas' absence to attack the Trojan camp. He tries to provoke the Trojans by burning their ships *(Iliad 16: Hector sets fire to one of the Greek ships)*, but these are miraculously turned into sea-goddesses. As Turnus presses his attack, two Trojans, Nisus and his beloved young friend Euryalus, propose to Ascanius, who is temporarily in charge, that they should go on a night-mission through the enemy lines to carry a message to Aeneas. *(Iliad 10: the night foray by Odysseus and Diomedes into the Trojan camp.)* This goes wrong when the two of them take the opportunity to kill some of the sleeping enemy. They are discovered and killed. Next day there is a fierce battle round the camp, at the end of which Turnus is trapped inside its gates. He escapes by diving off the walls into the river.

Book 10 begins with an angry debate in heaven, Venus protesting at war being raised against the Trojans, Juno at the Trojan invasion of Italy. Jupiter decides to let the war take its own course: fate shall decide. The Trojans in camp are holding out with difficulty as Aeneas approaches with his Etruscan allies, who are now listed by Virgil. Battle is for a while dominated by the youngest warriors, Pallas son of Evander and Lausus son of Turnus' fiercest ally Mezentius. But Turnus kills Pallas *(Iliad 16: Hector kills Patroclus)* and takes his sword-belt. Now Aeneas comes to the rescue. Juno temporarily saves Turnus from him by creating an Aeneas-image which runs away from Turnus and hides on a moored ship. *(Iliad 21: Apollo turns into one of the Trojans who runs away from Achilles.)* Turnus boards the ship, which Juno drives out to sea. Mezentius now leads the fighting, but is wounded. Lausus helps his father, but is killed by Aeneas, who goes on to kill Mezentius also.

Book 11. Aeneas laments the death of Pallas, and sends his body back to Evander in a long mourning procession including human victims for sacrifice. *(Iliad 23: Achilles slaughters young Trojans at Patroclus' pyre.)* A truce is agreed with the Latini and used by each side for burying its dead. There is a debate in Latinus's city about continuing the war. Allies have been approached and have refused to help. The king proposes peace and offers the Trojans territory to settle in. But a speech in support of this made by Drances, an enemy of Turnus, provokes Turnus to a furious 'no surrender' response, and when news arrives that the Trojans and their allies are renewing the war, the Latins follow Turnus into battle. Turnus himself goes to ambush Aeneas, who is leading a flanking attack over the hills. He entrusts the defence of the city to the virgin warrior Camilla. For a while Camilla carries all before her, but she has been stealthily tracked by Arruns, who brings her down with a spear-cast. Dying, she sends a message begging Turnus to return. He is forced to abandon his ambush just before Aeneas reaches the pass and comes safely through.

Book 12. Turnus now decides to accept a challenge to single combat made by Aeneas at the beginning of Book 11. Latinus and Aeneas meet in mid-battlefield, where they decide the terms of this combat and swear to stand by them. *(Iliad 3-4: the Achaeans and Trojans agree to a truce and a single combat between Paris and Menelaus; it is disrupted by the Trojans at Athena's suggestion.)* But before the ceremony is completed, the Latins, persuaded by Juturna, Turnus' nymph-sister, begin the fight anew. In the confusion Aeneas is wounded, and Turnus dominates the fighting until, after some difficulty, Aeneas is healed. Now Juturna takes over the reins of Turnus' chariot and keeps him clear of Aeneas in a last attempt to save him. But Aeneas assaults the city and Latinus' wife hangs herself. Hearing of this, Turnus dismisses his sister, halts the fighting and faces Aeneas on his own. *(Iliad 22: Hector faces Achilles.)* As their combat progresses, Jupiter and Juno talk. Juno at last agrees that the Trojans may settle in Italy, and Jupiter accepts her condition that in all but ancestry they should become Latins, Italians. Now Juturna leaves Turnus, who, after a brief struggle, falls wounded. *(Iliad 22: Apollo abandons Hector.)* Aeneas is about to spare him, but then he sees that Turnus is wearing the sword-belt which he took from the dead Pallas. He kills him in a fit of vengeful rage.

6. The Sixth Book

Book 6 brings the '*Odyssey*-half' of the *Aeneid* to an end. The Trojans have landed in Italy, but they do not reach their proper destination until the beginning of Book 7, so the book is transitional. Its longest episode, the descent to the underworld, also marks a personal transition for Aeneas. In it, Aeneas is carrying out his father's instructions to visit him in the underworld, where 'you will hear about all your descendants and about the city you are given' (5.737).

i. The setting: Cumae (1-235)

6.i.a. At the beginning, Aeneas lands on the shore at Cumae. There is a great temple to Apollo there, presided over by the Sibyl Deiphobe.

('Sibyl' seems originally to have been the name of an individual and later to have become the title of a number of prophetesses in various places.) There is also the cave where the Sibyl utters her prophecies. Apollo shares the shrine with his sister Diana, who is here above all a goddess of the dark powers and the underworld, and known by her other names Hecate and Trivia. Close by on the coast there is the headland which will become known as Misenum, after Aeneas' friend who will be buried there. All the hinterland is covered in great forested hills, and somewhere among these is the dark lake Avernus with its sulphurous fumes and its own cave, the entrance to the underworld.

6.i.b. Cumae is a real place, one with which Virgil was very familiar. A few miles west of Virgil's home on the edge of Naples, it faces the open sea and not the bay. Between Naples and Cumae lies the volcanic area called the Phlegraean Fields. It is dotted with craters, some of them active enough to give off fumes which on a still day make the whole region smell of sulphur. Lake Avernus lies in one such crater, nearer Cumae than Naples. One approaches it through the crater rim and sees a still round lake with forested slopes to the west, though to the north east runs the main road from Naples to the coast, and to the east there is a hill which appeared only in 1538 as the result of a volcanic eruption.

6.i.c. There is no archaeological evidence to suggest that there was ever a cave at the lake. But at Cumae the remains are striking. It was the first of the many places settled by Greeks on the Italian mainland, in the eighth century BCE. There is a citadel with two summits, a higher one to the north and a lower one to the south. The Temple of Apollo stands on the lower of the two. A few yards further south is the entry to the Sibyl's cave, a long gallery delved into the hill. As you walk into it there are several windows to the open air on the right and several artificial caves opening on the left.

6.i.d. These buildings were old in Virgil's day. But Cumae and the area was the scene of enormous activity in the 30s BCE. Octavian, the later Augustus, was facing a serious threat from Sextus Pompeius, son of Pompeius Magnus (see **1b**) who was occupying Sicily and whose ships controlled most of the western Mediterranean, cutting Rome off from its essential sources of imported grain. Octavian's fleets were twice crushed in 38, and he set his colleague Marcus Agrippa to create a huge landlocked naval training zone. Agrippa made the modern access to Avernus by cutting through the crater, thus joining it to the Lacus Lucrinus and the bay of Naples. He built a tunnel through the ridge from

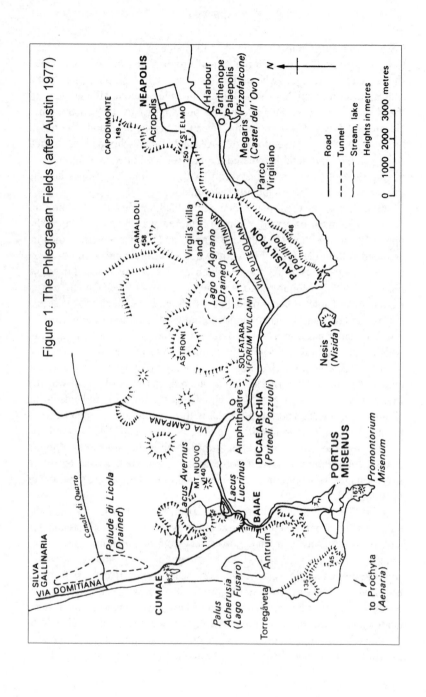

Figure 1. The Phlegraean Fields (after Austin 1977)

Avernus to Cumae and several elaborate underground constructions at Cumae itself. He then used Avernus and the Lacus Lucrinus to train in safety the ships with which he defeated Sextus in 36. Virgil must have been well aware of all this activity (even now it is very conspicuous!) and of the reconstruction of the Temple of Apollo at Cumae undertaken by Augustus. And not only Virgil. The Bay of Naples and the cities round it were famous for their climate, their wealth and their amenities; they were almost the first place for a Roman to think of going if he could get away from Rome. So we are concerned with an area which is well-known, important in Virgil's modern world and full of ancient memories.

6.ii. Virgil and the world of the dead (236-678)

In the mythology familiar to Virgil and his readers there were several stories of visits by heroes to the underworld.[39] Aeneas refers to four in lines 119-123.[40] But in this poem with its deliberate references to Homer, it is the memory of Odysseus which Virgil wishes in particular to evoke.

6.ii.a. At the end of *Odyssey* 10, Odysseus is told by Circe that he cannot get home without visiting the underworld on the way, and there consulting the ghost of the prophet Tiresias. He duly makes this visit: it involves a journey to the farthest west, where the mysterious Cimmerians live in perpetual darkness. Here he must make a sacrifice and offer the ghosts blood to drink; only so will they be able to speak. Odysseus will not allow any to drink before Tiresias. But the first of the ghosts to appear is his unburied companion Elpenor, who died as Odysseus was setting out from Circe's island. Presumably because he has not been buried and therefore has not yet fully departed this life, Elpenor is able to speak without drinking blood. Then Odysseus sees his mother Anticleia. She has to wait until Tiresias has spoken. The prophet appears, and advises him about his journey, about the state of affairs he will find at home, and about what he must do after his return. Now Odysseus speaks to his mother, who has much to tell Odysseus about his family. When she has gone, he sees first a series of women out of legend, then he talks to some of his colleagues from the Trojan war. The last of these is Ajax, who does not answer when Odysseus speaks to him. He had a bitter dispute with Odysseus over the ownership of Achilles' armour, and it remains unresolved even in the underworld. Next there is Minos, the legendary King of Crete and judge among the dead, then Orion the hunter, the great sinners Tityos, Tantalus and Sisyphus, and finally

Hercules. After all this, Odysseus, who is telling the story, says that the spirits of the dead came at him in their thousands, that he was overwhelmed with fear and that he made for his ship.

6.ii.b. Even from this summary, one can see something of how Virgil has made use of Homer. Elpenor appears as Palinurus and also as Misenus who died while Aeneas was preparing for his underworld journey. Circe's role is taken over and extended by the Sibyl. Anchises plays the combined role of Odysseus' mother and of Tiresias. The place of Homer's legendary women is taken in Virgil by the occupants of the Fields of Mourning; immediately after them come in both poets the colleagues from recent wars. In Homer Ajax is unreconciled, in Virgil Dido. The sinners in torment follow the warrior colleagues in both. In Homer, Hercules appears as climax and conclusion. Virgil's hero at this point is not a single person but the whole Roman nation as portrayed in its various representatives (756-886).

6.ii.c. In accommodating these details to his own scheme, Virgil has divided Aeneas' visit to the underworld into three parts. First, a long passage (235-415) of preparation in which sacrifice is made; we are introduced to the darkness and to the shadowy terrors of the world of the dead; Aeneas and the Sibyl make their way to the crossing-point of the river Styx. Secondly (417-636) there is the traditional underworld, the permanent home of the dead, a place at best of regret and resignation, at worst of fearful punishment. Third (637-892) is Elysium, which looks forward to a future life and beyond. The division is not rigid. In the first place, the death and burial of Misenus, which are part of the preparation, take place among the events in the upper world on the shore at Cumae, with the search for the golden bough neatly placed among them. Secondly, one of the themes of the journey is Aeneas' meetings with those whom he has known, Palinurus, Dido and Deiphobus. The order in which he meets them is the reverse of the order in which he knew them in life, and so it is suggested that Aeneas is reaching an accommodation with the events of his own past in order to confront his future. On this scheme, Palinurus from before the Styx plays his part in a series with Dido and Deiphobus from after it. Then there are the warriors whom Aeneas meets in the first part of Elysium (642-59). Their existence in a place of light and happiness separates them from all that has gone before, yet in another sense they are the conclusion of what has gone before – as Aeneas goes back into a Trojan past before the miseries of his own times.

6.iii. Purification and rebirth (679-751)

6.iii.a. In the underworld so far, every person or group of people mentioned has been considered in the context of life lived in the past – unburied, untimely dead, killed in battle, sinners and heroes – and it seems that they remain for ever in the part of the underworld to which they were first assigned. There are one or two hints that this may not be a world of unmitigated darkness and misery. The birds in the simile of 310-12 are travelling to 'sunny lands'. The souls stretch out their hands in passionate longing to reach the further shore of Styx (314). Dido and Sychaeus continue to share their love (474). But the overwhelming impression is of gloom. Even in the 'Farthest Fields', where war-heroes dwell (477-534) the predominant emotions are fear, horror and longing for the world above. But from 679 onwards, Virgil offers an entirely different view of the underworld. From now on life after death is looking to the future, to rebirth and beyond. In laying the foundations for this, Virgil develops a theory of the personality. First, the soul is seen as distinct from the body. Secondly, the rewards after death, and more particularly the punishments, are shown to be not merely retribution, but rehabilitation of the soul. Thirdly, rebirth is possible. Finally, rebirth itself is seen as a preparation for ultimate perfection in eternity.

6.iii.b. At this point Virgil ceases to depend upon Homer and turns to philosophy and mysticism, a combination of teaching current in his own day with thinking and inspiration dating back over the previous five centuries of Greek ideas.

6.iii.c. *The human soul:* Anchises' version of this derives from the Stoic philosophy. This was first propounded in about 300 BCE, and remained an important influence until well into the first centuries CE. (It took its name from the Stoa – 'gallery' – where its founder Zeno taught his pupils.) It was particularly practised by members of the Roman aristocracy, which is to say it would be familiar to many of Virgil's readers. According to Stoicism the universe consists of matter activated by mind. Mind is a pervading element akin to fire. Reason is the activity of the mind; a human being is most fulfilled when his whole life is guided by reason; the enemies of reason are the distractions of the body: fear, desire, grief, joy. After death the soul is reabsorbed into the spirit of heavenly fire from which it came.

6.iii.d. *Rehabilitation, rebirth and eternity.* These come originally from a variety of sources, but to Virgil himself principally from Plato, an

Athenian philosopher of the fifth-fourth centuries BCE. Plato's thinking was inspired by his teacher and friend Socrates, executed in 399 BCE for 'crimes' which, as represented by Plato, amount to thinking independently, standing up for the law, and refusing to compromise on what he regarded as right. Plato established a school of philosophy called 'The Academy' (again, after the precinct, a shrine of the hero Akademos, where he first taught). The Academy had its followers at Rome, and Plato was much read. Cicero, a leading figure of the generation before Virgil, calls Plato *deus noster*, and wrote Latin works based on some of Plato's principal writings. In his own works (especially *Phaedo* and *Republic*) Plato returns several times to the question of an afterlife, the consequences in it of good and bad behaviour in this life, and the possibility of reaching perfection over a series of lives.[41]

6.iii.e. Plato may well have been influenced by Pythagoras, a philosopher of the late sixth century BCE whose ideas included reincarnation, vegetarianism and a belief in the mystic significance of number and the power of music. Pythagoras too had his followers in Rome in Virgil's day. Ideas about the progress of the soul after death and its relation to the universe and eternity were also attributed to the followers of Orpheus, though the membership and activities of this cult (if it was a cult) are as obscure as its origins. Nevertheless Virgil makes a clear signal of acknowledgement to it by putting Orpheus and his son or pupil Musaeus in places of conspicuous importance in Elysium.

6.iii.f. For Virgil the most obvious value of the doctrine of rebirth is that it allows him to present Aeneas with a whole array of great men from Roman history before his eyes, waiting for the call to life (756-886). In combining it with Stoicism he appeals to the beliefs of the Roman aristocracy by whom he is read and about whom he is about to write. But in imaginative power this passage goes far beyond a mere literary device.

6.iii.g. For the form in which this is all presented, Virgil is heavily indebted to Lucretius, whose didactic poem *On the Nature of the Universe* had set a standard for presenting philosophical ideas in hexameter verse. His ideas were those of the Stoics' great rivals, the Epicureans, who believed in a purely material universe, maintaining that death was final and no after-life possible. Matter, even the matter of which the human soul and the gods are made up, consists of atoms (*semina*), which are separated as readily as they combine. In Lucretius, death and perpetual dissolution are presented as a truth which should bring gladness and consolation because there is nothing to fear, no afterlife, no punishment. Virgil's atoms are the elements of an undying soul, and the gladness (745-7) comes from a conclusion the contrary of Lucretius'. There is a paradox, that while Virgil's expression is Lucretian, his ideas would doubtless have been regarded by Lucretius with ridicule and horror.[42]

6.iv. Anchises and the catalogue of Alban and Roman heroes (752-886)

6.iv.a. Anchises and Aeneas watch a long line of their descendants going past on the way to the world above. The parade falls in to three sections: 756-807, leading up to Augustus; 808-53, leading up to the lines which lay down the guiding principles for the Roman nation; and 854-92, a lament for the young Marcellus. There is a very rough overall chronological sequence, in that the first part covers the pre-history of Rome, the second part the period of the Kings and the Republic (753 to about 50 BCE), and the third refers to events of the very recent past.

6.iv.b. The first part is devoted to the kings of Alba and the foundation of the tiny communities which represent the first stage of national expansion. Romulus, the link between Alba and Rome, appears to be forming a climax to this passage. But as he looks at Romulus, Anchises is carried on to the contemplation of the City herself (781-7), and then, in a 700-year historical leap, to a greater Romulus (789-807), Augustus, the new founder of the city, a new Hercules (see above, **5.ii**), a new Dionysus.

6.iv.c. The second part deals with Republican[43] heroes and itself falls into three sections. Lines 808-23 tell of the Kings of Rome down to the first days after the last King was expelled and the Republic established in 510 BCE. The leading figure in this revolution was Lucius Brutus, from whom Marcus Brutus, the murderer of Julius Caesar, claimed descent. Virgil pauses at the mention of this Brutus and reflects uneasily on similarities between him and his descendant. In a second part, 824-35, Anchises describes a tumultuous throng of heroes from the Republic, but he is checked by the unsettling sight of Julius Caesar and his great rival Pompeius, who between them could be held responsible for much of the civil strife of the first century BCE. Line 835 forms a very startling end to this passage – see the note on it. Now Anchises is carried away by the sight of a new crowd of heroes, conquerors of the great enemies of Rome, Greece and Carthage. Anxiety is set aside as Virgil concludes the description with a resounding quotation from his predecessor Ennius and makes Anchises deliver his great statement of mission for the Roman people.

6.iv.d. In a third section, Anchises seems to be going on in the same vein, as he sees the hero Marcellus. But he breaks off, and it is left to Aeneas to ask about Marcellus' companion. It is a younger Marcellus, Augustus' nephew, who married Augustus' daughter, and on whom Augustus had set his hopes for a successor. He died in 23 BCE. Augustus himself delivered the funeral oration which Virgil seems to recall in 867-86. The deep sadness of this last section seems to call into question the promise of empire which precedes it, and to prepare the way for the strange ending to the book which follows.

6.iv.e. The parade is a *tour de force*. In context, it inspires Aeneas. It is a celebration of Roman people and Roman achievements. It is praise of Augustus and his family, the Julii (see the notes for some contemporary references which are not covered here). It deals sensitively with some troubling events and people. It is optimistic but not blindly so – triumphant but not triumphalist. It makes humanity and empire seem, perhaps only for a moment, compatible.

6.v. Leaving the underworld: the Gate of Ivory and the Gate of Horn

6.v.a. After Anchises has finished mourning in advance for the premature death of Marcellus, there begins a puzzling and evocative conclusion to the book. 'Thus they roam everywhere throughout that region in the broad plains of the air, surveying all' (886-7).[44] This curiously insubstantial idea is immediately followed by a very down-to-earth sentence in which Anchises instructs Aeneas in detail about the difficulties he is due to face and the methods he should use to get the better of them. And now Anchises takes Aeneas and the Sibyl to the way out from the underworld: the twin gates of Sleep, the one made of ivory, the other of horn. Through the horn gate, we are told, pass 'genuine shades'; through the ivory gate 'falsehoods, nightmares'. Anchises shows Aeneas and the Sibyl out through the ivory gate.

6.v.b. Why is the underworld equated with sleep? Why is it given these two exits? Why does Virgil choose the ivory gate? No answer to these questions, especially the third, has ever seemed entirely satisfactory. Servius had a simple solution: 'Virgil wishes us to understand that everything he says is false.'[45]

6.v.c. The underworld is a place like no other, indeed is not like a place at all, and the normal rules of time and space do not operate. (535ff. remind us forcefully of the difference between the upper world and underworld.) The passage from upper to lower is marked by strange experiences, and the return from lower to upper needs also to be remarkable.

6.v.d. It is also important to establish that experiences in the underworld are different from those in the upper world. On the face of it, Aeneas has been given a clear view of what the future holds and a precise plan for how to reach it (888-92). But for him to act on this knowledge would deprive the second half of the poem of all narrative force. It is true that in the later books he shows none of the self-doubt which he showed in earlier ones, especially Book 4. But he seems to have no detailed memory of his experiences in the underworld. He never refers to Anchises' advice. On his shield at 8.678-9 he fails to recognise Augustus whom he has seen at 6.792.[46] It is indeed almost as if the underworld experience has been a dream.

6.v.e. Virgil's Homeric model does not offer a helpful precedent. Odysseus (*Odyssey* 11.632-7) is prompted to leave the underworld merely by a random and sudden onrush of the spirits of the dead which fills him with terror and moves him to run to his ship. Afterwards, though he knows well what he has been told (it is after all from his own words that we hear of his experiences), he makes no use of it.[47]

6.v.f. But Virgil finds an idea from a different part of the *Odyssey* to cover Aeneas' return to the upper world. In Book 19.535-67, Penelope tells the disguised Odysseus of a dream. Odysseus interprets it as foretelling his own return and triumph. Penelope is sceptical. 'There are two Gates of Dreams, one of horn, for true dreams, one of ivory, for false: one cannot tell which dream comes through which Gate.' This device provides a setting of suitable solemnity and antiquity for Aeneas' return journey. It also serves well to establish the difference between the two worlds. But it does not account for the choice of the ivory gate.

6.v.g. It is already clear (136ff., 722ff.) that Virgil was greatly influenced by Plato. One of Plato's writings (*Phaedo*) takes the form of a discussion between Socrates and his friends just before Socrates has to submit to the death penalty. Socrates convinces his friends that there is an afterlife and a reward there for goodness in this life. He concludes, 'It would not be proper for a sensible man to insist that these things are as I have described them',[48] but argues that to believe something of this sort is a risk worth taking. In another context he argues thus: 'when we make the false as like the truth as possible, are we not doing something useful?'

6.v.h. Other passages in the *Aeneid* are anchored as firmly as possible into the world the Romans knew. Palinurus, Misenum and Gaieta[49] are real places with commonly known stories behind them. Cumae is there. The Sibyl is there. In his account of the underworld, Virgil ventures further into imaginative fiction than anywhere else. The ivory gate may be his acknowledgement that he is so doing. He also seems to make some claim to the importance of his own work (see note on 676 and 847ff.). The ivory gate may be his request, no more than a hint, that in writing fiction he should be thought to have done something worth while. In a sense Servius (**6.v.b**) was right.

7. Metre

'Metre' refers to the rhythmic pattern of the verse.

7a. Rhythm, stress, long and short syllables.

Take the English lines:

> The tómb's a fíne and prívate pláce,
> But nóne, I thínk, do thére embráce.

There are four accented or stressed syllables in each line. Stressed and unstressed syllables come alternately.

> Yoúng Lochinvár is come oút of the Wést,
> Through áll the wide Bórder his steéd was the bést.

Here too each line has four stressed syllables, but between each stressed syllable there are two unstressed syllables.

Roughly speaking, each syllable in English takes the same length of time to say. (Thus, in terms of musical rhythm, one could say that the first quotation is in 2/8 time and the second in 3/8.)

Virgil writes a line which has six stressed syllables. Latin syllables do not all take the same length of time to say. They are either full-length ('long') or half-length ('short').

Take the English line:

Glóry to yoú, great Lórd, from the eárth and the skíes you creáted.

Say it in such a way that the stressed syllables are pronounced in a regular beat. Between each pair of stressed syllables there is either one long syllable or two short syllables, while after the last stressed syllable there is one extra syllable of uncertain length. This is exactly the pattern of Virgil's line – the *hexameter* – which could be described in musical terms as 6 bars of 4/8.

Virgil uses this rhythm for many effects, and it makes him much more rewarding to read if one can hear the words in the rhythm which he intended. The following notes are designed to help with this. Like all manuals of instruction, they risk making something essentially straightforward look tangled and complicated.

7b. Hexameter, feet, quantity, dactyl, spondee, trochee.
Virgil's line is called a hexameter ('six-measure').

Glóry to |yoú, great |Lórd, from the |eárth and the |skíes you cre|áted.

A line of identical rhythm in *Aeneid* 6 is

    1   2   3   4   5   6
sédibus |ópta|tís gemin|á super |árbore |sídunt (203).

There are six 'feet', each containing a stressed syllable (always long) and after it either one long syllable or two short ones – except for the last foot, which contains only two syllables, the second of which may be either long or short. The term for such an unprescribed syllable is 'anceps'. The scheme can be set out thus, where the signs represent 'quantity': – represents 'long' and ˘ represents 'short':

    1   2   3   4   5   6
– ˘˘ | – ˘˘ | – ˘˘ | – ˘˘ | – ˘˘ | – ˘

A foot containing one long and two shorts (– ˘ ˘)is called a 'dactyl'.
A foot containing two long syllables (– –) is called a 'spondee'.
A foot containing only one long and one short syllable (– ˘: only possible in the sixth foot) is called a 'trochee'.

7c. Scansion.

Working out the pattern of long and short syllables, hence the rhythm, is called 'scansion'.

(i) The last five syllables of a line are almost always – ˘ ˘ | – ˘ . (Very occasionally, hexameters end – – | – – . There are no such lines in *Aeneid* 6.)

(ii) The first syllable of the line is always long.

(iii) Now determine which other syllables must be long. A few rules go some way to establishing this:

- Where two vowels are pronounced together as a single syllable (a 'diphthong'), that syllable is long: *Romae, aurum*. (Where they are pronounced separately, the first is short: *puella, subeunt*.)[50]
- Where a vowel is followed by two consonants, the syllable is almost always long. (The exception is when the second of the two consonants is 'l' or 'r' – *patr*em. Then the syllable may be short, but is not always so.) Where a vowel is followed by 'll' or 'rr', or if the two consonants are in separate words, the syllable is always long.

> 18   tĭbĭ,| Phoēbĕ, *săcr*|āvĭt
> 21   C*ēcrŏ*pĭd|aē iūss|ī
> 128   s*ēd rĕ*vŏc|*āre grăd*|um

- The first syllable of a foot is always long.
- Where a syllable of unknown quantity comes on its own between two long syllables, that syllable must itself be long. (This is because shorts come in pairs, except in the sixth foot.)

(iv) Elision. Where a word ending in a vowel (or vowel + 'm') is followed by a word beginning with a vowel (or 'h'), the vowel at the end of the first word is not pronounced (it is 'elided', i.e. struck off).[51] In other circumstances, 'm' is an ordinary consonant.

> 384   ērg(o) ĭtĕr | īncēpt|ūm pĕrăg|ūnt
> 390   ūmbrār(um) | hīc lŏcŭs | ēst

(v) Some notes:

The following vowel combinations normally sound together as a single syllable: ae, au, oe. The combination 'eu' forms a single syllable in names derived from Greek: *Teucri, Orpheus*; otherwise the vowels are separate – *deus*. In all other combinations vowels form two separate syllables. The separation is sometimes also indicated by a diaeresis mark: *Minoïa*.

The combination 'qu' counts as a <u>single</u> consonant. So do 'gu' in *sanguis* and 'su' in *adsuesco, desuetus* and other compounds of *suesco*.

The letter 'h' is disregarded for the purpose of scanning.

The letter 'i' . This is usually a vowel (*dominus*), but often a consonant sounding 'y' (*iam*). Regularly you will find it as both in a single word (*iacio*) – rather as English 'yearly'.

'v' and 'u'. In many Latin texts (not this one) you will find 'u' printed instead of 'v'. The same principle then applies to 'u' as to 'i' here: it is sometimes vowel and sometimes consonant.

(vi) When you have scanned a line according to these rules, you will often find some syllables left unmarked for quantity. Given that they all have to be accommodated within six feet, no more, no less, it is usually easy to work out the quantity of the remaining syllables. For example:

```
        1              3      4      5      6
29   Daēdalus ipse do|lōs tēc|t(i) āmbā|gēsquĕ rĕsōlvit.
```

If you try making any of the unmarked syllables long, you will find that the line has to have more than six feet, which is impossible. They must therefore all be short, and the line must scan

```
        1      2      3      4      5      6
29   Daēdălŭs | īpsĕ dŏ|lōs tēc|t(i) āmbā|gēsquĕ rĕ|sōlvit.
```

Above all, read the lines out loud and learn to *trust your ear*. It is in order to establish the sound of the line that one scans it in the first place.

Consider line 24. Following the rules so far, you get:

```
        1              3      4   5      6
24   hīc crudelis am|ōr taūr|ī sūp|pōstăquĕ | fūrto
```

From a mechanical point of view, there are two possible ways of dealing with the 1st and 2nd feet. One is right and the other wrong.[52] If you are in doubt, read the line in both ways and see which sounds the more natural pronunciation. There is a mass of rules explaining which vowels[53] are long by nature and which short (see Kennedy para. 473), but with a little practice it is possible to be confident about one's decisions.

7d. Caesura

Where a break between two words occurs inside a foot, the break is called 'caesura' ('cutting'). In the line

337   ēccĕ // gŭ|bērnā|tōr // sē|sē // Pălĭ|nūrŭs // ă|gēbăt

caesura occurs four times, at the places indicated by //.[54] But in hexameters in general there is a strong tendency for caesura to occur after the first syllable of the third foot; if not there, then after the first syllable of the second or fourth foot, often both. These are often called 'principal caesura'. In writing out a line with its scansion, one is normally expected to indicate only the principal caesuras, thus

       1   2   3   4   5   6
337   ēccĕ gŭ|bērnā|tōr // sē|sē Pălĭ|nūrŭs ă|gēbăt

8. Virgil's use of metre and language

8a. Quantity

Virgil varies the number of short and long syllables in a line:

268   ībānt | ōbscū|rī // sō|lā sūb | nōctĕ pĕr | ūmbrăm

The line has the greatest possible number of long syllables. Aeneas and the Sibyl are making their slow and weary way through the darkness.

269   pērquĕ dŏ|mōs Dī|tīs // văcŭ|ās ĕt ĭnānĭă | rēgnă

This is the next line, and, surprisingly, it has nearly the largest possible number of short syllables – only one spondee, in the 2nd foot. The underworld is dark, but it is empty and insubstantial: the short syllables give a light effect.

34

8b. Ictus and accent

Consider a few lines from *Julius Caesar:*

And whén you sáw his cháriot bút appéar,
Have yoú not raísed an únivérsal shoút,
That Tíber trémbled úndernéath his bánk
To héar the réplicátion óf your soúnds
Made ín his cóncave shóres?

The Shakespearean line has five stresses, on alternate syllables. If one read it without thinking, applying the five-stress rule, it would come out as above. There are only three places where such a reading would sound seriously clumsy: the stress on 'you' in line 2, the stress on 'of' in line 4, and the stress on 'in' in line 5.

Now consider a line from later in the play:

Friends, Rómans, coúntrymén, lend mé your eárs.

It is, formally, a five-stress line like any other. But to read it so would make a nonsense of it. Shakespeare is not being a clumsy poet, he is representing a man (Mark Antony) struggling to make himself heard above a noisy and hostile crowd. In the clash between the formal rhythm and the way the line must actually be said we hear the tension of the event. But by the next line,

I cóme to búry Caésar, nót to praíse him.

the crowd has gone quiet, Antony can speak easily, and the line can be said in its five-stress pattern.

This clash between the natural stress of the words ('accent') and the rhythm of the line ('ictus') is much used by Virgil. For example:

érg(o) omnés magnó circúm clamóre fremébant

The accent over the vowel indicates the ictus (the first syllable of each foot, where the stress lies); the underlining indicates the accent (how the word would be accented in normal pronunciation).[55] As in Antony's first line, the two stress-systems are in conflict. The line represents a troubled scene: the confusion and grief following the discovery of the dead body of Misenus.

On the other hand, in

165   aére ciére virós Martémque accéndere cántu

there is hardly any clash between ictus and accent.

In nearly every line the words in the last two feet are arranged so that ictus and accent coincide. If there is tension at the beginning of the line, it is resolved at the end. Exceptions to this are rare and striking:

    únus quí nobís cunctándo réstituís rem

This is a near-quotation from the early poet Ennius, and the lumpy long syllables recall his old-fashioned style (in fact Virgil's adaptation makes the line even more Ennius-like than the original in Ennius). The line is about Fabius Maximus, who famously wore Hannibal down by delaying tactics. The monosyllabic ending creates an awkward rhythm which reflects Fabius' deliberate awkwardness.

A more common variation is when the line ends in a four-syllable word. In *Aeneid* 6 this is done only with Greek words or Greek names (apart from one exception: animumque (11, see note)). The suggestion is that Virgil is deliberately reminding us of the style of his Greek predecessors (393, 447, 483 etc).

8c. Onomatopoeia ('making pictures with words'): alliteration, assonance, elision.

Consider a line discussed above:

165   aērĕ cĭ|ērĕ vĭ|rōs // Mār|tēmqu(e) āc|cēndĕrĕ | cāntū

The line represents Misenus playing proudly and delightedly on his trumpet. It goes with an appropriate ease and swing. Hard consonants and the letter 'r' also represent the sound of the trumpet. Also:

520   tūm mē | cōnfēc|tūm cūr|īs sōm|nōque gră|vātum

The slow rhythms represent Deiphobus' mental and physical exhaustion as he goes to sleep on the last night of Troy.

314   tēndē|bāntquĕ mă|nūs rīp(ae) | ūltĕrĭōris ă|mōre

which refers to the souls gathered on the bank of the Styx, begging to be taken across. The stressed long 'o's at the end could represent the crying of the helpless dead.

644   pǻrs pědibús plaudúnt choreás et carmina dicunt

The 'p's represent the feet of the dancers as they drum the ground, the 'c's perhaps the clapping of their hands. The clash of ictus and accent shows that it is a pretty lively dance with a complicated rhythm perhaps more like what one might hear and see today in a South Indian dance than on a Western dance-floor.

Sounds repeated for effect are said to be in 'assonance' (the 'o's in 314); when the assonance comes in the form of repeated first letters of words ('p's and 'c's in 644), there is said to be 'alliteration'.

655   quinquagint(a) atris immanis hiatibus Hydra

Virgil is describing the Hydra's gaping snake-jaws. With the long 'a' at the end of *quinquaginta* elided against the long 'a' of *atris* it is impossible to say the line without opening one's own mouth wide.

8d. Syntactical structure and verse structure. Caesura, diaeresis, enjambement, end-stopping.

236   his ac|tis // proper(e) |exsequi|tur // prae|cepta Si|byllae.
237   spelunc(a) | alta fu|it // vas|toqu(e) im|manis hi|atu,
238   scrupea, | tuta la|cu nig|ro // nemo|rumque te|nebris.[56]

'Caesura', as explained (**7d**), refers to a word-break occurring within a foot. When a word-break corresponds with the end of a foot, the term is 'diaeresis'. In all these lines caesura corresponds to natural breaks within or between sentences. A comfortable rhythm is created, where, with caesura in the 3rd or 4th foot (237, 238), the second half of a line is a sort of answer to the first; or, with caesura in the 2nd and 4th (236), a pattern is created within the line of three units increasing in length.

In 238 above, although there is caesura in the 3rd foot, the more marked break in the line is the diaeresis after *scrupea*. It creates a rather odd effect: a single word abruptly cut off and surrounded by longer and more imposing phrases.

A much more intense passage is

494 atqu(e) hic | Priami|den // lani|atum | corpore | toto
495 Dēipho|bum // videt | et lace|rum // cru|deliter | ora,
496 ora ma|nusqu(e) am|bas, // popu|lataque | tempora | raptis
497 auribus | et trun|cas // inho|nesto | vulnere | nares.[57]

The calm flow of the hexameters with their regular caesura is upset by the torrent of words which conveys this dreadful description. It begins harmlessly (break at *Priamiden*). Then we see that *Priamiden* is an adjective referring to *Deiphobum*, so that the reading must continue into the next line without a pause. (When one line runs into another like this, there is said to be 'enjambement'; conversely, when there is a strong pause at the end of the line, it is said to be 'end-stopped'.) Then *vidit* brings the sentence to what seems a firm halt, except that now begins a build of four phrases describing Deiphobus over two and a half lines of mounting pathos and horror. In 496 there is a solid pause in the 3rd foot, but no pause at all at the end of the line. In 497, there is diaeresis after *auribus,* making a harsh division between the two words of the ablative absolute phrase over the end of the line. Then, although there is, formally speaking, a caesura after *truncas*, in fact there can be no stopping anywhere in the phrase *truncas ... vulnere*, so that, if there is a pause, it comes before *nares* – appropriately, as Aeneas attempts to look Deiphobus straight in his fearfully disfigured face.

Virgil is making sentences, clauses, phrases which sometimes fit easily within the rhythm of the hexameter and sometimes do not. It is helpful to be sensitive to these patterns and to try to appreciate the effect at which he is aiming.

9. Metre and syntax

Another advantage of an understanding of the metre is that one can see when the length of a syllable determines case, tense or meaning:

Case: ēt răbīē fĕră | cōrdă tŭmēnt (49), where the second syllable of *fera* must be short (the foot must be a dactyl); the word therefore agrees with *corda*.

Tense: ēt vīrĭdī sē|dērĕ sŏ|lō (192); where the first syllable of *sedere* must be long. It cannot therefore be the present infinitive, which has a short first syllable. It therefore comes from the perfect tense and must be the short form of the 3rd plural, in place of *sederunt*.

Meaning: sēd mē | cūm lū|cīs Hĕcă|tē prae|fēcĭt Ă|vērnīs (564).
At first glance *lucis* might be genitive singular of *lux*. But the long second syllable indicates that it must be dative plural of *lucus*.

10. Metrical rarities

Book 6 includes a number of metrical rarities: unfinished lines (94, 835), synizesis (33, 280, 412, 678), lines ending in 4-syllable words (11, 393, 445, 483, 484, 601, 623, 802, 895), line ending in a monosyllable (846), hypermetric line (602), correption (507), lengthening in arsis (254). These are further discussed in the notes to those lines, and the terms are explained in Index 1.

Some reading

Editions of Aeneid VI in English

P. Vergili Maronis *Aeneidos* Liber Sextus, edited by R.G. Austin, Oxford 1977
Vergil: Aeneid, edited by R.D. Williams: 2 vols: *Books I-VI*; *Books VII-XII*, Macmillan 1972 / BCP 1996
Virgil: Aeneid VI, edited by H.E. Gould and J.L. Whiteley, Macmillan 1946 / BCP 1991

Virgil in general

Camps, W.A.: *An Introduction to Virgil's Aeneid*, Oxford 1969
Gransden, K.W.: *Virgil: the Aeneid* in the series Landmarks of World Literature, Cambridge 1990
Griffin, Jasper: *Virgil*, Oxford 1988 / BCP 2001
Otis, Brooks: *Virgil: A Study in Civilised Poetry*, Oxford 1964
Quinn, Kenneth: *Virgil: A Critical Description*, Routledge 1968

Virgil: Aeneid 6

Translations

Sisson, C.H.: *Virgil: The Aeneid,* Everyman 1998
West, D.A.: *Virgil: The Aeneid,* a new prose translation, Penguin 1990

The history and archaeology of the period

Scullard, H.H: *From the Gracchi to Nero: A History of Rome from 133 BC to AD 68*, Methuen 1959, Routledge 1988 etc.
Claridge, Amanda: *Rome* in the series *Oxford Archaeological Guides*, Oxford 1998
(On the archaeology of Cumae Austin's introduction is full.)

Other works of reference

Oxford Classical Dictionary, Oxford 1948 and later editions
March, Jenny: *Dictionary of Classical Mythology*, Cassell 1998
Allen, W. Sidney: *Vox Latina*: The Pronunciation of Classical Latin, Cambridge 1965 etc.
B.H. Kennedy, *Kennedy's Revised Latin Primer*, Longman 1965

Notes

1. *non mos, non ius:* Tacitus, *Annals* 3,28,2.

2. Livy, *Praefatio* 9.

3. *Laudatio Turiae*: 'A speech in praise of Turia'. It survives as a huge inscription, now in fragments. Turia was the wife. The speaker's name is never given. It used to be supposed, but is now doubted, that he was one of the consuls of 19 BCE.

4. Law, society, religion: could be summed up as *res publica restituta* – 'the republic restored'. On this, see Scullard pp. 231-6; and note that it was Augustus' proudest boast, set as the climax of the *Res Gestae* (34,1).

5. See paragraph **1b**.

6. From Augustus' time, non-Roman Italians become conspicuous in the governing class at Rome. As an ideal: *Aeneid* 12.821, 'May the Roman race grow strong with the heroism of Italy.'

7. See paragraph **3a.**

8. Claridge, 62f.

9. *Res Gestae* 20, 4 (temples), 5 (roads).

10. Aqueducts: Frontinus *On Aqueducts* 1, 9-12; Sewers: Dio Cassius 49, 43,1. Augustus' colleague Agrippa went by boat along the Cloaca Maxima ('Great Drain') under the Forum and out into the Tiber.

11. Scullard: pp. 175-80, 231-3.

12. As a conspicuous example, the sculptures on the Altar of Peace: Claridge 187-9.

13. Horace, Propertius and Tibullus are the most conspicuous of the surviving poets (other than Virgil) who celebrated the Augustan achievement. Ovid, on the other hand, made fun of it and paid the penalty in being sent into exile.

14. Conveniently translated in Camps, pp. 115-20.

15. Appendix Virgiliana, *Catalepton* 5.

16. Pollio: *Eclogues* 3.84; 4.12 (40 BCE); other patrons: the general Varus (*Ecl.* 6.7) the general and poet Gallus (*Ecl.* 6.64; 10.2 etc.)

17. By 38 BCE, to judge by Horace, *Satires* 1.6,55 (Virgil was one of those who introduced Horace to Maecenas) and *Satires* 2.6, 40 & 53 (53 dates the poem to 30 BCE, 40 dates Horace's introduction to Maecenas at nearly eight years before that).

18. There was dispute in antiquity: *Life of Virgil,* 19.

19. Also called *Bucolics* – a Greek word which means 'pastoral pieces'.

20. For example, Eclogues 1 and 9 deal with the troubles associated with the redistribution of land to retired soldiers following the civil wars of the late 40s; 5 with the death and deification of Julius Caesar.

21. *Life of Virgil* 27.

22. Rather surprisingly, there is no ancient term for this type of poem.

23. See especially *Georgics* 1.505-8 on how badly things have gone wrong, 2.458-74 on how they might be otherwise.

24. Between two and three lines a day ... assuming he did nothing else. But the *Life* describes Virgil as comparing his careful revision of his own verses to a she-bear licking her cubs into shape (Camps 117).

25. For signs of incompleteness in the poem, see Camps 127-31.

26. Propertius 2.34.65-6.

27. For Virgil's use of Homer, see Griffin p. 14 and ch. 4, and follow the references under 'Homer' in the Index in Camps.

28. *Iliad* 20.307-8

29. Aeneas' rescue of his father Anchises was a popular image in Italy from the sixth century BCE. The third-century Greek historian Timaeus is recorded as having described a Roman cult as having a Trojan origin, and the third/second-century Roman authors Fabius Pictor, Naevius and Ennius all speak as if Romulus was a descendant of Aeneas.

30. In a funeral speech for his aunt Julia, Suetonius *Divus Julius* 6.

31. 1.279.

32. 6.756-886.

33. 8.102-584.

34. 8.626-728. The climax of the scene is Augustus in front of his own new-built temple to Apollo.

35. 4.622-9.

36. E.g. the funeral ritual in 6.212-31.

37. *pius* is an important word in the *Aeneid*. It means 'dutiful to the gods, to one's native land, to one's friends and particularly to one's family'.

38. 2.721-3 & 804, see also 6.110-11 and note.

39. The word for such a visit is 'katabasis' – 'a going-down' (Greek).

40. Orpheus, Castor & Pollux, Theseus & Pirithous, Hercules.

41. *Phaedo* 113-14 has some striking points of similarity with Virgil's account.

42. See Appendix 2(b) for a passage of Lucretius with which *Aeneid* 724-51 can be instructively compared.

43. 'Republican' refers to the period 510-31 BCE.

44. 'The air' represents *aer* – but see note. 'Surveying' represents *lustro* – but see note.

45. Other explanations: (i) It was believed that true dreams come before midnight, false dreams after. Virgil is showing that Aeneas left the underworld after midnight. (ii) Aeneas and the Sibyl are not in fact 'shades' at all, therefore they have to go out through the other exit. (iii) The ivory gate is the same as Orcus' porch, where empty dreams reside (283). (iv) For *eburna* read *Averna:* they go out, as they came in, 'by the gate at Avernus'.

46. He is *ignarus rerum* (8.730) – ignorant of these truths.

47. Tiresias has told him of the danger from the Sun-god's cattle, but so has Circe (*Odyssey* 12, 271-4). Tiresias has told him that his house will be occupied by strangers, but he forgets this and has to be reminded by Athene (*Odyssey* 13, 383-5).

48. *Phaedo* 114d.

49. For Palinurus see on 383, for Misenus / Misenum on 235. Gaieta (900) where A sails from Cumae, commemorates in its name A's aged nurse, who died there (7.2).

50. This rule does not apply with Greek names: Aēnēās, Dēīphŏbŭs.

51. Probably the elided vowel was not totally disregarded, but slurred with the following vowel. As for vowel + 'm', it is likely that the 'm' gave the preceding vowel a nasal sound, as in French.

52.   1   2   3   4   5   6
The right version is: hīc crū|dēlīs ă|mōr taū|rī sūp|pōstăquĕ | fūrtō

53. It is of course possible for a short <u>vowel</u> to be part of a long <u>syllable</u>, if two consonants follow it. (Compare *dixit* in 231 – second syllable long – with the same word in 677 with the second syllable short). It is impossible for a long vowel to be part of a short syllable. (Though there is one exception in Book 6: see 507.)

54. Caesura is said to be 'strong' if it comes after the first syllable of a foot, 'weak' if it comes between the short syllables of a dactyl.

55. This assumes that Latin speech is like English in having the accent fall on the second last syllable of a word if that syllable is long, and on the third last if the second last is short. This principle is generally accepted in English and German-speaking countries!

56. 'This done, he speedily fulfilled the Sibyl's commands. There was a deep cave, huge, with a yawning mouth, stony, protected by a black lake and dark woods.'

57. 'And here he sees the son of Priam with his whole body torn open – (it was) Deiphobus – cut brutally about the face, his face and both his hands, his head ravaged where his ears had been taken off and his nose chopped away, a shocking wound.'

58. Conversely, when there is a strong pause at the end of the line, it is said to be 'end-stopped'.

AENEID BOOK 6

The Trojans land at Cumae, the site of a temple of Apollo and the residence of the Sibyl, Apollo's prophetess. They admire the strange stories carved on its doors by Daedalus, founder of the temple. The Sibyl comes to meet them.

Sic fatur lacrimans, classique immittit habenas,
et tandem Euboïcis Cumarum adlabitur oris.
obvertunt pelago proras; tum dente tenaci
ancora fundabat naves, et litora curvae
praetexunt puppes. iuvenum manus emicat ardens   5
litus in Hesperium; quaerit pars semina flammae
abstrusa in venis silicis; pars densa ferarum
tecta rapit silvas, inventaque flumina monstrat.
at pius Aeneas arces, quibus altus Apollo
praesidet, horrendaeque procul secreta Sibyllae,   10
antrum immane, petit, magnam cui mentem animumque
Delius inspirat vates aperitque futura.
iam subeunt Triviae lucos atque aurea tecta.
　　Daedalus, ut fama est, fugiens Minoïa regna,
praepetibus pennis ausus se credere caelo,   15
insuetum per iter gelidos enavit ad Arctos,
Chalcidicaque levis tandem super asitit arce.
redditus his primum terris tibi, Phoebe, sacravit
remigium alarum, posuitque immania templa.
in foribus letum Androgeo; tum pendere poenas   20
Cecropidae iussi – miserum! – septena quotannis
corpora natorum; stat ductis sortibus urna.
contra elata mari respondet Gnosia tellus:
hic crudelis amor tauri, suppostaque furto
Pasiphaë, mixtumque genus prolesque biformis   25
Minotaurus inest, Veneris monimenta nefandae;
hic labor ille domus et inextricabilis error;
magnum reginae sed enim miseratus amorem
Daedalus ipse dolos tecti ambagesque resolvit,
caeca regens filo vestigia. tu quoque magnam   30

partem opere in tanto, sineret dolor, Icare, haberes.
bis conatus erat casus effingere in auro,
bis patriae cecidere manus. quin protinus omnia
perlegerent oculis, ni iam praemissus Achates
adforet, atque una Phoebi Triviaeque sacerdos,   35
Deïphobe Glauci, fatur quae talia regi:
'non hoc ista sibi tempus spectacula poscit.
nunc grege de intacto septem mactare iuvencos
praestiterit, totidem lectas de more bidentes.'
talibus adfata Aenean (nec sacra morantur   40
iussa viri) Teucros vocat alta in templa sacerdos.

*In the temple, the Sibyl goes into a trance. Aeneas prays to her that the
Trojans may settle in Italy. In return, he promises to build a temple for
Apollo and a special shrine for the Sibyl.*

    Excisum Euboïcae latus ingens rupis in antrum,
quo lati ducunt aditus centum, ostia centum,
unde ruunt totidem voces, responsa Sibyllae.
ventum erat ad limen, cum virgo 'poscere fata   45
tempus' ait; 'deus ecce deus!' cui talia fanti
ante fores subito non vultus, non color unus,
non comptae mansere comae; sed pectus anhelum,
et rabie fera corda tument, maiorque videri
nec mortale sonans, adflata est numine quando   50
iam propiore dei. 'cessas in vota precesque,
Tros' ait 'Aenea? cessas? neque enim ante dehiscent
attonitae magna ora domus.'[et talia fata
conticuit. gelidus Teucris per dura cucurrit
ossa tremor, funditque preces rex pectore ab imo: 55
'Phoebe, graves Troiae semper miserate labores,
Dardana qui Paridis derexti tela manusque
corpus in Aeacidae, magnas obeuntia terras
tot maria intravi duce te, penitusque repostas
Massylum gentes, praetentaque Syrtibus arva: 60
iam tandem Italiae fugientes prendimus oras;
hac Troiana tenus fuerit fortuna secuta.
vos quoque Pergameae iam fas est parcere genti,
dique deaeque omnes, quibus obstitit Ilium et ingens

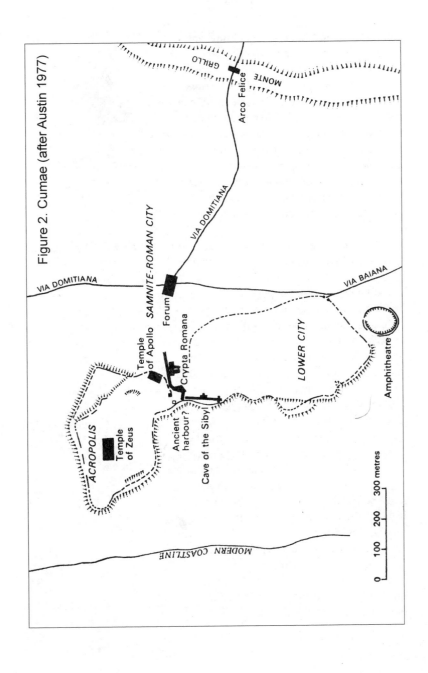

Figure 2. Cumae (after Austin 1977)

gloria Dardaniae. tuque, o sanctissima vates,   65
praescia venturi, da (non indebita posco
regna meis fatis) Latio considere Teucros
errantesque deos agitataque numina Troiae.
tum Phoebo et Triviae solido de marmore templum
instituam, festosque dies de nomine Phoebi.   70
te quoque magna manent regnis penetralia nostris:
hic ego namque tuas sortes, arcanaque fata
dicta meae genti, ponam, lectosque sacrabo,
alma, viros. foliis tantum ne carmina manda,
ne turbata volent rapidis ludibria ventis;   75
ipsa canas oro.' finem dedit ore loquendi.

The Sibyl answers: the Trojans will settle in Italy; they will face fearful
opposition but receive unexpected support.

   At Phoebi nondum patiens, immanis in antro
bacchatur vates, magnum si pectore possit
excussisse deum; tanto magis ille fatigat
os rabidum, fera corda domans, fingitque premendo.   80
ostia iamque domus patuere ingentia centum
sponte sua, vatisque ferunt responsa per auras:
'o tandem magnis pelagi defuncte periclis
(sed terrae graviora manent), in regna Lavini
Dardanidae venient (mitte hanc de pectore curam),   85
sed non et venisse volent. bella, horrida bella,
et Thybrim multo spumantem sanguine cerno.
non Simoïs tibi nec Xanthus nec Dorica castra
defuerint; alius Latio iam partus Achilles,
natus et ipse dea; nec Teucris addita Iuno   90
usquam aberit, cum tu, supplex in rebus egenis,
quas gentes Italum aut quas non oraveris urbes!
causa mali tanti coniunx iterum hospita Teucris
externique iterum thalami.
tu ne cede malis, sed contra audentior ito   95
qua tua te fortuna sinet. via prima salutis,
quod minime reris, Graia pandetur ab urbe.'

*Aeneas prays again – that the Sibyl will help him in his quest to descend
to the underworld and visit his father there.*

Talibus ex adyto dictis Cumaea Sibylla
horrendas canit ambages antroque remugit,
obscuris vera involvens; ea frena furenti   100
concutit et stimulos sub pectore vertit Apollo.
ut primum cessit furor, et rabida ora quierunt,
incipit Aeneas heros: 'non ulla laborum,
o virgo, nova mi facies inopinave surgit;
omnia praecepi atque animo mecum ante peregi.   105
unum oro: quando hic inferni ianua regis
dicitur et tenebrosa palus Acheronte refuso,
ire ad conspectum cari genitoris et ora
contingat; doceas iter, et sacra ostia pandas.
illum ego per flammas et mille sequentia tela   110
eripui his umeris, medioque ex hoste recepi;
ille, meum comitatus iter, maria omnia mecum
atque omnes pelagique minas caelique ferebat,
invalidus, vires ultra sortemque senectae.
quin, ut te supplex peterem et tua limina adirem,   115
idem orans mandata dabat natique patrisque,
alma, precor, miserere; potes namque omnia, nec te
nequiquam lucis Hecate praefecit Avernis.
si potuit manes accersere coniugis Orpheus
Threïcia fretus cithara fidibusque canoris,   120
si fratrem Pollux alterna morte redemit,
itque reditque viam totiens – quid Thesea, magnum
quid memorem Alciden? et mi genus ab Iove summo.'

*The Sibyl answers: to enter the underworld is permitted only to those
who have plucked the Golden Bough. Aeneas must in addition bury one
of his companions who has, unknown to him, been killed.*

Talibus orabat dictis, arasque tenebat,
cum sic orsa loqui vates: 'sate sanguine divum,   125
Tros Anchisiade, facilis descensus Averno;
noctes atque dies patet atri ianua Ditis;
sed revocare gradum superasque evadere ad auras,

hoc opus, hic labor est. pauci, quos aequus amavit
Iuppiter, aut ardens evexit ad aethera virtus, 130
dis geniti potuere. tenent media omnia silvae,
Cocytusque sinu labens circumvenit atro.
quod si tantus amor menti, si tanta cupido est
bis Stygios innare lacus, bis nigra videre
Tartara, et insano iuvat indulgere labori, 135
accipe quae peragenda prius. latet arbore opaca
aureus et foliis et lento vimine ramus,
Iunoni infernae dictus sacer; hunc tegit omnis
lucus, et obscuris claudunt convallibus umbrae.
sed non ante datur telluris operta subire, 140
auricomos quam quis decerpserit arbore fetus.
hoc sibi pulchra suum ferri Proserpina munus
instituit. primo avulso non deficit alter
aureus, et simili frondescit virga metallo.
ergo alte vestiga oculis, et rite repertum 145
carpe manu; namque ipse volens facilisque sequetur,
si te fata vocant. aliter non viribus ullis
vincere, nec duro poteris convellere ferro.
praeterea iacet exanimum tibi corpus amici
(heu nescis) totamque incestat funere classem, 150
dum consulta petis nostroque in limine pendes.
sedibus hunc refer ante suis, et conde sepulcro.
duc nigras pecudes; ea prima piacula sunto.
sic demum lucos Stygis et regna invia vivis
aspicies.' dixit, pressoque obmutuit ore. 155

*It is Misenus who has died, killed by the sea-god Triton for his boast of
superior skill on the trumpet.*

Aeneas, maesto defixus lumina vultu,
ingreditur linquens antrum, caecosque volutat
eventus animo secum. cui fidus Achates
it comes, et paribus curis vestigia figit.
multa inter sese vario sermone serebant, 160
quem socium exanimum vates, quod corpus humandum
diceret. atque illi Misenum in litore sicco,
ut venere, vident indigna morte peremptum,

Misenum Aeoliden, quo non praestantior alter
aere ciere viros, Martemque accendere cantu.   165
Hectoris hic magni fuerat comes, Hectora circum
et lituo pugnas,insignis obibat et hasta.
postquam illum vita victor spoliavit Achilles,
Dardanio Aeneae sese fortissimus heros
addiderat socium, non inferiora secutus.   170
sed tum, forte cava dum personat aequora concha,
demens, et cantu vocat in certamina divos,
aemulus exceptum Triton, si credere dignum est,
inter saxa virum spumosa immerserat unda.
ergo omnes magno circum clamore fremebant,   175
praecipue pius Aeneas. tum iussa Sibyllae,
haud mora, festinant flentes, aramque sepulcri
congerere arboribus caeloque educere certant.
itur in antiquam silvam, stabula alta ferarum;
procumbunt piceae; sonat icta securibus ilex;   180
fraxineaeque trabes cuneis et fissile robur
scinditur; advolvunt ingentes montibus ornos.

While they are in the forest gathering wood for the funeral pyre, Aeneas
is guided to the Golden Bough.

Nec non Aeneas opera inter talia primus
hortatur socios, paribusque accingitur armis.
atque haec ipse suo tristi cum corde volutat,   185
aspectans silvam immensam, et sic forte precatur:
'si nunc se nobis ille aureus arbore ramus
ostendat nemore in tanto! quando omnia vere
heu nimium de te vates, Misene, locuta est.'
vix ea fatus erat, geminae cum forte columbae   190
ipsa sub ora viri caelo venere volantes,
et viridi sedere solo. tum maximus heros
maternas agnoscit aves, laetusque precatur:
'este duces, o si qua via est, cursumque per auras
derigite in lucos, ubi pinguem dives opacat   195
ramus humum. tuque, o, dubiis ne defice rebus,
diva parens.' sic effatus vestigia pressit,
observans quae signa ferant, quo tendere pergant.

pascentes illae tantum prodire volando
quantum acie possent oculi servare sequentum.   200
inde ubi venere ad fauces grave olentis Averni,
tollunt se celeres, liquidumque per aëra lapsae
sedibus optatis gemina super arbore sidunt,
discolor unde auri per ramos aura refulsit.
quale solet silvis brumali frigore viscum   205
fronde virere nova, quod non sua seminat arbos,
et croceo fetu teretes circumdare truncos,
talis erat species auri frondentis opaca
ilice, sic leni crepitabat brattea vento.
corripit Aeneas extemplo avidusque refringit   210
cunctantem, et vatis portat sub tecta Sibyllae.

Misenus' funeral.

   Nec minus interea Misenum in litore Teucri
flebant, et cineri ingrato suprema ferebant.
principio pinguem taedis et robore secto
ingentem struxere pyram, cui frondibus atris   215
intexunt latera, et ferales ante cupressos
constituunt, decorantque super fulgentibus armis.
pars calidos latices et aëna undantia flammis
expediunt, corpusque lavant frigentis et unguunt.
fit gemitus. tum membra toro defleta reponunt,   220
purpureasque super vestes, velamina nota,
coniciunt. pars ingenti subiere feretro,
triste ministerium, et subiectam more parentum
aversi tenuere facem. congesta cremantur
turea dona, dapes, fuso crateres olivo.   225
postquam conlapsi cineres et flamma quievit,
reliquias vino et bibulam lavere favillam,
ossaque lecta cado texit Corynaeus aëno.
idem ter socios pura circumtulit unda,
spargens rore levi et ramo felicis olivae,   230
lustravitque viros, dixitque novissima verba.
at pius Aeneas ingenti mole sepulcrum
imponit, suaque arma viro remumque tubamque,
monte sub aërio, qui nunc Misenus ab illo

dicitur, aeternumque tenet per saecula nomen. 235

*Aeneas and the Sibyl perform a midnight sacrifice at a cave by Lake
Avernus in preparation for the journey below.*

His actis propere exsequitur praecepta Sibyllae.
spelunca alta fuit vastoque immanis hiatu,
scrupea, tuta lacu nigro nemorumque tenebris,
quam super haud ullae poterant impune volantes
tendere iter pennis: talis sese halitus atris 240
faucibus effundens supera ad convexa ferebat
[unde locum Grai dixerunt nomine Aornum].
quattuor hic primum nigrantes terga iuvencos
constituit, frontique invergit vina sacerdos,
et summas carpens media inter cornua saetas 245
ignibus imponit sacris, libamina prima,
voce vocans Hecaten caeloque Ereboque potentem.
supponunt alii cultros, tepidumque cruorem
succipiunt pateris. ipse atri velleris agnam
Aeneas matri Eumenidum magnaeque sorori 250
ense ferit, sterilemque tibi, Proserpina, vaccam.
tum Stygio regi nocturnas incohat aras,
et solida imponit taurorum viscera flammis,
pingue super oleum fundens ardentibus extis.
ecce autem, primi sub lumina solis et ortus, 255
sub pedibus mugire solum, et iuga coepta moveri
silvarum, visaeque canes ululare per umbram,
adventante dea. 'procul, o procul este, profani,'
conclamat vates, 'totoque absistite luco;
tuque invade viam, vaginaque eripe ferrum; 260
nunc animis opus, Aenea, nunc pectore firmo.'
tantum effata, furens antro se immisit aperto;
ille ducem haud timidis vadentem passibus aequat.

The poet invokes the powers of the underworld.

Di, quibus imperium est animarum, umbraeque silentes,
et Chaos, et Phlegethon, loca nocte tacentia late, 265
sit mihi fas audita loqui, sit numine vestro

51

pandere res alta terra et caligine mersas.

As they enter the House of Dis they encounter, personified, the grim causes of death and the shadowy shapes of the monsters of legend.

    Ibant obscuri sola sub nocte per umbram,
perque domos Ditis vacuas et inania regna:
quale per incertam lunam sub luce maligna   270
est iter in silvis, ubi caelum condidit umbra
Iuppiter, et rebus nox abstulit atra colorem.
vestibulum ante ipsum primisque in faucibus Orci
Luctus et ultrices posuere cubilia Curae;
pallentesque habitant Morbi, tristisque Senectus,   275
et Metus, et malesuada Fames, ac turpis Egestas,
terribiles visu formae, Letumque Labosque;
tum consanguineus Leti Sopor, et mala mentis
Gaudia, mortiferumque adverso in limine Bellum,
ferreique Eumenidum thalami, et Discordia demens,   280
vipereum crinem vittis innexa cruentis.
    In medio ramos annosaque bracchia pandit
ulmus opaca, ingens, quam sedem Somnia vulgo
vana tenere ferunt, foliisque sub omnibus haerent.
multaque praeterea variarum monstra ferarum,   285
Centauri in foribus stabulant, Scyllaeque biformes,
et centumgeminus Briareus, ac belua Lernae
horrendum stridens, flammisque armata Chimaera,
Gorgones Harpyiaeque, et forma tricorporis umbrae.
corripit hic subita trepidus formidine ferrum   290
Aeneas, strictamque aciem venientibus offert,
et ni docta comes tenues sine corpore vitas
admoneat volitare cava sub imagine formae,
inruat, et frustra ferro diverberet umbras.

They come to the river Styx, where the dead are gathering in crowds before the crossing. Charon the ferryman forbids the unburied dead to cross.

    Hinc via Tartarei quae fert Acherontis ad undas.   295
turbidus hic caeno vastaque voragine gurges

aestuat, atque omnem Cocyto eructat harenam.
portitor has horrendus aquas et flumina servat
terribili squalore Charon, cui plurima mento
canities inculta iacet; stant lumina flamma;   300
sordidus ex umeris nodo dependet amictus.
ipse ratem conto subigit velisque ministrat,
et ferruginea subvectat corpora cumba,
iam senior, sed cruda deo viridisque senectus.
huc omnis turba ad ripas effusa ruebat,   305
matres atque viri, defunctaque corpora vita
magnanimum heroum, pueri innuptaeque puellae,
impositique rogis iuvenes ante ora parentum:
quam multa in silvis autumni frigore primo
lapsa cadunt folia, aut ad terram gurgite ab alto   310
quam multae glomerantur aves, ubi frigidus annus
trans pontum fugat et terris immittit apricis.
stabant orantes primi transmittere cursum,
tendebantque manus ripae ulterioris amore.
navita sed tristis nunc hos, nunc accipit illos,   315
ast alios longe summotos arcet harena.
Aeneas miratus enim motusque tumultu
'dic,' ait, 'o virgo, quid vult concursus ad amnem?
quidve petunt animae? vel quo discrimine ripas
hae linquunt, illae remis vada livida verrunt?'   320
olli sic breviter fata est longaeva sacerdos:
'Anchisa generate, deum certissima proles,
Cocyti stagna alta vides Stygiamque paludem,
di cuius iurare timent et fallere numen.
haec omnis, quam cernis, inops inhumataque turba est;   325
portitor ille Charon; hi, quos vehit unda, sepulti.
nec ripas datur horrendas et rauca fluenta
transportare prius quam sedibus ossa quierunt.
centum errant annos volitantque haec litora circum;
tum demum admissi stagna exoptata revisunt.'   330
constitit Anchisa satus et vestigia pressit,
multa putans, sortemque animo miseratus iniquam.
cernit ibi, maestos et mortis honore carentes,
Leucaspim, et Lyciae ductorem classis Oronten,
quos simul a Troia ventosa per aequora vectos   335

obruit Auster, aqua involvens navemque virosque.

*Aeneas meets his helmsman Palinurus, who was lost at sea. Palinurus
begs to be taken across the Styx, though unburied. The Sibyl sternly
refuses, but consoles him with the knowledge that the place where he
swam to shore and was murdered will bear his name.*

Ecce gubernator sese Palinurus agebat,
qui Libyco nuper cursu, dum sidera servat,
exciderat puppi mediis effusus in undis.
hunc ubi vix multa maestum cognovit in umbra,   340
sic prior adloquitur. 'quis te, Palinure, deorum
eripuit nobis medioque sub aequore mersit?
dic age; namque mihi, fallax haud ante repertus,
hoc uno responso animum delusit Apollo,
qui fore te ponto incolumem, finesque canebat   345
venturum Ausonios. en haec promissa fides est?'
ille autem: 'neque te Phoebi cortina fefellit,
dux Anchisiade, neque me deus aequore mersit.
namque gubernaclum, multa vi forte revulsum,
cui datus haerebam custos cursusque regebam,   350
praecipitans traxi mecum. maria aspera iuro
non ullum pro me tantum cepisse timorem,
quam tua ne, spoliata armis, excussa magistro,
deficeret tantis navis surgentibus undis.
tres Notus hibernas immensa per aequora noctes   355
vexit me violentus aqua; vix lumine quarto
prospexi Italiam summa sublimis ab unda.
paulatim adnabam terrae; iam tuta tenebam,
ni gens crudelis madida cum veste gravatum,
prensantemque uncis manibus capita aspera montis,   360
ferro invasisset praedamque ignara putasset.
nunc me fluctus habet, versantque in litore venti.
quod te per caeli iucundum lumen et auras,
per genitorem oro, per spes surgentis Iuli,
eripe me his, invicte, malis: aut tu mihi terram   365
inice, namque potes, portusque require Velinos.
aut tu, si qua via est, si quam tibi diva creatrix
ostendit (neque enim, credo, sine numine divum

flumina tanta paras Stygiamque innare paludem),
da dextram misero, et tecum me tolle per undas, 370
sedibus ut saltem placidis in morte quiescam.'
talia fatus erat, coepit cum talia vates:
'unde haec, o Palinure, tibi tam dira cupido?
tu Stygias inhumatus aquas amnemque severum
Eumenidum aspicies, ripamve iniussus adibis? 375
desine fata deum flecti sperare precando.
sed cape dicta memor, duri solacia casus:
nam tua finitimi, longe lateque per urbes
prodigiis acti caelestibus, ossa piabunt,
et statuent tumulum, et tumulo sollemnia mittent, 380
aeternumque locus Palinuri nomen habebit.'
his dictis curae emotae, pulsusque parumper
corde dolor tristi; gaudet cognomine terra.

*Charon the ferryman is at first hostile, but the Sibyl shows him the
Golden Bough. Relenting, he takes her and Aeneas over the river.*

Ergo iter inceptum peragunt, fluvioque propinquant.
navita quos iam inde ut Stygia prospexit ab unda 385
per tacitum nemus ire pedemque advertere ripae,
sic prior adgreditur dictis atque increpat ultro:
'quisquis es, armatus qui nostra ad flumina tendis,
fare age quid venias, iam istinc, et comprime gressum.
umbrarum hic locus est, somni noctisque soporae: 390
corpora viva nefas Stygia vectare carina.
nec vero Alciden me sum laetatus euntem
accepisse lacu, nec Thesea Pirithoümque,
dis quamquam geniti atque invicti viribus essent.
Tartareum ille manu custodem in vincla petivit 395
ipsius a solio regis, traxitque trementem;
hi dominam Ditis thalamo deducere adorti.'
quae contra breviter fata est Amphrysia vates:
'nullae hic insidiae tales (absiste moveri),
nec vim tela ferunt. licet ingens ianitor, antro 400
aeternum latrans, exsangues terreat umbras;
casta licet patrui servet Proserpina limen.
Troïus Aeneas, pietate insignis et armis,

ad genitorem imas Erebi descendit ad umbras.
si te nulla movet tantae pietatis imago,   405
at ramum hunc' (aperit ramum qui veste latebat)
'agnoscas.' tumida ex ira tum corda residunt;
nec plura his. ille admirans venerabile donum
fatalis virgae longo post tempore visum,
caeruleam advertit puppim ripaeque propinquat.   410
inde alias animas, quae per iuga longa sedebant,
deturbat laxatque foros; simul accipit alveo
ingentem Aenean. gemuit sub pondere cumba
sutilis, et multam accepit rimosa paludem.
tandem trans fluvium incolumes vatemque virumque   415
informi limo glaucaque exponit in ulva.

*Cerberus, the guard-dog of the underworld, is pacified with a drugged
titbit.*

Cerberus haec ingens latratu regna trifauci
personat adverso recubans immanis in antro.
cui vates, horrere videns iam colla colubris,
melle soporatam et medicatis frugibus offam   420
obicit. ille, fame rabida tria guttura pandens,
corripit obiectam, atque immania terga resolvit
fusus humi, totoque ingens extenditur antro.
occupat Aeneas aditum custode sepulto,
evaditque celer ripam inremeabilis undae.   425

*They pass through the first two regions of the underworld proper,
inhabited by those who died in infancy and those who were unjustly
condemned to death.*

Continuo auditae voces, vagitus et ingens,
infantumque animae flentes, in limine primo
quos, dulcis vitae exsortes at ab ubere raptos,
abstulit atra dies et funere mersit acerbo.
hos iuxta falso damnati crimine mortis.   430
nec vero hae sine sorte datae, sine iudice, sedes.
quaesitor Minos urnam movet; ille silentum
consiliumque vocat vitasque et crimina discit.

proxima deinde tenent maesti loca, qui sibi letum
insontes peperere manu, lucemque perosi   435
proiecere animas. quam vellent aethere in alto
nunc et pauperiem et duros perferre labores!
fas obstat, tristisque palus inamabilis undae
alligat, et novies Styx interfusa coercet.

*In the Fields of Mourning dwell those who died of unhappy love. Aeneas
meets the ghost of Dido, who rejects his efforts to justify his conduct in
leaving her.*

  Nec procul hinc partem fusi monstrantur in omnem   440
Lugentes Campi – sic illos nomine dicunt.
hic quos durus amor crudeli tabe peredit
secreti celant calles, et myrtea circum
silva tegit; curae non ipsa in morte relinquunt.
his Phaedram Procrimque locis maestamque Eriphylen,   445
crudelis nati monstrantem vulnera, cernit;
Euadnen et Pasiphaën; his Laödamia
it comes, et iuvenis quondam, nunc femina, Caeneus
rursus et in veterem fato revoluta figuram.
inter quas Phoenissa recens a vulnere Dido   450
errabat silva in magna. quam Troïus heros,
ut primum iuxta stetit agnovitque per umbras
obscuram, qualem primo qui surgere mense
aut videt aut vidisse putat per nubila lunam,
demisit lacrimas dulcique adfatus amore est.   455
'infelix Dido, verus mihi nuntius ergo
venerat exstinctam, ferroque extrema secutam.
funeris heu tibi causa fui? per sidera iuro,
per superos, et si qua fides tellure sub ima est,
invitus, regina, tuo de litore cessi.   460
sed me iussa deum, quae nunc has ire per umbras,
per loca senta situ cogunt noctemque profundam,
imperiis egere suis. nec credere quivi
hunc tantum tibi me discessu ferre dolorem.
siste gradum, teque aspectu ne subtrahe nostro.   465
quem fugis? extremum fato quod te adloquor hoc est.'
talibus Aeneas ardentem et torva tuentem

lenibat dictis animum, lacrimasque ciebat.
illa solo fixos oculos aversa tenebat,
nec magis incepto vultum sermone movetur,   470
quam si dura silex aut stet Marpesia cautes.
tandem corripuit sese, atque inimica refugit
in nemus umbriferum, coniunx ubi pristinus illi
respondet curis aequatque Sychaeus amorem.
nec minus Aeneas, casu percussus iniquo,   475
prosequitur lacrimis longe, et miseratur euntem.

*Aeneas comes to the 'Farthest Fields' occupied by those who died
gloriously in battle. The Trojans welcome Aeneas, but the Greeks cower
away. There too is his cousin Deiphobus, hideously mutilated and
murdered by the Greeks on the night Troy was captured.*

    Inde datum molitur iter, iamque arva tenebant
ultima, quae bello clari secreta frequentant.
hic illi occurrit Tydeus, hic inclutus armis
Parthenopaeus, et Adrasti pallentis imago,   480
hic multum fleti ad superos belloque caduci
Dardanidae, quos ille omnes longo ordine cernens
ingemuit, Glaucumque Medontaque Thersilochumque,
tres Antenoridas, Cererique sacrum Polyboeten,
Idaeumque etiam currus, etiam arma tenentem.   485
circumstant animae dextra laevaque frequentes.
nec vidisse semel satis est; iuvat usque morari
et conferre gradum et veniendi discere causas.
at Danaum proceres Agamemnoniaeque phalanges,
ut videre virum fulgentiaque arma per umbras,   490
ingenti trepidare metu. pars vertere terga,
ceu quondam petiere rates; pars tollere vocem
exiguam: inceptus clamor frustratur hiantes.
    Atque hic Priamiden laniatum corpore toto
Deïphobum vidit, lacerum crudeliter ora,   495
ora manusque ambas, populataque tempora raptis
auribus, et truncas inhonesto vulnere nares.
vix adeo agnovit pavitantem ac dira tegentem
supplicia, et notis compellat vocibus ultro.
'Deïphobe armipotens, genus alto a sanguine Teucri,   500

quis tam crudeles optavit sumere poenas?
cui tantum de te licuit? mihi fama suprema
nocte tulit fessum vasta te caede Pelasgum
procubuisse super confusae stragis acervum.
tunc egomet tumulum Rhoeteo in litore inanem   505
constitui, et magna manes ter voce vocavi.
nomen et arma locum servant. te, amice, nequivi
conspicere et patria decedens ponere terra.'
ad quae Priamides: 'nihil o tibi, amice, relictum;
omnia Deïphobo solvisti et funeris umbris.   510
sed me fata mea et scelus exitiale Lacaenae
his mersere malis; illa haec monimenta reliquit.
namque ut supremam falsa inter gaudia noctem
egerimus, nosti; et nimium meminisse necesse est.
cum fatalis equus saltu super ardua venit   515
Pergama, et armatum peditem gravis attulit alvo,
illa, chorum simulans, euhantes orgia circum
ducebat Phrygias; flammam media ipsa tenebat
ingentem, et summa Danaos ex arce vocabat.
tum me confectum curis somnoque gravatum   520
infelix habuit thalamus, pressitque iacentem
dulcis et alta quies placidaeque simillima morti.
egregia interea coniunx arma omnia tectis
emovet, et fidum capiti subduxerat ensem.
intra tecta vocat Menelaum, et limina pandit,   525
scilicet id magnum sperans fore munus amanti,
et famam exstingui veterum sic posse malorum.
quid moror? inrumpunt thalamo; comes additus una
hortator scelerum Aeolides. di, talia Grais
instaurate, pio si poenas ore reposco.   530
sed te qui vivum casus, age fare vicissim,
attulerint. pelagine venis erroribus actus,
an monitu divum? an quae te fortuna fatigat,
ut tristes sine sole domos, loca turbida, adires?'

The Sibyl hurries Aeneas on.

Hac vice sermonum roseis Aurora quadrigis   535
iam medium aetherio cursu traiecerat axem;

59

et fors omne datum traherent per talia tempus,
sed comes admonuit breviterque adfata Sibylla est:
'nox ruit, Aenea; nos flendo ducimus horas.
hic locus est, partes ubi se via findit in ambas,   540
dextera quae Ditis magni sub moenia tendit,
(hac iter Elysium nobis), at laeva malorum
exercet poenas et ad impia Tartara mittit.'
Deïphobus contra: 'ne saevi, magna sacerdos;
discedam, explebo numerum, reddarque tenebris.   545
i decus, i nostrum; melioribus utere fatis.'
tantum effatus, et in verbo vestigia torsit.

They pass the walls which surround the pit of Tartarus, the place of
punishment. The Sibyl tells Aeneas how the goddess Hecate had once
shown her those imprisoned there and their fate.

Respicit Aeneas subito, et sub rupe sinistra
moenia lata videt, triplici circumdata muro,
quae rapidus flammis ambit torrentibus amnis   550
Tartareus Phlegethon, torquetque sonantia saxa.
porta adversa ingens, solidoque adamante columnae,
vis ut nulla virum, non ipsi exscindere bello
caelicolae valeant; stat ferrea turris ad auras,
Tisiphoneque sedens, palla succincta cruenta,   555
vestibulum exsomnis servat noctesque diesque.
hinc exaudiri gemitus, et saeva sonare
verbera, tum stridor ferri, tractaeque catenae.
constitit Aeneas, strepitumque exterritus hausit.
'quae scelerum facies? o virgo, effare; quibusve   560
urgentur poenis? quis tantus plangor ad auras?'
tum vates sic orsa loqui: 'dux inclute Teucrum,
nulli fas casto sceleratum insistere limen.
sed me cum lucis Hecate praefecit Avernis,
ipsa deum poenas docuit, perque omnia duxit.   565
Cnosius haec Rhadamanthus habet durissima regna,
castigatque auditque dolos, subigitque fateri
quae quis apud superos, furto laetatus inani,
distulit in seram commissa piacula mortem.
continuo sontes ultrix accincta flagello   570

Tisiphone quatit insultans, torvosque sinistra
intentans angues vocat agmina saeva sororum.
tum demum, horrisono stridentes cardine, sacrae
panduntur portae. cernis custodia qualis
vestibulo sedeat, facies quae limina servet?   575
quinquaginta atris immanis hiatibus Hydra
saevior intus habet sedem. tum Tartarus ipse
bis patet in praeceps tantum tenditque sub umbras,
quantus ad aetherium caeli suspectus Olympum.
hic genus antiquum Terrae, Titania pubes,   580
fulmine deiecti, fundo volvuntur in imo.
hic et Aloïdas geminos immania vidi
corpora, qui manibus magnum rescindere caelum
adgressi, superisque Iovem detrudere regnis.
vidi et crudeles dantem Salmonea poenas,   585
dum flammas Iovis et sonitus imitatur Olympi.
quattuor hic invectus equis, et lampada quassans,
per Graium populos mediaeque per Elidis urbem
ibat ovans, divumque sibi poscebat honorem,
demens, qui nimbos et non imitabile fulmen   590
aere et cornipedum pulsu simularet equorum.
at pater omnipotens densa inter nubila telum
contorsit, non ille faces nec fumea taedis
lumina, praecipitemque immani turbine adegit.
nec non et Tityon, Terrae omniparentis alumnum,   595
cernere erat, per tota novem cui iugera corpus
porrigitur, rostroque immanis vultur obunco,
immortale iecur tondens fecundaque poenis
viscera, rimaturque epulis habitatque sub alto
pectore, nec fibris requies datur ulla renatis.   600
quid memorem Lapithas, Ixiona Pirithoümque?
quos super atra silex iam iam lapsura cadentique
imminet adsimilis; lucent genialibus altis
aurea fulcra toris, epulaeque ante ora paratae
regifico luxu; Furiarum maxima iuxta   605
accubat, et manibus prohibet contingere mensas,
exsurgitque facem attollens atque intonat ore.
hic, quibus invisi fratres, dum vita manebat,
pulsatusve parens aut fraus innexa clienti,

aut qui divitiis soli incubuere repertis,   610
nec partem posuere suis, quae maxima turba est,
quique ob adulterium caesi, quique arma secuti
impia, nec veriti dominorum fallere dextras,
inclusi poenam exspectant. ne quaere doceri
quam poenam, aut quae forma viros fortunave mersit.   615
saxum ingens volvunt alii, radiisque rotarum
districti pendent; sedet aeternumque sedebit
infelix Theseus, Phlegyasque miserrimus omnes
admonet, et magna testatur voce per umbras:
"discite iustitiam moniti et non temnere divos."   620
vendidit hic auro patriam, dominumque potentem
imposuit; fixit leges pretio atque refixit.
hic thalamum invasit natae vetitosque hymenaeos.
ausi omnes immane nefas, ausoque potiti.
non, mihi si linguae centum sint oraque centum,   625
ferrea vox, omnes scelerum comprendere formas,
omnia poenarum percurrere nomina possim.'

They reach the entrance to Elysium, where Aeneas deposits the Golden Bough.

Haec ubi dicta dedit Phoebi longaeva sacerdos,
'sed iam age, carpe viam et susceptum perfice munus.
acceleremus,' ait. 'Cyclopum ducta caminis   630
moenia conspicio, atque adverso fornice portas,
haec ubi nos praecepta iubent deponere dona.'
dixerat, et pariter gressi per opaca viarum
corripiunt spatium medium, foribusque propinquant.
occupat Aeneas aditum, corpusque recenti   635
spargit aqua, ramumque adverso in limine figit.

The first part of Elysium is occupied by happy warriors of former times, priests, poets and others who have done good service to humankind. Aeneas and the Sibyl are directed to where they will find Anchises.

His demum exactis, perfecto munere divae,
devenere locos laetos, et amoena virecta
fortunatorum nemorum, sedesque beatas.

largior hic campos aether et lumine vestit   640
purpureo, solemque suum, sua sidera norunt.
pars in gramineis exercent membra palaestris,
contendunt ludo et fulva luctantur harena;
pars pedibus plaudunt choreas et carmina dicunt.
nec non Threïcius longa cum veste sacerdos   645
obloquitur numeris septem discrimina vocum,
iamque eadem digitis, iam pectine pulsat eburno.
hic genus antiquum Teucri, pulcherrima proles,
magnanimi heroes, nati melioribus annis,
Ilusque Assaracusque et Troiae Dardanus auctor.   650
arma procul currusque virum miratur inanes.
stant terra defixae hastae, passimque soluti
per campum pascuntur equi. quae gratia currum
armorumque fuit vivis, quae cura nitentes
pascere equos, eadem sequitur tellure repostos.   655
conspicit, ecce, alios dextra laevaque per herbam
vescentes, laetumque choro paeana canentes
inter odoratum lauris nemus, unde superne
plurimus Eridani per silvam volvitur amnis.
hic manus ob patriam pugnando vulnera passi,   660
quique sacerdotes casti, dum vita manebat,
quique pii vates et Phoebo digna locuti,
inventas aut qui vitam excoluere per artes,
quique sui memores aliquos fecere merendo.
omnibus his nivea cinguntur tempora vitta.   665
quos circumfusos sic est adfata Sibylla,
Musaeum ante omnes (medium nam plurima turba
hunc habet atque umeris exstantem suspicit altis):
'dicite, felices animae, tuque, optime vates,
quae regio Anchisen, quis habet locus? illius ergo   670
venimus, et magnos Erebi tranavimus amnes.'
atque huic responsum paucis ita reddidit heros:
'nulli certa domus. lucis habitamus opacis,
riparumque toros et prata recentia rivis
incolimus. sed vos, si fert ita corde voluntas,   675
hoc superate iugum, et facili iam tramite sistam.'
dixit, et ante tulit gressum, camposque nitentes
desuper ostentat. dehinc summa cacumina linquunt.

*Aeneas and Anchises greet each other. Anchises is looking at the spirits
of those due to return to life as his descendants. Aeneas cannot
understand why anyone should wish to live again.*

At pater Anchises penitus convalle virenti
inclusas animas superumque ad lumen ituras   680
lustrabat studio recolens, omnemque suorum
forte recensebat numerum, carosque nepotes,
fataque fortunasque virum, moresque manusque.
isque ubi tendentem adversum per gramina vidit
Aenean, alacris palmas utrasque tetendit,   685
effusaeque genis lacrimae, et vox excidit ore:
'venisti tandem, tuaque exspectata parenti
vicit iter durum pietas? datur ora tueri,
nate, tua, et notas audire et reddere voces?
sic equidem ducebam animo rebarque futurum,   690
tempora dinumerans, nec me mea cura fefellit.
quas ego te terras et quanta per aequora vectum
accipio! quantis iactatum, nate, periclis!
quam metui ne quid Libyae tibi regna nocerent!'
ille autem: 'tua me, genitor, tua tristis imago   695
saepius occurrens haec limina tendere adegit.
stant sale Tyrrheno classes. da iungere dextram,
da, genitor, teque amplexu ne subtrahe nostro.'
sic memorans largo fletu simul ora rigabat.
ter conatus ibi collo dare bracchia circum,   700
ter frustra comprensa manus effugit imago,
par levibus ventis volucrique simillima somno.
    Interea videt Aeneas in valle reducta
seclusum nemus et virgulta sonantia silvae,
Lethaeumque domos placidas qui praenatat amnem.   705
hunc circum innumerae gentes populique volabant,
ac velut in pratis ubi apes aestate serena
floribus insidunt variis et candida circum
lilia funduntur, strepit omnis murmure campus.
horrescit visu subito, causasque requirit   710
inscius Aeneas, quae sint ea flumina porro,
quive viri tanto complerint agmine ripas.

tum pater Anchises, 'animae, quibus altera fato
corpora debentur, Lethaei ad fluminis undam
securos latices et longa oblivia potant.   715
has equidem memorare tibi atque ostendere coram
iampridem, hanc prolem cupio enumerare meorum,
quo magis Italia mecum laetere reperta.'
'o pater, anne aliquas ad caelum hinc ire putandum est
sublimes animas, iterumque ad tarda reverti   720
corpora? quae lucis miseris tam dira cupido?'
'dicam equidem, nec te suspensum, nate, tenebo'
suscipit Anchises atque ordine singula pandit.

Anchises explains how the human soul is purified over several cycles of
life and death, until it finally becomes once again the heavenly fire which
is its original essence.

'Principio caelum ac terram camposque liquentes
lucentemque globum lunae Titaniaque astra   725
spiritus intus alit; totamque infusa per artus
mens agitat molem, et magno se corpore miscet.
inde hominum pecudumque genus vitaeque volantum
et quae marmoreo fert monstra sub aequore pontus.
igneus est ollis vigor et caelestis origo   730
seminibus, quantum non noxia corpora tardant
terrenique hebetant artus moribundaque membra.
hinc metuunt cupiuntque, dolent gaudentque, neque auras
dispiciunt, clausae tenebris et carcere caeco.
quin et supremo cum lumine vita reliquit,   735
non tamen omne malum miseris nec funditus omnes
corporeae excedunt pestes, penitusque necesse est
multa diu concreta modis inolescere miris.
ergo exercentur poenis, veterumque malorum
supplicia expendunt: aliae panduntur inanes   740
suspensae ad ventos, aliis sub gurgite vasto
infectum eluitur scelus aut exuritur igni:
quisque suos patimur manes. exinde per amplum
mittimur Elysium, et pauci laeta arva tenemus,
donec longa dies, perfecto temporis orbe,   745
concretam exemit labem, purumque reliquit

aetherium sensum atque auraï simplicis ignem.
has omnes, ubi mille rotam volvere per annos,
Lethaeum ad fluvium deus evocat agmine magno,
scilicet immemores supera ut convexa revisant   750
rursus, et incipiant in corpora velle reverti.'

*Anchises shows Aeneas his descendants, who will eventually become
Romans. He does so in three stages. First are the founders and kings of
Alba Longa until the time of Romulus. The sight of Romulus and the
thought of Rome carry Anchises forward in a long leap over time to
Augustus.*

  Dixerat Anchises, natumque unaque Sibyllam
conventus trahit in medios turbamque sonantem,
et tumulum capit, unde omnes longo ordine posset
adversos legere, et venientum discere vultus.   755
  'Nunc age, Dardaniam prolem quae deinde sequatur
gloria, qui maneant Itala de gente nepotes,
inlustres animas nostrumque in nomen ituras,
expediam dictis, et te tua fata docebo.
ille (vides?) pura iuvenis qui nititur hasta,   760
proxima sorte tenet lucis loca, primus ad auras
aetherias Italo commixtus sanguine surget,
Silvius, Albanum nomen, tua postuma proles,
quem tibi longaevo serum Lavinia coniunx
educet silvis regem regumque parentem,   765
unde genus Longa nostrum dominabitur Alba.
proximus ille Procas, Troianae gloria gentis,
et Capys, et Numitor, et qui te nomine reddet,
Silvius Aeneas, pariter pietate vel armis
egregius, si unquam regnandam acceperit Albam.   770
qui iuvenes! quantas ostentant (aspice!) vires,
atque umbrata gerunt civili tempora quercu!
hi tibi Nomentum et Gabios urbemque Fidenam,
hi Collatinas imponent montibus arces,
Pometios Castrumque Inui Bolamque Coramque.   775
haec tum nomina erunt, nunc sunt sine nomine terrae.
quin et avo comitem sese Mavortius addet
Romulus, Assaraci quem sanguinis Ilia mater

educet. viden, ut geminae stant vertice cristae,
et pater ipse suo superum iam signat honore?   780
en huius, nate, auspiciis illa incluta Roma
imperium terris, animos aequabit Olympo,
septemque una sibi muro circumdabit arces,
felix prole virum: qualis Berecyntia mater
invehitur curru Phrygias turrita per urbes,   785
laeta deum partu, centum complexa nepotes,
omnes caelicolas, omnes supera alta tenentes.
huc geminas nunc flecte acies, hanc aspice gentem
Romanosque tuos. hic Caesar et omnis Iuli
progenies, magnum caeli ventura sub axem.   790
hic vir, hic est, tibi quem promitti saepius audis,
Augustus Caesar, divi genus, aurea condet
saecula qui rursus Latio, regnata per arva
Saturno quondam, super et Garamantas et Indos
proferet imperium; iacet extra sidera tellus,   795
extra anni solisque vias, ubi caelifer Atlas
axem umero torquet stellis ardentibus aptum.
huius in adventum iam nunc et Caspia regna
responsis horrent divum et Maeotia tellus,
et septemgemini turbant trepida ostia Nili.   800
nec vero Alcides tantum telluris obivit,
fixerit aeripedem cervam licet, aut Erymanthi
pacarit nemora et Lernam tremefecerit arcu;
nec, qui pampineis victor iuga flectit habenis,
Liber, agens celso Nysae de vertice tigres.   805
et dubitamus adhuc virtutem extendere factis,
aut metus Ausonia prohibet considere terra?

Second, the kings and heroes of Rome itself down to the present time.

quis procul ille autem, ramis insignis olivae,
sacra ferens? nosco crines incanaque menta
regis Romani primam qui legibus urbem   810
fundabit, Curibus parvis et paupere terra
missus in imperium magnum. cui deinde subibit
otia qui rumpet patriae, residesque movebit
Tullus in arma viros et iam desueta triumphis

agmina. quem iuxta sequitur iactantior Ancus,   815
nunc quoque iam nimium gaudens popularibus auris.
vis et Tarquinios reges, animamque superbam
ultoris Bruti, fascesque videre receptos?
consulis imperium hic primus saevasque secures
accipiet, natosque pater, nova bella moventes,   820
ad poenam pulchra pro libertate vocabit,
infelix! utcumque ferent ea facta minores.
vincet amor patriae laudumque immensa cupido.
quin Decios Drusosque procul, saevumque securi
aspice Torquatum, et referentem signa Camillum.   825
illae autem, paribus quas fulgere cernis in armis,
concordes animae nunc et dum nocte premuntur,
heu quantum inter se bellum, si lumina vitae
attigerint, quantas acies stragemque ciebunt,
aggeribus socer Alpinis atque arce Monoeci   830
descendens, gener adversis instructus Eois!
ne, pueri, ne tanta animis adsuescite bella,
neu patriae validas in viscera vertite vires;
tuque prior, tu parce, genus qui ducis Olympo,
proice tela manu, sanguis meus! –   835
ille triumphata Capitolia ad alta Corintho
victor aget currum, caesis insignis Achivis.
eruet ille Argos Agamemnoniasque Mycenas
ipsumque Aeaciden, genus armipotentis Achilli,
ultus avos Troiae, templa et temerata Minervae.   840
quis te, magne Cato, tacitum, aut te, Cosse, relinquat?
quis Gracchi genus, aut geminos, duo fulmina belli,
Scipiadas, cladem Libyae, parvoque potentem
Fabricium, vel te sulco, Serrane, serentem.
quo fessum rapitis, Fabii? tu Maximus ille es,   845
unus qui nobis cunctando restituis rem.
excudent alii spirantia mollius aera
(credo equidem), vivos ducent de marmore vultus,
orabunt causas melius, caelique meatus
describent radio, et surgentia sidera dicent: 850
tu regere imperio populos, Romane, memento
(hae tibi erunt artes), pacique imponere morem,
parcere subiectis et debellare superbos.

Third, Marcus Marcellus and his identically named descendant,
Augustus' son-in law and nephew, prematurely dead in 23 BCE.

   Sic pater Anchises, atque haec mirantibus addit:
'aspice, ut insignis spoliis Marcellus opimis   855
ingreditur, victorque viros supereminet omnes.
hic rem Romanam, magno turbante tumultu,
sistet eques, sternet Poenos Gallumque rebellem,
tertiaque arma patri suspendet capta Quirino.'
atque hic Aeneas (una namque ire videbat   860
egregium forma iuvenem et fulgentibus armis,
sed frons laeta parum, et deiecto lumina vultu)
'quis, pater, ille, virum qui sic comitatur euntem?
filius, anne aliquis magna de stirpe nepotum?
qui strepitus circa comitum! quantum instar in ipso!   865
sed nox atra caput tristi circumvolat umbra.'
tum pater Aeneas lacrimis ingressus obortis:
'o nate, ingentem luctum ne quaere tuorum.
ostendent terris hunc tantum fata, neque ultra
esse sinent. nimium vobis Romana propago   870
visa potens, superi, propria haec si dona fuissent.
quantos ille virum magnam Mavortis ad urbem
campus aget gemitus! vel quae, Tiberine, videbis
funera, cum tumulum praeterlabere recentem!
nec puer Iliaca quisquam de gente Latinos   875
in tantum spe tollet avos, nec Romula quondam
ullo se tantum tellus iactabit alumno.
heu pietas, heu prisca fides, invictaque bello
dextera! non illi se quisquam impune tulisset
obvius armato, seu cum pedes iret in hostem,   880
seu spumantis equi foderet calcaribus armos.
heu, miserande puer, si qua fata aspera rumpas!
tu Marcellus eris. manibus date lilia plenis,
purpureos spargam flores, animamque nepotis
his saltem accumulem donis, et fungar inani   885
munere.'

The Underworld journey is over. Anchises gives Aeneas some final advice. He and the Sibyl leave the underworld by the Gate of Ivory and return to Cumae, from where Aeneas continues his voyage.

   sic tota passim regione vagantur
aëris in campis latis atque omnia lustrant.
quae postquam Anchises natum per singula duxit,
incenditque animum famae venientis amore,
exim bella viro memorat quae deinde gerenda,   890
Laurentesque docet populos urbemque Latini,
et quo quemque modo fugiatque feratque laborem.
  Sunt geminae Somni portae, quarum altera fertur
cornea, qua veris facilis datur exitus umbris,
altera candenti perfecta nitens elephanto,   895
sed falsa ad caelum mittunt insomnia manes.
his ibi tum natum Anchises unaque Sibyllam
prosequitur dictis portaque emittit eburna.
ille viam secat ad naves sociosque revisit.
  Tum se ad Caietae recto fert litore portum.   900
ancora de prora iacitur. stant litore puppes.

Notes on the Text

Reading Virgil requires and rewards patience. But the difficulty does not lie in complex syntax, as it tends to do with prose authors. It lies (i) in the extensive vocabulary, (ii) in the adventurous word-order, and (iii) in the fact that Virgil pressed vocabulary and grammar to perform services which they could only just manage (see line 646 and note).

There are four indexes: (1) explanation of linguistic and literary terms, (2) names appearing in the text, (3) names and historical topics mentioned in the notes but not appearing in the text, (4) abbreviations.

These Notes often contain expressions of doubt – 'perhaps, 'probably' etc. In most instances, of course, the matter could have been discussed further. For those who would like to pursue individual points the modern editions available in English are those by Austin and Williams.

Asterisks refer to topics mentioned in the Indexes.

1. **fatur**: 'he speaks'. It is Aeneas who speaks. At the end of Book 5 the Trojans were sailing peacefully from Sicily towards Italy when Palinurus, the helmsman of Aeneas' ship, fell asleep and was lost overboard. The last words of Book 5 are spoken by Aeneas: *nudus in ignota, Palinure, iacebis harena*: 'You will lie naked, Palinurus, on an unknown strand.' Hence his tears (**lacrimans**).

   immittit habenas: 'flings out the reins'. The fleet is seen as a chariot with Aeneas as its rider, who slackens off the reins to allow the horses to set off at speed. The fleet has come to a halt, but now Aeneas sets it going again. *mitto* often means 'throw' (compare the English word 'missile').

   classi: loosely, 'for the fleet' (dative of 'reference'*).

2. **tandem**: 'finally', after all the anguish Aeneas has suffered in trying to reach Italy. (For this, see the summary of Books 1-5 in Intro. **5**.)

   Euboicis ... oris: (dat.) 'to the Euboean shores of Cumae'. Cumae, a city on the coast near Naples (see map), was founded by Greeks from the island of Euboea in about 750 BCE (see Intro. **6.i**). The adj. 'Euboean' is transferred* from 'Cumae' to 'the shores'. The dative ('dative of motion') means 'towards'; in prose the idea would normally be given by **ad** + the accusative.

adlabitur: of the smooth motion of the ships after the oarsmen cease to row and the sails are furled; the two elisions* in this line add to the effect.

3-4. As the ships approach the shore, the oarsmen stop rowing. They throw out the anchors from the bow. (Virgil leaves us to understand this.) The weight of the anchor slows the bow, thus the crew 'makes the ship swing round to face' the open sea (**obvertunt**) while still moving towards the shore. This puts the strain on the anchor cable so that the anchor hooks into the seabed and begins to hold (**fundabat**) the ship.

fundabat: the imperf. is used here, as often, to give the idea 'began to'. (See the note above.) The use is called 'inceptive'*.

4-5. **litora ... praetexunt puppes**: the shore is seen as a piece of cloth with the ships attached to it like a fringe. Some idea of the beautiful curved sterns of Roman galleys can be gained from the reliefs of Trajan's column.

There are three striking metaphors* in these first lines: the fleet seen as a chariot (**habenas**, line 1), the anchor seen as a biting animal (**dente**, line 3), and the shore with the ships seen as a tasselled fringe on cloth (**praetexunt**, line 5). Metaphorical language is not always so frequent or so striking and will not always receive comment, but it is an important part of Virgil's technique.

5. **emicat:** the simple verb *mico* means 'glitter'; *emico* gives the idea of the flashing reflections on the young men's armour as they come quickly ashore.

6. **Hesperium**: 'western'. Aeneas received his first instruction to travel 'to the Western land' from his wife Creusa at 2,781. Now finally he is reaching it.

pars ... pars: 'one part (of the band of young men) ... another part', i.e. 'some ... others'.

semina: 'seeds' regularly means also 'particles' – the atoms of the Epicurean world-view (see Intro. **6.iii.g**). Here it refers to sparks, which can be seen also as the 'seeds' from which grows a flame.

7-8. **densa**: 'Some plunder the woods, the impenetrable lairs of the beasts'. **silvas** and **tecta** are both object of **rapit**, in the sense 'plunder' rather than 'seize'. **silvas** simply explains what is meant by **ferarum tecta** and is said to be in 'apposition*' to it. The plunder consists of wood for fire or of the wild animals themselves.

9-11. **at pius Aeneas ... petit.** Take the sentence thus: **Aeneas arces** (*et*) **secreta Sibyllae petit.** 'Aeneas made for the citadel and the Sibyl's private place.' He was told to do this by Anchises in 5.731-6.

9. **at:** the word marks a strong transition to something different.

> **pius:** the word which is most regularly associated with Aeneas, indicating loyalty to family, country and gods. Here he shows himself **pius** in obeying the instructions given to him by his father's spirit.

> **arces:** perhaps singular for plural (tr. 'citadel'), or perhaps Virgil wants to remind us of the two citadels at Cumae, the higher with the temple of Zeus, the lower with the temple of Apollo.

> **altus:** Apollo is high perhaps because his temple is built on a hill or perhaps because his statue here actually was high – at least 5 metres according to Servius, who wrote a commentary on Virgil in the late fourth century CE.

10. **horrendae:** the word is a gerundive – 'deserving terror' – 'terrifying'. The Sibyl is so described because of her strange appearance when she is in a trance and because of the sense of the god's presence which surrounds her. Note the wide separation between adj. and noun, common in Virgil. Here it calls attention to the adj., creates suspense about what is to be the noun agreeing with it, and thus emphasises this first mention of the Sibyl.

> **procul:** 'at a distance, the dreadful Sibyl's separate place, a monstrous cave'. This is probably the long gallery which still survives, cut into the rock below the temple of Apollo and some 100 metres from it.

11. **cui:** refers back to the Sibyl, 'into whom the Delian prophet breathes a great spirit.'

12. **inspirat:** all the verbs so far have been in the present tense except *fundabat* (4: see note). They are almost all 'historic* presents', designed to make us focus on each event as it happens. But *praesidet, inspirat, aperit,* though present, are not quite the same, because these are not events happening as the story goes on. They are universally true, 'now' (for Virgil) as then.

> **vates:** Apollo is especially the prophet-god, most famously with his oracle at Delphi, but he had many other sacred places, and one of them was the island of Delos (hence **Delius**), where he was born.

futura: acc. n. pl. of the fut. part.: 'things which will be'.

13. **iam:** 'right now'. Virgil fixes this in our mind as the point which the story has reached while he goes into the digression which follows.

subeunt: now we see that Aeneas has some companions with him, one of whom is Achates* (34).

Triviae: *Trivia* ('she of the crossroads') is Apollo's sister Diana. Like many gods, Diana is called by different names when she is performing different functions. *Trivia* is appropriate for her when she is the goddess of witchcraft and the powers of the world below. The Sibyl is priestess to both Apollo and Diana / Trivia (35). In her capacity as Apollo's servant she delivers to Aeneas the prophecy recorded in 83-97; in her capacity as Diana's, she will later be his guide to the underworld.

lucos ... tecta: the 'golden roofs' belong to Apollo's temple, as appears from the following lines, where the Trojans appreciate the relief carving on the doors. But woods and temple are evidently common to both divinities.

14. **Daedalus** was the great craftsman of legend. Athenian by birth, he lived in Crete, but offended King Minos and was forced to flee. He made wings for himself and his son Icarus. The wax which held Icarus' wings together melted when he flew too near the sun; he fell into the sea and was lost. There were different stories of Daedalus' journey (see, e.g., March), but Virgil appears to have him going to Cumae (line 18) by a flight which took him either very high or far to the north. (**gelidas ad Arctos** can give either idea – see on 16.)

ut fama est: 'as the story goes'. Nothing in the book so far has prepared us for Daedalus. He is a new character and one out of a different story. Thus the first four words of this line mark a completely fresh start in a way which the actual first words of the book (*sic fatur lacrimans*) definitely do not. Virgil arouses our curiosity to see how Daedalus will be made relevant to Aeneas' story. The story of Daedalus and Icarus is told at length by Ovid (*Metamorphoses* 8.183-235).

15. **ausus se credere:** 'daring to entrust himself ...'.

16. **enavit:** 'swam' or 'floated'. This and the next three main verbs are all in the perfect tense. These past events are the background. When Virgil returns to description of the carvings which the Trojans are inspecting, he reverts to the historic present with *stat* in 22. He is there describing a scene which catches the attention of the Trojans.

gelidas ... ad Arctos: *Arcti* (Gk: 'the Bears') refers to the constellations, Great and Little Bear. The Great Bear suggests the North by its proximity to the Pole Star. 'Chilly' perhaps because high up, perhaps because it gets cooler as one goes north, as Naples is further north than Crete.

17. **Chalcidica:** Chalcis was one of the cities of Euboea. Cumae is 'Euboean' (see note on line 2).

 levis: translate 'lightly'; adj. for adv. as in, e.g., *laetus feci* – 'I did it gladly'.

 tandem: it had been a long and difficult journey.

18. **redditus ... terris:** 'restored to land here', as if by a guardian spirit.

 tibi: when an author addresses one of the characters in his own book, it is called apostrophe*. Daedalus offers his wings to Phoebus (Apollo) as those retiring from a trade often offered the tools of their trade.

19. **remigium alarum:** 'the rowing equipment of his wings'; better 'the wings with which he had rowed'. Note the two metaphors for flying: swimming (**enavit** 16) and rowing.

 posuit: 'placed there' – 'established'.

 templa: plur. for sing. This is common in poets. We are talking about one temple, as is clear from what follows.

20. **in foribus ...:** 'on the doors the death of Androgeos (is illustrated)'. Androgeos was the son of King Minos. He was killed on a visit to Athens. Minos punished the Athenians by demanding seven boys each year as an offering for the Minotaur, a monster with a human body and a bull's head, who lived in the Labyrinth, a maze specially constructed to contain it.

 There were various versions of this story (see March: 'Theseus').

 At several points in the *Aeneid* Vergil holds up the action to give a detailed description, usually of a natural scene or a work of art (1.159-69: a sheltered bay; 1.466-93: the doors of the temple at Carthage). Such description is called 'ecphrasis*'. It creates a pause in the action, and the description illustrates ideas relevant to the action. The relevance of the Daedalus scenes to the action of the *Aeneid* may be in calling our attention to this first overseas foundation in Italy, founded by an refugee in distress (**fugiens**, 14) like Aeneas, who is described in 1.2 as *fato profugus* – 'a refugee by destiny'.

20-1. tum ... natorum: 'Next (on the doors are depicted) the Athenians, ordered to pay as a penalty (dreadful thing!), seven bodies of their sons each year'. **Cecropidae** = the sons of Cecrops, i.e. the Athenians. Cecrops was the legendary founder-king of Athens.

22. corpora is in apposition* to **poenas**.

    stat ... urna: *sortes ducere* is 'to draw lots'. The lots evidently take the form of names written down somehow and put into an urn. The decision as to who shall go to Crete has already been made; the miserable Athenians are standing around, but our attention is focused on the urn which seems to have condemned them. Virgil does this by using the harsh monosyllable *stat* and by placing it harshly straight after the caesura* (see Intro. **7d**).

23. contra: on the other leaf of the double doors.

    elata mari: 'rising from the sea'. Virgil invites us to think how this looks both in reality and in the gold relief.

    respondet: 'corresponds'.

    Cnosia: 'from Cnossus'. Cnossus was the chief place of Crete, the site of the huge palace said to have belonged to Minos.

24. hic: in this line and in 27 means 'here (is)', referring to different places on the sculptured doors where the story is told in stages.

    crudelis ... tauri: Minos, seeking to prove his claim to the kingdom of Crete, prayed to Poseidon to send him something from the sea which he would then sacrifice. Poseidon sent a bull so fine that Minos would not sacrifice it. The god sent the bull wild and made Minos' wife Pasiphae fall in love with it. **crudelis** can be taken as nom. with **amor** – 'a cruel passion' (cruelty on the part of Poseidon) or as gen. with **tauri** – 'a savage bull'.

    suppostaque furto: Pasiphae was 'laid secretly beneath' the bull thanks to Daedalus, who constructed an artificial cow into which Pasiphae climbed and in this guise offered herself to the bull. **supposta** is a shortened form of *supposita*, nom. fem. sing. perf. part. of *suppono*.

25. mixtum ... biformis: 'a mixed family and a two-shaped offspring'. The first phrase refers to the parents, human and animal, the second to the Minotaur's appearance as man / bull.

26. inest: 'is contained', i.e. in the relief.

    Veneris: 'passion' represented as Venus the goddess of love (metonymy*).

    monimenta: nom., in apposition* to **Minotaurus**.

27. **labor ... domus:** 'the famous problem of the palace – the windings which could not be disentangled'. (For the Labyrinth, see on line 20.) **ille** here, as often, means 'that (well known) person / thing'.

   domus: note that the metre demands that *-us* is long and therefore gen. sing., and not nom. sing., where *-us* is short.

28. **reginae:** not so much 'queen' here 'as 'princess' (cf. 1.273). She is Ariadne, Minos' daughter. Theseus, son of King Aegeus of Athens, offered himself as one of the seven annual victims of the Minotaur. When he arrived in Crete, Ariadne fell in love with him, and persuaded Daedalus to show him a way of escaping from the Labyrinth – a ball of wool which he unwound as he went along and could rewind on his return.

   miseratus: 'taking pity on'.

   Note **magnum**, widely separated from **amorem**. The two first words of the line carry emphasis, as they are Daedalus' reasons: she was after all a princess, and so very much in love. Daedalus is given the hint of a character: a fond old man.

29. **ipse:** emphasised because it was Daedalus who had made the puzzle in the first place.

   dolos ... ambagesque: lit. 'the tricks and winding ways', but translate it e.g. 'the tricky winding ways' (hendiadys*).

   resolvit: it isn't clear whether the tense is perfect, in which case we are simply being given background information, or present. If present, we should think of Daedalus as visible in the sculptured relief, presiding in some way over the thread-trick.

30. **caeca:** grammatically going with *vestigia* but referring to Theseus. 'Unseeing' is used both because of the darkness and because of Theseus' ignorance.

   tu: the apostrophe* (see 18) emphasises the pathos* of Icarus' fate: a father brings about the death of his own son. If Augustus is in Virgil's mind here (see on 31), he may be thinking of Augustus' loss of his son Marcellus, the theme of lines 863-86.

31. **opere:** the 'work' is the relief sculpture on the gates.

   sineret dolor: it is as if Virgil had simply left out the word 'if' in 'if your grief had permitted you'. English idiom permits this omission of 'if': 'did but his grief allow'. The imperf. subj. is commonly used to imagine possibilities for the present ('would *now* be').

There is an empty space on the doors where there might have been an illustration of the fate of Icarus. Thus Daedalus comes to the successful end of an epic journey – but is overwhelmed by grief at the loss which he has caused and suffered on the way. Thus Aeneas comes to the successful end of an epic journey – and he too has to face his grief at the damage he has caused and suffered on the way, the death of Dido being so far the most obvious instance. Thus too Augustus, Aeneas' heir and successor (see Intro. **4a**), completes the task of rebuilding the Roman nation, but has to face the death and destruction he has caused in achieving it.

32. **bis:** the word used at the beginning of two successive sentences connects the sentences (anaphora*) and adds pathos*.

33. **cecidere:** short form of *ceciderunt*, 3rd pl. perf. indic. *cado*. This abbreviation is found very frequently; it is useful for the metre.

> **quin** here means not much more than 'in fact'.
>
> **omnia:** this word, normally of three syllables, here has two ('synizesis'*). The 'i' sounds as a 'y'.

34. **perlegerent:** only now are we told that the Trojans were looking at these sculptures of Daedalus'. One might have expected *perlegissent*, giving the idea of 'would have ...'; Virgil's intention is no doubt to make the ideas more vivid by talking about them as if they were present: 'they would be reading them right through'.

> **iam**: with **praemissus**.

35. **una:** 'together (with Achates)'.

36. **Deiphobe Glauci:** 'Deiphobe, daughter of Glaucus'. Glaucus is appropriate as a father for the Sibyl: he is a sea-god with prophetic powers, whose home is opposite Chalcis (see on 17). Note the scansion **Dēïphŏbē**.

> **quae**, referring to the Sibyl, is subj. of **fatur**.
>
> **regi :** the king is Aeneas.

37. **non hoc ... poscit:** 'this time does not demand that (sort of) sightseeing for itself', i.e. 'this is no time for you to be hanging around staring at things like that'. The Sibyl is abrupt, almost schoolmistressly. Her impatience is shown in the two monosyllables **non hoc**, and by the separation of **hoc** from **tempus** and **ista** from **spectacula**.

> **ista:** possessive pronoun of the 2nd person, i.e. 'that (of yours)'; it often carries with it a reproachful overtone.

38. **intacto:** 'untouched' by the yoke.

39: **praestiterit:** perf. subj. The form is regularly used to make a polite suggestion – 'it would really be better'. The Sibyl is more friendly, since she has now got their attention – unless this is the sarcastic politeness of the sergeant-major. Either way, she is an impressive, commanding character.

de more: take closely with **lectas**: 'chosen according to established custom'.

bidentes: *bidens* is used for a sheep old enough to have lost its two front milk teeth and grown two large adult teeth in their place, giving the impression that it only has two teeth anyway. The word establishes the youth of the sheep as **intacto** does that of the bullocks.

40. **talibus:** understand *verbis*.

morantur: 'hesitate (to obey)'.

41. **Teucros:** *Teucri* is another word for 'Trojans'.

42. **excisum:** understand *excisum est*, perf. pass. 'A side of the Euboean cliff has been carved out into a huge cavern.' For 'Euboean' see on line 2. **ingens** could go with **latus** or with **antrum**; perhaps better with **antrum**.

43. **quo:** 'whither', 'to which'.

centum: 'a hundred', vaguely for 'a very large number', the idea of its largeness increased by the repetition. For the present appearance of the Sibyl's cave, see Intro. **6.i.c**. There are six openings – but to one standing in the cave it seems a large number, and Virgil capitalises on this.

44. **responsa:** 'answers' to the questions and requests put to the Sibyl by the worshippers at the shrine.

45-6. **ventum erat:** impersonal passive* ('it had been arrived'), indicating that something has been done, with only the context to indicate who has done it. We have to translate 'they had arrived ...'; French manages better with *on était arrivé*.

poscere ... tempus: understand *est*: 'it is time to demand ...'.

fata: the word is connected with *for fari* 'say', and means literally 'utterances', then 'utterances of a god', 'oracles', then 'the destined future', 'fate' as conveyed by the oracle.

46-8. **deus ecce deus:** more like an inarticulate cry than a sentence; it contains the terror and the joy which the Sibyl feels as the god draws near.

cui talia fanti ...: 'And in her, as she spoke these words (standing) before the doors' (see on *ora* in 53) '(there was) no single expression, no single colour, nor did her hair stay in place'. **cui:** When it begins a sentence, the relative pronoun can be translated as 'and (she)'; it is called the 'connecting* relative'. The dative here is 'reference'*.

The repetition of **non**, connecting the three phrases, is called 'anaphora'*; it asks us to see very clearly how *nothing* remained the same.

48. **mansere:** short form of *manserunt* (see on 33).

    pectus anhelum (*est*).

49. **corda:** plural form, singular meaning.

    fera: *ferus* refers to wild animals, those which humans <u>cannot</u> <u>control</u>. So 'Her heart, now out of control, swells with madness'. Her heart beats impossibly fast and she feels a crushing pressure within her chest, no doubt as the god's words begin to force their way out.

    Note that the second syllable of **fera** must be short, so that the word must agree with **corda**.

    maiorque videri (*est*): 'she is greater to look upon'. The infin. <u>explains how</u> the Sibyl is 'greater'; the usage is called 'explanatory' or 'epexegetic' (cf. 165).

50-1. **nec mortale sonans:** *mortale* is acc. sing. n. – 'adverbial accusative'*. Translate 'and sounding inhumanly'. Presumably we think of the Sibyl speaking louder and more penetratingly than usual in what she says in 51-3.

    adflata est ...: take **quando** first – 'since she was inspired by the spirit of the god, even now drawing near'.

51. **cessas in vota:** lit. 'are you dawdling towards your prayers', a slightly odd expression for 'why are you being slow to get down to prayer?'

    vota precesque: *preces* are the prayers you make to a god requesting a service; *votum* is the promise you make to him on the assumption that he will do it.

52. **cessas:** the repetition indicates a slightly indignant reproach on the part of the Sibyl. **Tros ... Aenea** (both voc.) explains the reproach. The idea is 'being, as you are, a Trojan and none other than Aeneas, you should know better'.

    neque ... ante: i.e. not before Aeneas says a prayer. **ante** is adv.

53. **attonitae ... domus** (genitive – the subject is **ora**): the Sibyl's house
is the cave (42). It is personified here: it has 'mouths' and it is
'dumbstruck' (**attonitae**). The Sibyl is standing in front of the
doors (47). By 77 she is 'in the cave'. Presumably she goes into the
cave after she 'falls silent' in 54. The doors mentioned in 47 (**fores**)
are not the same as the **ostia**, or **ora**, which open (52, 81) when the
Sibyl speaks in answer to Aeneas' prayer. A touch of magic is
added by the fact that when Aeneas is speaking, he addresses not
the Sibyl, but the *domus*, which lies in front of him like a living
impersonation of the god, its mouth ready to open in answer.

 fata: this is nom. fem. sing. of the perf. part. of *for* (= 'I speak'),
and refers to the Sibyl; **talia** is acc. n. pl., direct object of **fata**.

54-5. **Teucris:** dative of reference*: 'for the Trojans, a chill shudder
passed right through their bones'.

 gelidus ... dura: notice that these adjectives are both separated
from their nouns, **gelidus** by a long way. The separation
concentrates our attention on the adjectives. The shivering shakes
even the hard, rigid bones; the chilling effect goes deep down
inside. **imo** is also stressed, coming at the end of the line.

56. Aeneas adopts a traditional form of prayer, in which the god's
favours (here three of them) are first listed as a justification for
whatever new request the person praying makes.

 miserate: vocative of the perf. part., agreeing with **Phoebe**.
This grand language is almost impossible to translate into modern
English. C.H. Sisson (Everyman) tries. 'Phoebus, you whom the
heavy griefs of Troy have ever moved to pity ...', but it seems
clumsy. The sixteenth-century language of the *Book of Common
Prayer* is equal to it. 'O Lord our heavenly Father, ... who dost
from thy throne behold all the dwellers upon earth ....' but West
(Penguin) is wiser simply to translate **miserate** as if it were a main
verb. 'Phoebus Apollo, you have always pitied the cruel sufferings
of the Trojans.'

 Apollo was the most important of the three Olympian gods who
constantly supported the Trojans in the *Iliad*.

57-8. **Dardana ... Aeacidae:** 'You who guided the Dardanian weapons
of Paris and (his) hands against the body of Aeacus' descendant'.
Dardana agrees with **tela** but should be thought of as going with
Paridis (transferred epithet*). **tela manusque** come in the opposite
order to that which one might expect: first the aiming hand and

then the flying arrow. Putting ideas thus 'the wrong way round' is called 'hysteron proteron'*. The effect here is that we see the arrow strike and only then think of the hand which sent it.

derexti: short form of *derexisti*.

corpus in Aeacidae: *Aeacides* is a Greek word with the common termination *-ides* = 'descendant of'. The reference is to Achilles, greatest of the Greek heroes, grandson of Aeacus king of Aegina. Achilles was killed almost at the end of the Trojan war, shot by Paris in the heel according to the legend, since he was elsewhere invulnerable. Note that neither Homer nor Virgil makes use of this invulnerability of Achilles, presumably because it would detract from his humanity.

58. **magnas ... terras: terras** is the object of **obeuntia,** which agrees with **maria**. 'I have entered upon so many seas which touch huge territories'. 'So many seas': there are some eight different named seas traversed by Aeneas. (For his journey from Troy, see the summary of *Aeneid* 1 and 3 in Intro. **5**). But 'huge territories' seems to refer only to Africa, which is in any case the most outlandish and intimidating of the places Aeneas has visited.

duce te: 'with you as leader' 'under your leadership' – ablative absolute. (One normally expects a participle in abl. abs. – 'with you *being* leader' – but there is no pres. part. of *sum*.) Aeneas has on four recorded occasions received instructions and advice from Apollo: at Delos from Apollo himself, in Crete through the Penates, later through the Harpy queen and then through Helenus, all in Book 3 (Intro. **5**).

59-60. **Massylum:** gen. pl. (old form, frequent in verse). The 'y' is scanned* long. The Massyli were a group of African tribes. According to Virgil here, they are **penitus repostas** 'set deep in the fastnesses (of Africa)'. **gentes** is another object of **intravi.**

repostae: from *repostus*, short form of the perf. part. of *repono* (cf. *supposta* 24).

praetenta ... arva: 'territory stretched before the Syrtes'. 'Syrtes' refers to the huge bay in the centre of the coastline of North Africa. Africa is dangerous both for the shallow seas off its coast and the fierce tribes of its hinterland.

61. **Italiae ... oras:** lit. 'we are grasping the shores of Italy as they run away'. Aeneas' experience has been that whenever he thinks he is reaching Italy (as he very nearly did at the beginning of Book 1),

he finds that he has still further to go. It is as if Italy was a prey always on the point of escaping the hunter's grasp. (See Book 1, Intro. **5**.)

62. **hac ... tenus:** these two words are often written as one and should be taken together here: 'as far as here (and no further)'.

 fuerit: perfect subjunctive; take it closely with **secuta** as a tense of *sequor*. Lit. 'let the ill-luck of Troy have followed us thus far'. The subjunctive is jussive*.

63. **vos** is accusative, subject of **parcere**, in the acc. and infin. expression following **fas est.** *parco* requires the dative (**genti**) after it. 'It is right that you spare the people of Troy.'

64. In high poetic style, where -**que** follows two successive words, it very often means 'both ... and'. (See too 113 and 116.)

65-8. **Dardaniae:** Dardania is the land of Troy, named after Dardanus, ancestor of the Trojan kings. But Virgil wants to remind us of the legend that Dardanus himself came originally from Italy, becoming the founder-king of Troy (see 650) when he married the daughter of Teucer, then ruler of the land (see in March). Thus Aeneas' journey to Italy is a return to the family home. The Trojans are sometimes called 'sons of Dardanus' – *Dardanidae*.

 tuque ... da ... considere: 'And you, prophetess, (please) grant that the Trojans may settle ...'. **tu** is at the beginning to mark the change from the others whom Aeneas has been addressing, Phoebus and 'all the gods and goddesses'. The priestess thus, in this company, acquires almost the status of a goddess, and so can be asked to grant a god's favour. **Teucros ... considere** is accusative and infinitive.

66. **praescia venturi: venturi** is gen. sing. n.: 'that which will come' i.e. 'the future'. So 'with foreknowledge of the future', 'prophetic'.

67. **regna:** plural for singular 'a kingdom'. **non indebita:** lit. 'not un-owed to my destiny'. The double negative makes a strong positive: '... a kingdom which is only my destiny's rightful due'.

68. **errantes ... agitata:** The gods are the Penates (household spirits) of Troy. Aeneas rescued them from Troy in Book 2. They are 'wandering' and 'harassed' because they have been with Aeneas, chased around the world by the fury of Juno. The two phrases **errantes deos** and **agitata numina** repeat the same idea in different words to add emphasis and intensity (theme and variation*).

69. **templum:** Virgil's readers will think of the great temple to Apollo on the Palatine Hill in Rome, built by Augustus and dedicated in 28 BC, just as Virgil was beginning the Aeneid. There was a statue of Diana alongside Apollo outside the temple. 'Solid' marble is especially splendid: many temples had pillars of brick faced with plaster decorated as marble.

70. **instituam:** 'I will set up'. He has made his prayer (62, and 66-8), now he makes his vow (cf. 51) He cannot fulfil this vow, because he himself will never settle in Rome. He does not yet know it, but it will be fulfilled by Augustus, the second Aeneas.

    festos dies: the 'games of Apollo' (*Ludi Apollinares*), a nine-day festival of theatre, wild-beast hunts and horse-racing, were established in 212 BC. **de:** 'called after'.

71. **te ... manent:** 'a shrine waits for you', i.e. 'you will have a shrine'. Aeneas is addressing the Sibyl again. **nostris:** 'my kingdom': Aeneas here (and in **meae** (73)) proudly assumes that his prayer (66-8) will be granted.

72. **hic:** 'here', i.e. in the shrine. **namque:** translate this first in the sentence. 'For here I will lay the prophecies and the secret destinies delivered to my people'. Prophecies attributed to the Sibyl were collected in books, stored in Rome, and consulted on urgent matters by a specially chosen group of fifteen nobles (*quindecimviri*). The legend was that the books had been brought to Rome by the Sibyl and offered for sale to King Tarquin the Proud. (For the story, see March under 'Sibyl'.) They were originally kept in the basement of the temple of Jupiter on the Capitol. This was burned down in 83 BC. Later a new collection was made, which Augustus moved to his temple of Apollo. The natural interpretation of **magna penetralia** is that it is different from the temple itself; if so, the 'shrine' is perhaps the cabinet at the foot of the statue of Apollo where the books were stored (Suetonius, *Augustus* 31.1).

73-4. **lectos ... viros:** the 'chosen men' are the *quindecimviri* (see above).

    alma: 'kindly', 'giver of blessing': it is a word appropriate to a goddess. Aeneas has been treating the Sibyl almost as a goddess in the requests he makes of her (see on 65).

74-5. 'But please do not commit your songs to leaves, in case they may be muddled and fly around, playthings for the greedy winds.' It is surprising that she might be expected to do this. Aeneas was given his instruction to approach the Sibyl by Helenus in Book 3.441-52.

Helenus warned him that the Sibyl was liable to write her prophecies down on (palm-)leaves and leave them in order at first, but then to take no trouble to keep them so or to stop them being blown about. Such heedlessness does not seem in character for the powerful Sibyl of Book 6. Virgil is perhaps showing his appreciation of Augustus' reorganisation and relocation of the Sibylline prophecies (see note on 72).

ne ... manda: 'do not commit'; *ne* + imperative is more common in verse than *noli* + *infin.* The following **ne ... volent** is an ordinary purpose clause.

76. **ipsa ... oro:** 'I beg you to prophesy yourself'. Think of this as an abbreviated version of *oro ut canas* (indirect command), or as effectively two separate sentences *oro* 'I beg', and *canas* 'may you prophesy' (jussive* subjunctive).

finem ... loquendi: 'he made an end of speaking'. **loquendi** is genitive of the gerund.

ore: 'with his mouth' – 'aloud'.

77-80. These lines describe the Sibyl as she goes into her prophetic trance. The god Phoebus is taking possession of her. As he moulds and crushes her both physically and mentally, it is a painful experience; so painful in fact that she instinctively tries to escape. The sight and sound of her struggles is frightening.

77. **Phoebi ... patiens:** 'not yet tolerant of Phoebus': i.e. not yet willing to let him take control. Once he has established control, her own personality will be subordinated and she will calm down once more.

immanis: 'frightful' because weird and inexplicable to ordinary people, 'huge' because the presence of the god has already made her seem larger (49). **immanis** can bear both meanings. Easiest to translate as an adverb, perhaps 'terrifyingly'.

78. **bacchatur:** the word refers in origin to the ecstatic revelling of the followers of Bacchus. It is then used for the wild behaviour caused by the influence of any god.

si: here giving an idea of purpose: 'in case she may be able to ...'. But it also hints at the Sibyl's own wish 'if only I could ...'.

79. **excussisse:** perf. infin.: 'if only she could have shaken off the god' i.e. got the matter finished. Perhaps 'if only she could succeed in shaking ...'. Note also the three double s's in two successive words: the Sibyl gasps for breath (onomatopoeia*).

tanto magis: 'so much the more', 'all the more'.

79-80. **fatigat ... domans:** take these two together, with both **os** and **corda** as objects: 'he wears down and tames her wild features and her uncontrolled heart', though English may prefer 'he wears her down, taming her wild features ...'. Note the alliteration* in the three phrases beginning with f.

80. **fingit:** 'forms': the word is used of horse-training, and picks up the same general idea as **domans**.

   premendo: abl. of the gerund, 'by crushing'. It is a violent process.

81. **ostia:** the openings referred to in 43.

   patuere: short form of *patuerunt*. Note the switch to the perfect tense: 'suddenly they swung open'.

83. **defuncte:** voc. of the perf. part. The same sort of translation problem as in 56. Perhaps 'You have come to the end of the great dangers of the sea'. *defungor* takes the abl. (**periclis**) of what one has come to the end of.

84. **terrae:** genitive, like **pelagi**. 'Those of the land are worse.'

   in regna Lavini: 'to the kingdom of Lavinium' (**regna** is pl. for sing.). Lavinium is the city founded by Aeneas and named after his wife Lavinia, daughter of King Latinus (see Intro. **5**, Book 7). **Lavini** is a gen. of definition*, not usual in this sort of expression.

85. **Dardanidae:** see on 64. **mitte:** 'dismiss'.

86. **sed ... volent:** 'but they will actually (**et**) wish not to have arrived'.

87. **Thybrim** (acc.): *Thybris* is the Greek name for the Tiber: the Sibyl speaks as a Greek prophetess.

   multo: one may find 'much' a rather flat translation (though think of Wilfred Owen: 'Then, when much blood had clogged their chariot wheels ...'). Perhaps 'foaming high with blood' or 'with torrents of blood' (West).

88-90. **non Simois ... dea:** Simois and Xanthus are the rivers of Troy. 'Doric' here means 'Greek' (rather as 'English' has sometimes been used for 'British'). The Sibyl is saying that the war in Latium will be a re-run of the Trojan war. 'You will not lack the Simois, the Xanthus or the Greek camp' i.e. 'You will find that they were there again after all' ('after all' suggested by the future perfect **defuerint**: Aeneas is thought of as looking back on the events after them). The two Trojan rivers have their parallels in the Tiber and the Numicus of Latium*, the Greek camp in the army of Turnus, and Achilles in Turnus himself (see below). See the summary of Books 7-12 (Intro. **5**).

alius ... Achilles: 'another Achilles has been born in Latium', i.e. Turnus. For the story of Turnus' rejection and fury, see the summary of Book 7 (Intro. **5**).

Latio: 'in Latium': ablative without preposition; rare in prose, common in verse.

natus ... dea: 'he too born of a goddess'. **dea** abl. The idea is 'born <u>from</u> a goddess'. Turnus' goddess-mother is the nymph Venilia.

90-91. **nec ... aberit:** lit. 'nor will Juno, added to the Trojans (as an extra enemy) be absent (from them) anywhere'. Or 'There will be Juno too. She will not leave the Trojans anywhere.'

cum tu ... urbes: 'While you – what nations of the Italians and what cities will you not beseech as a suppliant in time of need?' **supplex** refers to one who throws himself on someone else's mercy. **in rebus egenis:** literally 'in needy circumstances', hence 'in time of need'. Perhaps translate 'While as for you – what nation or what city of all Italy will you pass without casting yourself on its mercy in your need?'

In Book 8, Aeneas leaves his companions, going on a mission to seek help from various sources (Intro. **5**, Book 8). Juno on the other hand never ceases to harass them. The contrast is made by the words **cum tu**, where **tu** is heavily stressed.

oraveris: fut. perf.; cf. on 88-90.

93. **causa mali tanti:** understand *erit*.

coniunx ... hospita: the 'foreign bride' is Lavinia (Intro. **5**, Book 7), whom Aeneas takes from Turnus as Paris once took Helen from Menelaus (Intro. **5**, para. 1). **externi ... thalami** (94) repeats the idea as theme and variation*.

94. The line is incomplete, as is 835. There are about 50 incomplete lines in the *Aeneid*. It has been suggested that these lines were deliberately left as part-lines. But the ancient tradition was that, when Virgil died, he thought the *Aeneid* still needed three years' work in revision, and it is much more likely that part of the revision would have been the completion of these lines.

95. **tu** is heavily stressed at the beginning of the line, marking the transition from background information to serious instruction.

ne cede: 'do not give in', like *ne manda* in 74.

contra ito: take the words together as from a verb *contra ire* 'go out to face'. *ito* is an old fashioned and solemn imperative; the normal form is *i*.

96-7. 'The road to safety will be revealed first from a Greek city – (a thing) which you hardly expect'. **reris** is 2nd sing. pres. indic. of *reor*. The antecedent* of **quod** is the whole sentence **via salutis Graia pandetur ab urbe**.

prima agrees with **via**, but should be taken as an adverb with **pandetur.**

Graia ab urbe: the 'Greek city' is Pallanteum, on the site of the future Rome. It was ruled by Evander, a Greek from Arcadia. It is one of the places visited by Aeneas in his quest for support (see on 92, and, for what happened at Pallanteum and after, Intro. **5**, Books 8 and 10).

99. **ambages:** all this is unintelligible to Aeneas, of course, especially the *coniunx hospita* (93).

100. **ea frena:** 'These reins Apollo shakes over (her) as she raves ...', i.e. 'This is the way Apollo controls her': by turning her raving into half-intelligible words. Virgil concludes the Sibyl's words by returning to the same idea with which he introduced them in 77-80: a rider controlling a wild horse. This use of similar ideas to frame a central piece is a feature of literary style; it is called 'ring composition'*.

102. **quierunt:** shortened form of *quieverunt*, perf. of *quiesco*.

rabida ora: her wild speech.

103-4. **non ulla ... surgit:** take it **non ulla facies laborum surgit mi nova inopinave:** 'No form of trouble rises before me new or unexpected'. The Sibyl could not predict anything which Aeneas had not suffered already or had not prepared himself to suffer in the future – as he explains in the next line.

virgo: the respectful tone of the word is perhaps represented by 'mother' as addressed to a nun, even if that is not necessarily an apt translation.

mi: shortened form of *mihi.*

105. **animo mecum:** 'in my mind, by myself'. Aeneas is seen as an isolated figure, wrestling with problems all on his own – (cf. 158, 185)

107. **dicitur:** understand *esse.*

inferni ianua regis: 'the gateway of the king (who lives) below'.

tenebrosa ... refuso: the 'gloomy swamp where Acheron overflows', if it is the same place as the 'gateway', is the lake of Avernus. There was also a lagoon called the Acherusian Swamp on the coast just south of Cumae (see the map on p. 22). Virgil seems to conflate them.

108-9. **ire ... contingat.** *contingit* (impersonal) is used of good things happening, and the subjunctive expresses a wish: 'may it be my good fortune to go'.

doceas: this goes with **oro** (106) in Indirect Command like *ipsa canas oro* (76). 'Please explain ....'

110. **illum:** strongly emphasised by being placed at the beginning of the line and next to **ego**; **ille** at the beginning of the next sentence (112) reinforces the emphasis (anaphora*). There is in fact a careful double anaphora: **illum ego** (object then subject) picked up by **ille meum** (subject then object). The scene of Aeneas carrying Anchises on his shoulders away from Troy is one of the most famous in ancient art; the story establishes Aeneas' *pietas* (Intro. **4b**).

113. **omnes ... minas:** as told in Book 3 (Intro. **5**).

ferebat: the imperf. gives a slightly different sense from the perf., which would simply comment on the fact that Anchises was present throughout. The imperf. suggests that he gladly bore the burden and contributed to the outcome: perhaps translate 'persisted in bearing ...'.

114. **vires ... senectae:** 'beyond his strength and the condition of old age', effectively 'beyond an old man's strength' (hendiadys*). West gives 'finding a strength beyond his years'.

115-16. **quin ... idem ... mandata dabat:** 'In fact he, the same person, used to give commands ...'. **idem** can be translated as 'he also' to give emphasis to this second point about Anchises. The imperf. **dabat** suggests that he kept on doing so, although Virgil mentions only one occasion, in Book 5 (Intro. **5**).

116-17. **alma:** see on 74.

miserere: imperative of *misereor*. **nati** and **patris** are gen. depending on it.

potes: understand *facere*.

118. **Hecate**, like *Trivia* (35), is a name given to Diana when she is seen as the goddess of the dark powers and the world below.

lucis ... Avernis: The woods and the lake of Avernus (**Avernis** is adj.) lie in a volcanic crater some two miles east of the Sibyl's temple. Some of the forest which surrounded it survives even today, though most was cut down in Virgil's time.

119-23. Aeneas, speaking the standard language of prayer (reference to favours done by a god in the past to justify a claim that he should do so again in the present), gives four instances of previous visits to the underworld. They were made by (i) **Orpheus**. He was a legendary Thracian singer who went to the underworld to recover his wife Eurydice, killed by a snake. He charmed Hades by his singing, and was permitted to take his wife back – provided he did not turn round to look at her on the way. At the last minute, he did so and lost her. (ii) **Pollux**. Castor and Pollux were twin sons of Jupiter*. Castor was mortal, Pollux immortal. As Castor lay dying after a battle, Pollux prayed that his immortality might be shared between them. So Pollux makes his daily journey to and from the underworld, and Castor does so too, in the opposite direction. (iii) **Theseus**. His friend Pirithous was determined to have as his bride Persephone, the wife of Hades. Theseus accompanied him on the downward journey. On arrival they were greeted by Hades and invited to sit – in seats from which it was impossible to stand up. They remained there till they were rescued by (iv) **Hercules** (here called **Alcides**), also a son of Jupiter. As the last of the tasks he performed for Eurystheus, Hercules was told to go down to Hades and kidnap the three-headed dog Cerberus. While in the world below, Hercules (according to one version) rescued Theseus but not Pirithous. Virgil mentions Orpheus and Pollux because they are both examples of the loyalty (*pietas*) which brings Aeneas himself to make the journey. He mentions Theseus and Hercules as great heroes who are also, as Aeneas is, descended from great gods, Hercules from Jupiter and Theseus from Neptune.

119. **si potuit:** the thought is 'take pity *on me as is only fair:* if Orpheus and Pollux were able to make the descent, why can't I?'

119-20. **Orpheus ... cithara:** 'Orpheus, relying on his Thracian lyre' (**fretus** 'relying on' takes the abl.)

    fidibus: from *fides fidium* pl.: 'the strings of an instrument'.

    'the strings and the lyre' is hendiadys* for 'the strings of the lyre'.

121. **alterna morte:** 'by alternating death' i.e. by each being dead on alternate days; see on 119-23 above.

122. **itque reditque viam:** 'and passes back and forth along the way'. **viam** is internal acc*.

122-3. **quid ... memorem:** 'why should I mention?' **memorem** is pres. subj. of *memoro* – 'deliberative' subjunctive. Both **Thesea** and **Alciden** are Greek accusatives, objects of **memorem**.

123. **Alciden:** Alcides means 'descendant of Alcaeus'. Alcaeus was Hercules' grandfather. It is impossible to fit the name 'Hercules' into hexameter* verse.

    mi: possessive dative*. 'To me also (there is) descent from Jupiter*', 'I also have a family (descended) from Jupiter on high'.

    ab Iove summo: Venus, Aeneas' mother, was daughter of Jupiter. On his father's side, his distant ancestor Dardanus* was son of Jupiter.

124. **orabat ... tenebat:** the imperfects suggest that, while he was speaking, the Sibyl cut in on his last words. **aras:** imagine an altar in front of the entrance to the Sibyl's cave, as if the cave were a temple. Those who pray touch the altar in token of the urgency of their prayers.

125. **orsa:** understand *est.*

    sate: voc. of the perf. part. *satus* (from *sero* (2)). Cf. 56 and 83.

    divum: genitive plural of *deus.*

126. **Tros Anchisiade:** voc. Aeneas is not named, but referred to by those whom he represents: his people (**Tros**) and his family ('son of Anchises'). The combination gives a tone of epic grandeur.

    facilis ... Averno: understand *est.* Avernus here is either (a) the lake near Cumae by which one reaches the underworld, or (b) the underworld itself. If (a), translate 'the way down from Avernus is easy' – *Averno* is ablative; if (b), 'the way down to Avernus is easy' – *Averno* is dative. A dative indicating movement towards somewhere is rare after a noun but not impossible. The current weight of opinion favours 'to Avernus'. But *Avernus* as noun or adj. are always used in Book 6 to refer to the place in the upper world, and this may encourage 'from Avernus'.

127. **noctes atque dies:** 'by night and day'. The acc. of time 'how long' is a little surprising, but perhaps the idea is 'for all time, both night and day'.

    Ditis: *Dis,* gen, *Ditis* is a Roman name for the god of the underworld. The name is used four times in Book 6; the only other name used for the god is another Roman one, *Orcus*. 'Hades' and 'Pluto', Greek names, are not used at all.

129-30. **revocare**: the infin. goes with **opus** and **labor** ('this is the task, this the labour: to retrace one's step ...'). **labor** is not mere repetition of the idea in **opus**. **opus** means 'the task', 'what one has to do'. **labor** is more exacting, more heroic. It reminds us of Hercules' labours: Aeneas will, in performing his task, be achieving something worthy of Hercules. **hoc:** the 'o' is short, but the syllable must be long (Intro. **7b**). Latin grammarians pointed out that the word should be pronounced (and originally was spelled) *hocc*.

  pauci ... potuere (= *potuerunt*): 'A few have succeeded, whom (even) impartial Jupiter has loved or who have been carried up to heaven by their own blazing excellence – sons of gods.' **aequus** = 'fair, impartial'. The 'few' prove their excellence by the fact that Jupiter, who normally shows no favour, loved them. The ones whose excellence carried them up to heaven were Pollux and Hercules (121, 123), who became gods. **dis geniti:** 'born of gods' (for the abl. see on 90): divine descent is necessary for permission to make the journey – but Aeneas has already emphasised his divine descent (123).

131. **tenent ...:** 'forests hold everything in the middle (of the underworld)' or 'forests hold everything between (here and the underworld)'.

132. **Cocytus:** the 'y' is scanned* long. One of the seven waters of the underworld whose names can be memorised in the hexameter *Styx Acheron Phlegethon Lethe Cocytus Avernus*. Cocytus is 'the River of Lamentation'. Perhaps Virgil intends something sinister in its movement: *sinus* can be used of the winding of a snake (*OLD* 10b) and *labor* of a snake's motion (*OLD* 1c).

133. **quod si:** 'but if'. **menti:** possessive dative*. 'If in your mind there is such passion, such eagerness.' **tantus amor, tanta cupido** simply emphasise each other as a repeated idea. Perhaps 'such intense passion'.

134. **innare** is transitive* here, like 'to swim the Channel'. Literally 'to swim in', it is also used of boats 'to float on'; only here of a passenger in a boat. Aeneas must cross the river Styx in the boat of the ferryman Charon (295-416). **bis** 'twice' because he will have to do so again after his death. (Some see in **bis** a reference to Aeneas returning over the Styx after his visit to the underworld on this

occasion. But this is not an easy way of understanding the account given by Virgil in lines 893-8, on which see Intro. **6.v.**)

Stygios lacus: 'the Stygian waters', but they are described as *palus* 'a marsh' in line 323, so perhaps one is meant to think of them as stagnant. We are used to confined rivers smoothly flowing along a defined channel. The Styx is like an unregulated river, intermittently marsh and lake – indeed like Virgil's home river the Mincius (*Georgic* 3.15).

135. **Tartara**: Tartarus is the deepest dungeon in Hades. The horrors there are described in lines 548-627. Virgil regularly uses a neuter plural form for it, as here.

    videre: in fact Aeneas does not 'see' Tartarus. He is not allowed to (563). The Sibyl is putting Aeneas' plan in such a way as to make it look outrageous, as she immediately goes on to suggest by her words **insano ... labori**: ('it gives (you) pleasure to give way to a wild and foolish undertaking'). She is being sarcastic about Aeneas' motives (cf. line 37), especially in the words **iuvat** and **indulgere**. (The oxymoron* might be illustrated thus: 'You are giving yourself trouble as a treat.') She does not encourage him, because the initiative must come all from Aeneas himself.

136. **accipe ... prius**: 'hear what things (are) first to-be-done'. The understood verb may be *sunt* (relative clause) or *sint* (indirect question).

    latet ... ramus: 'There is a branch hidden on a dark tree, golden both in its leaves and in its bending stem.' The ablatives **foliis** and **vimine** go closely with the adjective **aureus**.

    The Golden Bough is found nowhere else in classical literature: it seems to be Virgil's own invention. There has been a great deal of speculation about Virgil's source for the idea, of which our first record is a comment by the first-century CE freedman Cornutus: 'Poetic licence.' David West offers the following interpretation. (i) Why a branch? It is a token to offer to Proserpina*, entitling the bearer to safe passage in the underworld. Such a branch (not golden) was carried by those who were initiated into the mystery rites of Proserpina at Eleusis near Athens. Augustus was a member of this cult. The branch here alludes to the cult of Proserpina and is an oblique compliment to Augustus. (ii) Why is the branch golden? There was a literary anthology current in the first century BCE called *The Garland*. Each of the poets in the collection was represented in the introduction by a floral element as part of the 'Garland'. The philosopher Plato* was represented (for his poetry) by a golden bough. In the tenth book of Plato's *Republic* the story is told of the man Er who died and subsequently returned to life, having seen the destiny of the souls below. Several passages in Virgil recall Er's story. Thus the Golden Bough is a poetic acknowledgement of Plato – who is Virgil's pass to the world of the dead.

138. **Iunoni infernae:** 'to the Juno of the lower world', i.e. Proserpina. Juno herself is the wife of the supreme Jupiter; her counterpart below is Dis'* wife.

    dictus sacer: 'called sacred' i.e. 'consecrated'.

    tegit: 'hides' or 'protects'. 'The whole wood hides it', i.e. it is hidden away and protected in the very heart of the forest.

139. **obscuris ... umbrae:** 'shadows enclose it in dark glens'; a Virgilian way of saying 'dark glens enclose it with their shadows'.

140-1. 'But it is not permitted to go down into the hidden places of the earth until one has plucked from the tree its golden-haired growth.'

    Take **ante** and **quam** together as *antequam* 'until'. This separation of the word into its two components is very common in all Latin writers.

    operta: acc. n. pl. of the perf. part. Understand, e.g., *loca*.

    quis: here means 'anyone'. (An 'indefinite' pronoun.)

    auricomus: a word apparently invented by Virgil. It is a compound* adjective designed to remind us of epic style. Homer is full of such compounds.

    fetus: acc. pl. – plural with singular meaning.

142-3. 'Fair Proserpina ordained that that this her own gift should be presented to her.'

    instituit: 'established the custom that ...'.

143-4. 'When the first is broken off a second golden one does not fail,' i.e. there is never one missing. **avulso** is abl. of perf. part., *avello*.

145. **alte:** adverb: *deep* in the forest and *high* on the trees.

    vestiga: imperative of *vestigo*.

    rite: 'in proper form'; the adv. goes with both verbs. **repertum:** perf. part. 'When it has been found ....' Finding and picking the branch is an act of sacred ritual, and therefore must be done in exactly the right way. This includes picking the branch by hand.

146. **ipse:** 'by itself'. **volens facilisque:** the branch is personified*. **facilis** is regularly used of a person who can be easily persuaded – though this point is obscured by the natural translation 'easily'.

147-8. Read **non poteris ullis viribus vincere nec convellere** ....

149. **tibi:** dative of reference*, 'the body of one of your friends'. Aeneas may easily assume that the friend is Palinurus (see note on 337-83), though **heu nescis** (150) may raise a doubt. It is in fact Misenus, whose story is told in 162-74 below.

150. **incestat:** 'pollutes'. The presence of a dead body means that proper relations with the gods can only be re-established by proper ritual.

    funere: *funus* means here 'dead body' as quite frequently.

151. **pendes:** 'you are lingering'. The Sibyl reverts to her critical tone (37, 51, 135).

152. **sedibus ... suis:** 'Take him first to his proper resting place'. **ante:** (an adverb) 'beforehand'; i.e. before you set out to seek the Golden Bough. **suis** here does not refer to the grammatical subject, as reflexive pronouns normally do, but to Misenus, who is the chief topic of the sentence.

153. **duc:** imperative of *duco*.

    ea ... sunto: 'let them be the first offerings'. **sunto** is a 3rd person plural imperative, a rare and formal word. **piacula:** these are offerings made to the powers of the underworld (this is why the sheep are black) to secure Aeneas' passage.

154. **sic demum:** 'only thus'.

    invia vivis: '(realms) inaccessible to the living'.

155. **presso ore:** abl. abs.: 'her mouth pressed shut'.

156-7. **defixus lumina:** think of this expression as meaning 'having fixed his eyes downward'. In fact of course the participle is passive 'having been fixed'. **lumina** is said to be a 'retained accusative*': the acc. has been 'retained' as object <u>as if</u> the participle were active (cf 281). So 'Aeneas walks on, his eyes gazing down and his expression sorrowful ...'.

157-8. **caecosque ... secum:** 'and turns over by himself in his mind the dark outcome (of the Sibyl's prophecies)'. The two words **animo secum** emphasise how lonely are Aeneas' deliberations (105, 185). **caecos:** the word means 'blind, unseeing' but also 'dark, unseen' (30). Aeneas cannot see his way through to a happy outcome of what the Sibyl has told him.

158-9. **cui ... comes:** 'and to him (**cui** –connecting relative*) loyal Achates walks as comrade' – 'loyal Achates walks with him, keeping him company'.

　　paribus ... figit: 'places his steps with equal anxiety': this evidently means that Achates keeps in exact step with Aeneas, the identical pace showing that he shares Aeneas' concern.

160. **serebant:** from *sero serui* 'to join together'. *sermo* comes from the same root.

161-2. **quem ... diceret:** '(wondering) which companion was the prophetess talking of as dead?' The subjunctive **diceret** is in indirect question, though one has to provide a word to introduce it.

　　quod corpus: quod is acc. n. of *qui* (2) interrogative: 'what body did she say must be buried?'

　　humandum: gerundive; understand *esset*, again in indirect question.

162. **illi:** the pronoun is not absolutely necessary, because there is no change of subject between **serebant** and **vident**, but it creates the idea 'and in fact they did find one – it was Misenus'.

　　in litore sicco: i.e. where the shore was dry above the water-line. It appears (174) that he had been drowned by the god and thrown up on the shore. That he should lie so far up the shore suggests the violence of the wave which cast him up – and thus also the contemptuous anger of the god who killed him.

163. **venere:** short form of *venerunt*.

164. **Misenum:** the name is repeated for emotional effect: 'Can this really be ...?'

　　Aeoliden: the accusative in *-en* is Greek, as are all words in *-ides*.

　　quo ... alter: 'than whom (there was) no other man better ...'.

165. 'To call the men with the clarion, to set the battle ablaze by his bugle-play.'

　　A fine onomatopoeic* line, with the 'r's and hard consonants creating the sound of the trumpet.

　　The infinitives explain how he was 'better' ('epexegetic infinitive', cf. 49).

　　Martem: 'battle'. The god's name stands for the activity over which he presides ('metonymy'*).

166. **Hectora:** Greek accusative; the noun is acc. because it depends on *circum.*

167. Take the words **et lituo insignis et hasta** together: 'conspicuous both with his trumpet and his spear'. The *lituus* was a bronze instrument with a turned-up bell; it made an especially bright and piercing sound.

168. **illum:** Hector.

victor: 'Achilles in his triumph'.

169-70. **sese ... addiderat socium:** 'had added himself (as) companion' i.e. 'had joined Aeneas (as) companion'. Note that there is, as usual, no Latin word for 'as'. (**socium** is in apposition* to **sese**.)

socius denotes an associate of inferior not equal status. **fortissimus heros** asks us to see Misenus as a man of the highest standing – and therefore Aeneas as even higher. Hence **non inferiora secutus**: 'following (things) no lower (than Hector)', i.e. 'joining a hero just as great'.

171. **cava:** the metre requires the second syllable to be long, so that it cannot agree with **aequora** and must be taken as abl. with **concha**.

dum personat ...: 'while he was making the waters ring'. *dum* regularly takes the present indicative even when the surrounding tenses are past. So translate **personat** as past.

172. **demens:** Misenus was 'foolishly carried away' by the brilliance of his own playing and challenged the gods to do better. The god who took him on was Triton, a minor sea god, but one whose special instrument was famously the conch shell. Misenus' seemingly harmless arrogance is shockingly punished. For stories of this type see 'Arachne', 'Marsyas', 'Niobe', in March.

173. **aemulus exceptum Triton ... immerserat:** understand *Misenum*. 'Jealous Triton had drowned Misenus who-had-been-taken-on (as a competitor or as a challenger).'

virum presumably emphasises the difference between the man and the god.

si credere dignum est: There is doubt perhaps because Aeneas has this story only from the other people on the beach – and there is something mysterious about Misenus' death, corresponding in time with Aeneas' own determination to go to the world below. But Virgil seems to be distancing himself from some elements of his own story.

174. **spumosa:** on the face of it this could agree with either **saxa** or **unda**, acc. n. pl. or abl. fem. sing. But it certainly goes with **unda**:

(i) there is a natural break at the 3rd foot caesura* after **virum**; (ii) **unda** would look very bare without an adjective.

175. **circum:** adverb with **fremebant**: 'they were making a noise all around'.

176-7. **iussa ... festinant**: 'they perform quickly the Sibyl's orders'.

   haud mora: the words are in parenthesis*: 'and (there was) no delay'.

177-8. **aram ... certant:** 'and they compete to heap up with trees the altar of the tomb and to bring it up to the sky'. **aram sepulcri** is a strange phrase which baffled even ancient commentators. Perhaps 'the altar-tomb'. Austin suggests: 'the pyre is a tomb because it consumes the body and an altar in that it is heaped with offerings to the spirits of the departed'.

179-82. In this passage Virgil is imitating the early Roman poet Ennius* who was himself imitating Homer. For Ennius' lines and a discussion of how Virgil uses them, see Appendix.

179. **itur:** impersonal passive (cf. 45). 'Off they go.'

   alta: perhaps 'deep (in the forest)' or 'tall' because of the height of the trees or 'high' because they are in the mountains (182). Or all these meanings. (Cf. 145.)

   picea, 'a pine tree'; **ilex,** 'an ilex (holm oak) tree'; **fraxineus,** 'made of ash wood'; **robur,** 'an oak tree'; **ornus,** 'a manna-ash tree'.

181-2. **fraxineae ... scinditur:** the subjects are **fraxineae trabes** and **fissile robur**. The rest of the sentence **cuneis scinditur** is split so that one of the words goes next to one subject and the other next to the other – a common pattern. **scinditur** is singular because it is governed by the subject nearest to it – as often.

182. **advolvunt ... ornos:** note that these words consist largely of spondees* and that there are four double-consonants with 'n' as the first of the pair. Virgil is illustrating the heavy trundling as the great trees are rolled down (onomatopoeia*).

183. **nec non**: 'also'. The negatives cancel each other, but the result is more forceful than a mere 'and'.

   primus: take closely with **opera inter talia**: 'taking the lead in this work'.

184. **accingitur:** 'is equipped', or 'equips himself'.

paribus ... armis: 'similar tools' (not 'arms'). The tools are the axe, wedge and hammer as needed to do the work described in 179-82.

185. **ipse suo ... cum corde:** 'by himself in his own downcast heart'. Aeneas' isolation emphasised again (105, 158).

185-6. **haec:** take this as obj. of **volutat** and of **precatur**. 'He ponders these (i.e. the following) ideas and then utters them in prayer.'

187-8. **si:** 'if only', the following subjunctive **ostendat** expressing a wish. 'If only that golden branch would present itself on its tree in all this woodland.'

188. **quando:** 'since' or 'because'.

188-9. **vere heu nimium:** 'alas, only too truly'.

190. **forte:** 'by chance' – but of course here, as in 186, it only seems 'by chance' to Aeneas himself. His mother Venus is operating behind the scenes (Intro. **5**, Books 1, 4, 5, 8, 10), but we are able to share Aeneas' delight and surprise.

191. **caelo:** 'from the sky' **venere, sedere:** short form of *venerunt, sederunt*

193. **maternas:** 'his mother's'. Doves were sacred to Venus.

194. **este:** 2nd pl. imperative of *sum*. The word **o** here and in 196 can be taken as going with any of a number of different words and phrases in the surrounding sentences, and because of this very ambiguity emphasises Aeneas' pleading anxiety.

   qua: nom. sing. fem. of the indefinite adjective *qui*: 'any'.

196. **dubiis ... rebus:** 'do not fail (me) in difficult circumstances': **rebus** appears to be ablative, and one should understand an object for **defice.** Cf. *rebus egenis* (91) and translate 'in my time of trouble'.

197. **vestigia pressit:** 'he checked his steps' i.e. 'stood still'.

198. **ferant, pergant:** the subject is 'the doves'. The subjunctive is that of indirect question. After a main verb in the perfect (*pressit*), one might expect imperf. subj. The vivid present tense gives something of the tension in Aeneas' mind.

   tendere pergant: '(where) they were proceeding to go', but the Latin sounds less clumsy than this English, and it is a single idea 'where they were heading'.

199. **illae:** the doves.

   prodire: the infinitive is used as a main verb, the so-called 'historic infinitive' (also in 256). It means the same as the imperf.

indic: here 'kept on moving', and its subject is in the nominative (**illae**).

199-200. **tantum ... quantum:** 'only so far ... as' or 'as much ... as'.

> **volando:** abl. of the gerund: 'by flying'.

> **acie:** *acies* means 'an edge', then 'a line of battle', then 'a line of sight', and so here 'gaze'.

> **possent:** the subj. introduces the idea of a purpose clause. The doves were deliberately acting thus so that the followers could see them.

> **sequentum:** gen. pl. pres. part. It ends more usually *-ium*; the rarer form is more manageable in hexameters.

> 'As they fed, the doves kept moving ahead in flight only as far as the eyes of the followers could keep them in view.'

201. **venere:** for *venerunt*.

> **fauces:** 'jaws'. The word is used quite neutrally for the narrow entrance-passage to a building, so is a natural description for the approach to Lake Avernus, which is a long straight path between two forested slopes. But one is entitled also to see a lurking simile*: the jaws of a creature with its foul breath.

> **grave olentis Averni:** 'of evil-smelling Avernus'. **grave** is acc. n. sing. – 'smelling an unpleasant (smell)' or 'smelling unpleasantly' (adverbial accusative*).

> For the smell, see lines 239-41.

202. **celeres:** adverbial: 'swiftly'.

> **liquidum:** the adjective means both 'flowing' (the birds move like a boat slipping through water) and 'clear, bright'.

> **aëra:** Greek type acc. of the Greek word *aër*. Notice that there are three syllables.

> **lapsae:** 'gliding'. Perfect participles of deponent verbs can often be translated as if they were present. This reveals an ambiguity about the English participle, which can mean '*after* doing something' as well as '*while* doing something'. Here the idea is 'after gliding'.

203. **sedibus optatis:** 'in the longed-for place' – longed for by Aeneas in his prayer 187-8.

> **gemina ... arbore:** 'the twin-tree': 'twin' in that it was both wood and gold. Perhaps translate 'double-natured'.

204. **discolor auri aura:** 'the contrasting breath of gold'. 'The breath of gold' was a phrase which puzzled Roman commentators. Williams

connects it with an ancient theory of sight: atoms are thrown off by objects and activate the air between themselves and our eyes, which 'see' when they are struck by these activated atoms of air. Lucretius (4.246-52) refers to this intervening column of air as **aura**. This very mechanical explanation could well be at the back of Virgil's mind, though he will also be conscious of the more imaginative idea represented by 'the breath' of gold (the brightness of the gold is so intense that it makes on the eye the same effect as the physical touch of wind), and by the assonance* of **auri** and **aura** – words which unite in sound two utterly contrasting substances. **discolor** because the gold contrasts with the dark green of the branches through which it gleams.

    refulsit: perf.; one might have expected pres. (historic) or imperf. The perf. gives the idea that Aeneas just 'caught a sudden glimpse' of gold in among the branches of the tree.

205-9. A complicated simile*: 'Just as mistletoe, which its own tree does not generate, is accustomed to grow green with new leaves in the chill of winter, and to ring smooth tree-trunks with its yellow growth, such was the sight of the gold growing as leaves on the gloomy ilex, and so did its foil rustle in the gentle breeze.'

    A simplified version in the order it should be taken:
quale viscum solet frondere et circumdare truncos
Just as mistletoe is accustomed to grow leaves and to surround tree-trunks,
talis erat species auri, sic brattea crepitabat.
such was the appearance of the gold, so did the foil rustle.

205. **quale** is acc. n. sing. and adverbial like *grave* in 201. Take it with **solet frondere:** 'in-just-the-way-that it is accustomed to grow leaves ...'.

207. **croceo:** there are two sorts of mistletoe, one with white and the other with yellow berries. We tend to be more familiar with the white.

208-9. Virgil stresses the contrast between the bright gold and the dark tree by separating the adjective **opaca** from its noun **ilice** over the line-ending (enjambement*). **sic ... vento:** this description has nothing to do with mistletoe, but it captures brilliantly the uncanny presence of the gold branch in the green tree with the clattering onomatopoeia* of **crepitabat brattea.**

210. **avidus:** adverbial, 'impatiently'.

210-11. corripit, refringit: understand *ramum* as obj. of these verbs. **cunctantem** agrees with this understood word. 'Resisting' seems inconsistent with 146 'it will come of its own accord', but perhaps the resistance is imagined in Aeneas' impatient mind. Aeneas certainly is impatient: **corripit** and **refringit** are forceful words, conspicuously placed first and last in the line; **avidus** and **extemplo** add to the effect. But the branch (personified* as in 146 – see note) is perhaps being a little discouraging, like the Sibyl (note on 135).

212-35. The Funeral. Misenus is buried with full honours. Virgil is attributing to the legendary past (i) the Roman funeral ritual of his own day, (ii) the name of the place where Misenus is buried ('Punta di Miseno') and even its appearance. (The hill which forms the cape was held to look like a tomb.) Such explanations of existing features by reference to legendary antiquity are called 'aetiological*'.

212. nec minus: with **flebant**. 'They were weeping no less (bitterly).'
213. suprema: understand *dona*. 'Last offerings to ungrateful ashes' encapsulates the bitter but necessary futility of a funeral ritual. (Catullus 96.2; 101.4.)
214. pinguem ... secto: literally 'rich with pine and cut-down oak'. 'Rich' because resinous and so inflammable and scented. This strictly applies only to the pinewood, so the phrase **pinguem taedis** can be understood as equivalent to *pinguibus taedis* (transferred epithet*).
215. struxere: for *struxerunt*.
　　　　cui ... latera: 'on which they weave the sides with dark fronds', or 'whose sides they weave ...'; **cui** is dat. of reference*: 'on which'.
216. ferales: cypresses are 'associated with funerals' especially because of their dark colour.
　　　　ante: as a sort of screen 'in front of' the pyre.
217. constituunt: 'they set up'.
　　　　super: adv. 'above'.
　　　　armis: not Misenus' own, which are kept to adorn his tomb (233).
218. pars ... pars (222): 'some ... others'; the verb is plural, according to the sense. (Cf. 6-7, where the verb is singular.)

aëna: 'bronze (vessels)' (three syllables).

calidos ... flammis is both hendiadys* (They actually secure hot water *by* boiling cauldrons) and 'hysteron proteron'* (First you put the cauldron on the fire *then* you get the hot water). Possibly translate 'to get hot water, they set out cauldrons ...'.

219. **frigentis:** genitive. 'They wash the body (of him) now cold.' It is the person Misenus who is cold, not just the corpse. The loss of life is more intensely felt.

220. **fit gemitus:** 'lamentation is made'; 'the sound of mourning goes up'.

    toro: 'on the couch' abl. without prep. (89).

    defleta: agreeing with **membra.** *fleo* = 'I weep for'; *defleo* = 'I weep completely for'. 'When they have wept their fill for it, they lay the body on the couch.'

221. **purpureas:** a traditional colour for Roman aristocrats to be buried in. (See note on **more parentum** 223.)

    velamina nota: in apposition* with *vestes*: 'purple garments, a well-known covering'. 'Well-known' to Misenus, i.e. 'familiar'.

222. **pars:** see on 218.

    subiere: for *subierunt* from *subeo*. 'They went beneath the huge bier', i.e. lifted it up.

223. **triste ministerium:** 'a grim task', referring to **subiere feretro.** The phrase is acc., and the figure is called 'accusative in apposition to the sentence*'.

    subiectam: with **facem** (224). The torch is 'put downwards into' the pyre.

    more parentum: the phrase makes the listener think of *Roman* tradition, though Misenus' *parentes* were obviously Trojan. Virgil is providing the Roman custom with a yet more ancient origin.

224. **aversi:** they turn away so as not to see the dead man's spirit as it leaves.

    tenuere: for *tenuerunt*.

225. **dona:** the word goes closely with **turea,** but 'the gifts' are also the other items mentioned: food (**dapes:** perhaps a sacrificial cake) and olive oil.

    fuso ... olivo: '(bowls) with oil poured in'. **fuso** give the idea of oil poured 'lavishly' in.

    crateres: the last syllable is short, as it would be in Greek – *crater* is a Greek word.

226. **conlapsi** (*sunt*).

> **quievit:** 'died down'.

227-8. lit, 'They washed with wine the remains and the thirsty ash, and Corynaeus sealed the gathered bones in a brazen casket'. There is hendiadys* in that the 'remains' <u>are</u> the 'ash', and we should think of both 'ash' and 'bones' as objects of both 'washed' and 'sealed'. The ash goes into the casket as well as the bones. (**cineres** (226) refers to the ash of the pyre generally; **favillam** more particularly to the incinerated human remains.)

> **reliquias:** the first syllable is treated as if it were long here and on several other occasions in poetry; it cannot otherwise fit into a hexameter.

229. **idem:** 'He also' (see note on 116).

> **ter:** three is a significant number in many magical and religious contexts.

> **circumtulit:** Servius* explains this word as identical to *purgavit* 'purified' – it is, he says, an ancient usage. This makes sense of the object **socios** and the ablative **unda** 'with water'. Originally of course it meant simply 'carry round', then 'carry round someone for religious purposes' then 'purify someone'.

229-31. There are two ideas in the sentence so far: Corynaeus moves round the company, and he sprinkles them. The idea of sprinkling is then repeated in **spargens rore levi**, the idea of movement in **lustravit viros. rore et ramo:** hendiadys* for 'water on a branch'. The repetition (theme and variation*) slows down the movement of the passage and increases its solemnity. It also underlines the importance of **ramo ... olivae**.

> **felicis:** both 'fruitful' and 'fortunate'.

> **olivae:** in Virgil's day the tradition was to use a branch of bay, not olive. Servius* has a story that Augustus wished to dissociate the bay leaf from mourning because he was fond of a bay tree on the Palatine which sprouted on the day of his own birth. Thus Virgil's suggestion of 'olive' may be a compliment to Augustus.

> **novissima verba:** the traditional words, *ave atque vale*, 'hail and farewell'.

232. **at pius Aeneas:** cf. 9. Here he shows himself *pius* in working to preserve the memory of his friend.

> **ingenti mole sepulcrum:** 'a tomb of great mass', 'a massive tomb' – ablative of description.*

233. **imponit:** 'sets up upon (the remains of the pyre)'.

> **suaque arma viro:** 'and, for the hero, his own arms'. For the use of the reflexive **sua**, see note on 152.

> **remumque tubamque:** his arms and his trumpet because in life he had been conspicuous for skill with these (167); his oar reminds the reader of the funeral of Elpenor, the young companion of Odysseus whose story (*Odyssey* 10.552-60; 11.51-80; 12.8-15) suggested that of Misenus (see Intro. **6.ii.a**).

234. **aerio:** partly a poetic exaggeration – the hill is only 167 metres high. But it rises straight from the sea, impressively steep and isolated.

> **ab:** 'after' or 'from'.

235. **tenet:** the hill, Punta di Miseno, keeps its name even now. The place had its own great importance in Virgil's day as Augustus' naval base.

236. **praecepta:** the Sibyl (153) had given three instructions: find the bough, bury Misenus and make a sacrifice. Aeneas now performs the third of these.

237ff. The cave. It is the subject of a brief ecphrasis* which introduces some of the ideas of darkness and desolation which attend the first part of the journey to the underworld. Historically speaking, there is no evidence that there ever was a cave in the slopes surrounding Lake Avernus.

> **vastoque immanis hiatu:** 'awe-inspiring with (because of) its huge wide gape'. The 'breath' (240) and the 'throat' (241) combine to make this *hiatus* seem the yawn of a living creature's mouth (cf. 201). The long 'a's in the line ensure that one enacts the idea while saying the line (onomatopoeia*).

238. **nemorum tenebris:** 'the darkness of woods' equivalent to 'dark woods'.

239. **quam super:** 'over which'.

> **volantes:** an unusual use of the pres. part. as a noun: 'flying creatures'.

240. **tendere iter:** 'to go their way'.

> **talis ... ferebat:** take **sese** as object of both **effundens** and **ferebat**. 'Such a (foul) breath, pouring itself out of the dark throat, carried itself to the vault above' – 'So foul was the breath which poured up from that dark throat to the sky above'. As often in

verse, there is no preposition 'from' with the ablative **atris faucibus**.

242. 'From which the Greeks have called the place "Aornus" by name.' 'Aornus' means 'birdless' in Greek, but it is generally agreed that 'Avernus' is not in fact derived form 'Aornus'. The line appears in only one of the main manuscripts. Editors have concluded that it is not by Virgil. The square brackets mark it as an interpolation. It may well be, however, that Virgil knew of the bogus derivation and had it in mind when he described the place as bringing death to birds.

243-54. The priestess conducts the sacrifice. There are many victims – all black (243, 249) – and several gods involved: bullocks for Hecate (247), a lamb for Night and Earth (250), a cow for Proserpina (251) and bulls for Dis (252). It begins at midnight (note on *nocturnas* 252), and ends just before dawn (255) with a fearful earthquake. It is a long, arduous and disturbing procedure.

The priestess first has to get the victims to stand still (*constituo*) by the altar. In behaving passively, they show that they are willing victims. Wine is poured over their foreheads, the bristles between their horns are cut and burned as a preliminary offering (*libamen*), then their throats are cut and the blood collected in dishes. Meanwhile the priestess prays.

243-4. **hic**: 'here'.

sacerdos is subject of both **constituit** and **invergit**.

nigrantes ... iuvencos: 'bullocks black as to their hides', i.e. 'bullocks with black hides'. **terga** is acc. of respect*.

fronti: singular, but referring to all the bullocks.

245-6. **saetas** is object of both **carpens** and **imponit**.

media inter cornua: 'midway between the horns' – 'exactly between'.

libamina prima: 'as a first offering'; in apposition* to **summas saetas**, or rather the whole sentence **summas ... sacris** (cf. 223).

247. **voce vocans**: 'calling with the voice' or 'calling aloud on'; the phrase has a religious solemnity to it (also in 506).

Hecaten ... potentem: **Hecaten** is acc. from the Greek nom. *Hecate*. She is powerful 'both in the sky' as Diana, Apollo's sister, 'and in Erebus' as Trivia or Hecate. Erebus (connected with the Hebrew *erev* – 'darkness') is another name for the underworld; by a different route, the original word has become 'Europe', the land of evening, the West, 'Hesperia', in fact.

248. **supponunt ... cultros:** first the victim is stunned by a blow on the head. As it falls, the attendants 'put the knife in' to the throat.

249. **atri velleris agnam:** 'a lamb of black fleece' or 'a black(-fleeced) lamb'. Gen. of description*.

250. **matri Eumenidum:** 'for the mother of the Eumenides' as if the verb had been 'sacrifices'. The Eumenides (the word is Greek; the native Latin term is *Furiae*: the Furies) are the spirits of vengeance. They are the children of Night, herself a goddess born of the Emptiness (265) at the beginning of the universe, according to Homer's near-contemporary Hesiod*, author of a poem called *The Birth of the Gods*. Night is of course appropriate here; her offspring, the Eumenides, have no particular relevance, but their mention contributes to the frightening character of the occasion.

    magnaeque sorori: Night's sister is Earth, into which Aeneas is about to descend.

251. **Proserpina:** the apostrophe* means that Virgil does not have to use the dative Proserpinae, which would not fit into the verse; but it also makes poet and reader more nearly participants in the events.

252. **Stygio regi:** the King of the Styx is Dis (Roman name) or Pluto (Greek) (see on 127).

    nocturnas: 'night-time altars', or translate as adv. 'he set up at night'. Only now does Virgil actually tell us it was night.

    aras: probably to be translated as singular.

253. **solida ... viscera:** in sacrifices to the spirits below, victims were put on the fire 'whole' not carved up, and oil (254) was offered instead of wine.

254. **super:** take closely with **fundens** as a single word: 'pouring (oil) over (the entrails)'. The second syllable must, remarkably, be scanned as long (lengthening in arsis*.)

    It is called 'tmesis'* when a compounding prep. is separated from its verb, a common practice in Homeric hexameters.

    The oil would have contributed to a great blaze in the surrounding darkness.

255. **ecce autem:** taken together, these words regularly introduce a startling new event.

primi ... ortus: 'just before the light and rising of the earliest sun' (**ortus** is acc. pl.); a typical expression for 'just before sunrise'.

256. **mugire:** historic infinitive (see on 199), here 'began to groan'.

   coepta moveri: understand *sunt*. The verb *coepi* is active in form when the following infinitive is active, passive in form (*coeptus sum*) when the following infinitive is passive, as here – **moveri**.

256-7. **iuga ... silvarum:** 'the ridges of the woods', i.e. the woods on the ridges, visible in silhouette against the sky from down below.

   visaeque (*sunt*).

257. **dea:** this is Hecate, the Sibyl's patron goddess. Real dogs were thought to feel her presence and to howl at night; the goddess also had her own hounds in the spirit world.

258. **procul este:** 'Keep far off'. The instruction is addressed to the **profani**, 'those who are unconsecrated'. It is not addressed to Aeneas or his companions, who are consecrated by their presence at the sacrifice, but is a traditional and general warning designed to preserve the integrity and effectiveness of the ritual.

260. **tuque:** she is addressing Aeneas in contrast to the **profani**, but she leaves saying his name until the next line, when she uses it perhaps to bolster his courage.

261. **opus** (*est*): 'there is need of'. The ablative indicates what is needed – **animis** and **pectore firmo**. *animi* is often used as a plural for 'high spirits, courage'.

262. **furens:** because she is possessed by the goddess. Perhaps 'ecstatically'.

   antro ... aperto: until now the cave has stood before them dark, forbidding and emitting the foul fumes of 240-1. Now there is the sense that the way through it is open (**aperto**). Still the Sibyl has to fling herself at it (**immisit**) in order to overcome the horror.

263. **haud timidis passibus:** 'with no fearful steps' – i.e. 'very courageously'. Such understatement is called 'litotes*'. Aeneas 'equals' her both in pace and in courage.

264-7. Epic poets, speaking of the legendary or mythical past, rely on and invoke the Muses at the beginning of their poems. The Muses are to inspire them to tell what otherwise they could not know (*Aeneid* 1.8-11). It is a convention to make a renewed appeal to mark a crucial stage of the narrative (7.37-44, 7.641-6 etc.). Here Virgil makes such an appeal – but not to the Muses. He is entering a world of which the Muses, spirits of the light and the world above, cannot speak.

264. **Di** is voc., as are **umbrae, Chaos, Phlegethon** and perhaps **loca**.
    quibus: possessive dative*.
    imperium animarum: 'power over the spirits'.
265. **Chaos:** the Emptiness before the beginning of Creation. Out of it grew Erebus and Night.
    Phlegethon: the River of Fire, representing the rivers of the underworld (see 550-1 and the note on 132).
    loca ... late: 'regions lying silent in night over a wide space', or 'a vast region of darkness and silence'. **loca** is perhaps in apposition* to the preceding vocatives (though Phlegethon is neither dark nor silent (550-1)); or perhaps another vocative – but all the others are joined by 'and', while **loca** is not.
266. **sit mihi fas:** 'may it be lawful for me'. **sit numine vestro:** understand **sit** *mihi fas* **numine vestro pandere** .... Note **mihi** and **vestro** in contrasting positions at the beginning and end of the line: 'may it be <u>my</u> right to tell and to reveal by <u>your</u> will ...'.
    audita: acc. n. pl.; 'things heard'.
268. A very slow line: all spondees until the 5th-foot dactyl. The strangeness is increased by the fact that both adjectives are transferred*: the line might have been *ibant obscura soli sub nocte* ....
    nocte: you first think of this as being an extension of the night of the upper world they have just left. But the underworld as a whole is the region of night (265), such that even souls dwelling in the brightness of Elysium* can be said to be 'sunk in night' (827).
269. **domos vacuas, inania regna: inania** repeats and intensifies the idea of **vacuas**, as does the word-order, with the phrases set out in chiasmus*.
    domos: it is as if they were walking down a street. Is Virgil thinking in terms of the main roads into Rome, lined by magnificent tombs? Even now a walk along the Via Appia gives some idea of what it was like, and Petronius' tale of the werewolf (*Satyricon*, 62) suggests that such roads made for uneasy walking by night.

Ditis: gen. of *Dis*, the Roman name for the Lord of the Underworld (127, note).

270-1. **quale ...:** the expression is abbreviated; think, e.g., of (*tale erat iter eis*) **quale est iter in silvis:** lit. 'their walk was such as is a walk in the woods'.

per incertam ... maligna: 'by an uncertain moon under a grudging light' – a sort of hendiadys*: 'by the grudging light of a fitful moon'. It is a cloudy night; the moon is half-seen and even that only from time to time. 'In the woods' no doubt because of the sense of strange half-seen shapes impending.

272. **abstulit:** from *auferre*, to remove something (acc.) from something (dat.).

273. **vestibulum:** suddenly they are standing outside a house – a grand one with a porch, and in this porch, personified* as if they were the wild beasts which clustered round Odysseus' men outside Circe's palace in *Odyssey* 10.212ff., are the conditions and states of mind which bring death.

Orci: Orcus is another name for Dis (127, note).

274. **ultrices ... Curae:** 'tormenting Anxiety', traditionally explained as 'guilty conscience'.

277. **terribiles visu formae:** 'shapes terrible to behold', referring to all the conditions mentioned in 274-80. **visu:** the 4th principal part of most verbs ends in -*um* and is called the 'supine'. It is a noun used only in the accusative and an odd ablative ending -*u*, meaning (for *video*) 'seeing'. Here 'terrible in the seeing'.

278-9. **mala mentis Gaudia:** 'perverted pleasures' (West). Probably one should think of **mala** as transferred* – 'the pleasures of an evil heart'.

279-80. **adverso in limine:** 'in the doorway facing them', i.e. where they are most threatening. These three, War, Revenge (the Eumenides: see on 250), and Discord have been the especial agents of destruction in Virgil's Rome – and Augustus is especially proud of having tamed them (*Aeneid* 1.293-6, *RG* 13 on the closing of the temple of Janus, and Intro. 1).

280. **ferrei:** this word, normally of three syllables, here has two. The vowels *ei* are run together by synizesis*.

thalami: the word is very frequently used of marriage-chambers and regularly also of the rooms of young girls before marriage. The Eumenides were virgins and so may have **thalami**, but there is something rather disagreeable, perhaps deliberately so, in combining the idea of such rooms and the iron torture-chambers of the Furies (oxymoron*).

281. 'Having bound her snaky hair with bloody woollen bands.' **innexa,** nom. fem. agreeing with **Discordia. crinem,** acc. following the (passive) participle **innexa,** is retained* accusative as in 156.

Discord has snaky hair like other death-bringing creatures, the Gorgon Medusa or the avenging Furies.

vittis: *vittae* are strands of wool used in general to indicate consecration: of a priestess, of a sacrificial victim, of an altar. With them, the demon Discordia seems to appear as a hideous parody of a priestess.

282. **in medio:** 'in the middle' – of the space before the **vestibulum**? or of a court inside the house? Virgil is not concerned to be precise about it.

annosaque bracchia: no more than an expansion of **ramos,** with focus on the idea **annosa.**

283-4. 'an elm, which place they say that **(ferunt)** empty dreams occupy in crowds'; or '... a place which ...'. 'A place' is the antecedent* of the relative 'which'. In Latin the antecedent is often included within the relative clause ('which place ...').

No origin has been traced for the dream-haunted elm tree. It may be worth observing that the elm was felt to offer dark shade (it was planted along roads), and that its foliage was thick enough to hide in.

vulgo: probably with **tenere** ('they – i.e. the dreams – occupy in crowds') rather than with **ferunt** ('they – i.e. people – commonly say').

285. **multa ... variarum monstra ferarum:** 'many oddities consisting in different beasts', i.e. 'many different fantastic creatures'. The word *monstrum* refers to something significant sent by the gods, hence often something strange. **variarum ferarum** defines **monstra**: it is called the defining* genitive.

The following notes suggest rather well-defined appearances for most of the monsters – more literal than Virgil's own words really allow. His hints and suggestions are more frightening than any literal description.

286. **biformes** may well refer to both **Centauri** and **Scyllae.** Centaurs were half-man, half-horse. Scylla was the monster who ate several

of Odysseus' men in *Odyssey* 12; according to the mythological handbook attributed to Apollodorus she had a woman's head and shoulders, and dogs' heads growing around her waist. The plural **Scyllae** probably suggests 'creatures like Scylla'.

287. **Briareus:** a monster with 50 heads and 100 hands. **centumgeminus** ('hundredfold') may be an impressionistic way of describing him – it looked as if there were 100 of him.

> **belua Lernae**: the Lernaean Hydra, killed by Hercules. It is represented in art as a nine-headed snake.

288. **horrendum:** 'dreadfully'; adverbial* acc.

> **Chimaera:** a fire-breathing monster killed by the hero Bellerophon. It had the head of a lion, the hindquarters of a snake and the torso of a goat.

289. **Gorgones:** there were three Gorgon sisters, one of whom was Medusa, killed by Perseus. They are represented in art with lion-like faces, bared fangs and snaky hair.

> **Harpyiae:** the middle syllable *yi* is a diphthong, i.e. a single long syllable. The Harpies were half bird, half woman. They pestered Aeneas in Book 3.225-67.

> **forma ... umbrae:** 'the Shape of the Three-bodied Phantom'. 'Three-bodied' is an adj. appropriate to Geryon, the giant killed by Hercules on his journey to the far west. **forma** and **umbrae** make his appearance much more menacing.

290. **hic:** 'at this point', adv.

> **subita ... formidine:** 'agitated by sudden terror'. **trepidus** of the hastiness of Aeneas' action, **formidine** of the fear which inspires it.

291. **strictam:** – though he was told to draw it in 260.

> **aciem:** the edge of the sword, see on 200.

> **venientibus:** 'to (the creatures) as they came'.

292-4. '... and if his learned companion did not tell (him) that (these creatures), mere bodiless spirits, were fluttering-about with the empty appearance of shape, he would charge....' The verbs are pres. subj. One might have expected pluperf. subj. *admonuisset, inruisset* – 'if she had not told, he would have charged'. The pres. subj. is used for things which might still happen. Virgil wishes vividly to put us beside the Sibyl just before she utters her warning.

> **docta:** the Sibyl was 'learned' or 'well-informed', having been given an introductory tour of the underworld by Hecate at the time of her appointment (564-5).

There are some six ideas in the two lines 292-3 which give the idea of substancelessness. The last two, **sub imagine formae**, 'under the appearance of a shape' sum it up, presenting an idea like the Greek proverb 'man is the dream of a shadow'.

295. **hinc via:** understand *est*. 'From here is' (or 'starts') 'the road ....'
    fert: 'leads'

296. There are various ways of taking this sentence. Perhaps 'This (river), dark with mud, a flood with enormous depth, seethes ...'. **vasta voragine** goes closely with **gurges** as an ablative of description*. **gurges** suggests a whirling mass of water. **vorago** ('an abyss') is connected with the word *vorare*, to devour. One thinks of the whirlpool monster Charybdis from the *Odyssey*, the more so because of the open-mouthed assonance* **vastaque voragine**.

297. Aeneas comes to the point where Acheron and Cocytus meet. This is where Odysseus in the *Odyssey* was told to enter the underworld (10.514). There were in fact two real rivers Acheron and Cocytus in north-western Greece, and where they met there was a famous oracle for the consultation of the dead. Virgil's narrative depends on knowledge of geography, cult and literature.
    Cocyto: dative; in prose one would expect *in Cocytum*. For the character of the river, see on 132. The 'y' is scanned* long.

298. **portitor:** originally 'a harbour master', determining who passes through his port. Charon does this (315-16). But *portitor* came to be equivalent to *portator* 'a carrier', or 'a ferryman', and this too is Charon's function, to transport the souls of the dead to the place where they will receive judgment and a permanent place. In his description of Charon, Virgil combines the features of a coarse and filthy boatman with those of a demon of death. One aspect of the tradition – the toll paid by the passengers – Virgil omits.
    aquas et flumina: 'the waters of the river' – hendiadys*.

299 **terribili squalore:** take this as abl. of description* with **Charon**: 'C., (a figure) of terrifying filth'.

299-300. **cui:** 'on whose chin lies ...'. **cui** is dat. of reference*.
    plurima ... canities inculta: 'very much unkempt grey hair' or 'a long straggling grey beard'. **mento:** 'on his chin'; ablative without preposition.

300. **stant lumina flamma:** 'his eyes are fixed in flame'; perhaps 'his eyes are staring circles of fire'. Charon suddenly becomes a figure of fear, not simply of disgust.

301. **nodo:** 'by a knot'; this adds to the dishevelled impression – the usual fastening would be pin or brooch.

302. **ipse:** 'by himself'. He has no one to help him.

    conto ... velis: he punts the boat with his pole in the shallows and uses the sails for the deep water. **velis** is probably dat. 'sees to the sails', though *ministro* sometimes takes an accusative, in which case **velis** is abl. and the meaning is 'tends the boat with sails'. It is hard to see how Charon can sail a small boat (**cumba**) seeing to both pole and sails and still have room for passengers! It is thought that Virgil's Charon may represent an actual painting, as his 'Madness' did in 1.294.

303. **ferruginea:** the metre shows it to be abl., agreeing with **cumba**.

    corpora: simply 'the dead'; an oddly-chosen word when we have just been told (292) that the phantoms of 274-89 are 'lives without bodies'. But the underworld throughout is self-contradictory in simultaneously having and not having a physical existence (410-14, 489-93, 700-3).

304. Understand *est.* 'For a god, old age is fresh ....' **cruda** is a striking word, suggesting 'rude strength' (West) and adding to the coarseness of the characterisation (see 299).

305. **huc:** 'towards Charon'.

    omnis turba: 'the whole crowd' – explained by what follows.

    ad ripas effusa: 'streaming down to the banks'.

306-7. **defunctaque ... heroum:** 'the figures of great-hearted heroes who have ended their lives'. For **corpora**, see on 303. **magnanimum:** an archaic* gen. pl; **heroum:** also gen. pl.; **defuncta:** nom. pl. (short 'a'); **vita:** abl. sing., because **defuncta** (perf. part. of *defungor*) takes abl. (see on 83).

309-10. Start with **quam multa folia lapsa cadunt:** 'as many leaves as slip and fall ...' or 'as many as the leaves which slip and fall ...'.

310-12. Start with **quam multae aves glomerantur ad terram:** 'as many birds as come-flocking towards the land ...'. Understand *eas* as object of **fugat** ('drives') and **immittit. frigidus annus:** 'the chilly season'. The birds are arriving, yet it is winter, not spring. Virgil must be thinking of flocks of swallows on their way from northern Europe, clustering on the shores of Campania* before they set out again for Africa.

Similes* are used to intensify ideas and concentrate the imagination. Double similes are rare and carry correspondingly greater weight. These two are very carefully balanced in length and in the placing of the ideas within them. We think of the vast numbers of falling leaves, as of swarming birds; also of the way they move, both apparently at random – but the movement of the birds is shown at the end of the simile (**terris apricis**) to be governed by the aim and hope for something better.

313. **orantes ... cursum:** after **orantes** one would expect *ut primi transmitterent* (indirect command). The infinitive **transmittere** is a Greek construction, used by Virgil no doubt because it is briefer and balder. **transmittere** is here intransitive* 'cross over', and **cursum** an accusative ('internal'*) as in expressions like *ire iter* 'to make a journey'. So 'to make the crossing'.

314. **amore:** there is pathos* in the use of the word 'love' for the longing of the dead to reach the place where love is likely to have no meaning (see Intro. **6.iii.a**). The intensity of their pleas can be heard in the long and metrically stressed 'o's in **ulterioris amore**.

315. **nunc hos, nunc illos:** in the repeated **nunc** we see Charon making his seemingly arbitrary choice, pointing now to those near (**hos**), now to those further off (**illos**).

316. **ast alios ... arcet harena:** this is the most important clause in the sentence, alliterated* throughout (Romans argued about correct spelling: *arena* or *harena*? – see Allen p. 43). Thus attention is called to the intervening words **longe summotos**, all heavy long syllables, suitable for their depressing message 'pushed well away' – with the pole, no doubt.

317. **enim:** here 'indeed' not 'for'; it intensifies the preceding word.

318. **vult:** 'means' (cf. French *que veut dire?*)
    concursus means not only 'coming together' but 'running about in a confused way', picking up the idea of **ad ripas effusa** (305). **ad amnem** goes with the idea of movement (running) contained in **concursus**: 'all this running down to the river'.

319. **quid-ve:** 'or what ...?'
    discrimine: *discrimen* is 'a principle of division'. 'How is Charon deciding between those he takes and those he leaves?'

320. **hae ... illae:** fem. because of *animae* understood.

linquunt: i.e. move back up the shore. They are the *summoti* of 316.

verrunt: literally 'sweep', used of rowing. Charon's passenger-souls are propelling the boat for him. This sounds inconsistent with 302-3, where Charon is doing all the work on his own. As suggested on 302, Virgil may at that point have being thinking of a particular work of art, while here he turns to a different tradition about Charon. The fifth century BCE Athenian comic poet Aristophanes has Charon getting his passenger to row and then charging him for the passage (*Frogs* 197, 270)!

321. **olli:** an archaic* and solemn form of *illi* (dat.), which avoids three heavy 'i' sounds in succession, and also introduces a decidedly formal-sounding line, with the solemn epithet **longaeva**, also the adv. **breviter**, which seems regularly to refer to quite lengthy speeches and to suggest 'properly', 'in due form' at least as much as 'briefly' (398, 538 and *paucis* 672, *pauca* in 4.333). The Sibyl then speaks in the precise tones of a lecturer enunciating basic truths: **haec ... ille ... hi**.

322. **Anchisa:** abl.: 'born *from* Anchises', 'son of Anchises'.

    deum proles: 'offspring of the gods' (*deum* gen. pl., as often). Aeneas' mother was Venus (193) and his ancestor, maternal and paternal, was Jupiter (123).

    certissima: take as adv. 'most surely'. Aeneas could not otherwise have got so far (131).

323. Virgil does not trouble to make it clear how the Styx fits into the topography of Acheron and Cocytus already described in 295-7. It seems almost as if Cocytus and Styx are identical. But here too he is dealing with two traditions which he feels no need to harmonise precisely: (i) that the entrance to the underworld is at the confluence of Acheron and Cocytus (297, note); (ii) that souls entering the underworld were ferried by Charon across the Styx.

    Cocyti: the 'y' is scanned* long.

324. 'by whose divinity the gods fear to swear and to break their oath'. *iuro* takes the acc. (**numen**) of that by which one swears. In Ovid *Metamorphoses* 3.291-2 Jupiter swears by the Styx to grant Semele (March, p. 353) her wish. So solemn is the oath that although in granting it he will, as he knows, cause Semele's death, even he cannot do otherwise.

325. It is simplest to understand an extra word *turba* after **haec omnis**. Lit. 'this whole (crowd), which you see, is the helpless and

unburied crowd', or 'all those whom you see are the helpless mass of the unburied'.

326. **ille** (*est*), **hi** (*sunt*). **sepulti:** 'the ones who have been buried'.

　　quos vehit unda: 'whom the water carries'. i.e. who are in Charon's boat.

327-8. 'Nor is it permitted to ferry (the souls) across the dreadful banks and the roaring streams until ....' **datur:** 'it is permitted'. *transporto* takes two accusatives: (*animas*) **fluenta transportare** – 'to carry souls across the streams'.

　　prius quam: 'until'.

　　sedibus: abl. without prep. – 'in their proper place'.

　　quierunt = *quieverunt* from *quiesco*.

329. **centum ... annos:** 'for a hundred years'; acc. of time 'how long'.

　　errant: they move around aimlessly; **volitant:** they move restlessly. The careful choice of verbs makes more pathetic the hundred years of suspended existence which the unburied suffer.

　　circum: prep. 'around'; translate with **haec litora**.

330. **stagna exoptata:** 'the intensely-longed-for waters' or 'the waters for which they deeply long'. The prefix *ex-* gives the idea of intensity. For their longing, cf. *amore* in 314.

　　The idea that the unburied suffer as described is an expression of the importance attached to proper burial by every period of antiquity known to us. Aeneas is about to experience an instance of this in meeting (337-83) the ghost of Palinurus (see note on 1).

331. **constitit, vestigia pressit:** theme and variation*, both meaning 'stopped'.

　　Anchisa satus: 'the son of Anchises'; the phrase reflects *Anchisa generate* (322).

332. **putans:** *putare* means 'to get something sorted out in the mind'; **multa,** acc. n. pl., is object of **putans**.

　　miseratus: 'pitying' (see on 202).

333-4. **maestos, carentes:** acc. plur., agreeing with both the names in 333.

　　carentes: 'lacking'; what one lacks goes in the abl., i.e. **honore**. The 'due honour of death' is burial.

　　Orontes is mentioned in Book 1 as having been shipwrecked. Leucaspis is named only here, no doubt for the assonance with **Lyciae** which helps to divide the line into two unequal parts; thus Leucaspis whom we do not know prepares the way for the more important Orontes whom we do, and the still more important Palinurus. (For this technique of preparation see on 483.)

335-6. take the lines thus: **quos obruit Auster ...** 'whom the south wind overwhelmed ...' **simul a Troia vectos ...** 'having travelled together from Troy'. **involvens** agrees with **Auster:** 'the wind, rolling up ship and men ...'.

   vectos: *veho* = 'carry'. The passive *vehor* 'I am carried' is used generally for 'I ride', 'I travel'. Thus *vectus* 'having travelled' or often 'travelling'.

335-6. the frequent 'v' and 'u' sounds (identical in Latin) in these lines reinforce the idea of shipwreck in a howling wind. Notice also the harsh elision* **aqu(a) involvens.**

337-83. Among the unburied, Aeneas meets his former helmsman Palinurus, who fell overboard between Sicily and Italy, as is told at the end of Book 5. Palinurus now explains that, after he fell overboard, he struggled to shore, but was there murdered. He begs Aeneas to help him. But the Sibyl forbids it. She promises that he will be buried by those who live near where his body lies, and that the place will be called after him. The headland is in fact still called Capo Palinuro. The episode performs at least two functions: (i) it gives particular focus to the general matter of the fate of the unburied; (ii) it is an aetiological* passage (see on lines 212-35).

337. **sese agebat:** lit. 'was moving himself', but *se agere* is a standard colloquial equivalent to *ire*, so 'was coming (towards them)'.

338. **Libyco cursu:** 'during the African journey', i.e. the voyage from Africa. The abl. is a sort of abl. of time.

   dum sidera servat: 'while he was watching the stars'. For pres. translated as past with *dum*, see on 171. He watches the stars to work out a course as helmsman.

339. **effusus:** 'tumbling'. For *effusus* of rapid uncontrolled movement, cf. 305.

   mediis in undis: 'in mid-ocean'.

340. **vix:** with **cognovit;** 'recognized with difficulty'.

342. **nobis:** with **eripuit,** 'snatched you from us', but it is dat., the 'dat. of reference*' or 'disadvantage' regular with words for 'take away'.

343. **dic age:** 'come on, tell me'. Palinurus is evidently slow to respond, or Aeneas very anxious for his answer.

343-4. **mihi animum delusit Apollo:** 'Apollo deceived my mind', effectively 'deceived me'. **mihi** is dat. of reference*.

    fallax ... repertus: 'though not found (to be) deceitful before'.

    responso: *responsum* is an answer delivered by a god, so 'an oracle'. Virgil does not refer to this oracle elsewhere.

345. **fore:** fut. infin. of *sum*; acc. and infin. with **canebat**. 'He prophesied that you would be safe.'

    ponto: 'at sea'; abl. of place without prep.

345-6. **finesque ... Ausonios:.** 'to the Ausonian lands', acc. of motion without prep. 'Ausonia' is an ancient name for Italy. **venturum** (*esse*) fut. infin.

    canebat: *cano* = prophesy; 'he was continually prophesying'. Virgil tells us only of one prophecy by Apollo himself (3.94-8). That does not mention Italy, but several other prophecies do (2.780-2, 3.163-71, 3.254, 3.374ff.). Either we are to think of these, or Virgil, as quite often, refers back to an event which he did not mention in its time-context (409, 456).

    en: 'look!', like *ecce*, but here as very often with a note of protest.

347. **ille:** it is often appropriate to translate pronouns as names; here 'Palinurus'. Understand 'answered'.

    cortina: at Apollo's famous sanctuary at Delphi in Greece, oracles were delivered by the Pythia, Apollo's priestess, who sat in a bronze vessel on a tripod in the inner part of the temple. **cortina** is strictly the word for this vessel, but it comes to be used for the oracle itself.

348. **dux Anchisiade:** voc.

349-51. A natural order for Palinurus' narrative might be: 'I was in charge of the steering oar, and was guiding the ship with it, when suddenly it was broken off, and I fell with it and brought it down with me.' It may be that his actual order of narrative suggests his agitation. The bare facts are given by **gubernaclum revulsum praecipitans traxi mecum:** 'I dragged with me as I fell the steering oar which had been broken off ...'. Add to this: **multa vi forte:** 'violently and unexpectedly', and **cui ... regebam:** 'to which (i.e. the oar) I was holding-fast, having been appointed (as) supervisor, and guiding (our) course'. **cursus:** plural for singular.

351-4. The basic sentence is: **iuro** (*me*) **non cepisse tantum timorem pro me quam ne tua navis deficeret**. 'I swear that I did not feel so much fear for myself as that your ship would fail.' **maria aspera:** '(I swear) <u>by</u> the violent seas'. **ullum** intensifies: 'not any such fear at all'. **spoliata armis:** 'stripped of its equipment', i.e. of the steering oar; **armis** is abl. of separation – 'away from'. **excussa magistro:** one might expect *excusso magistro* abl. abs. 'the helmsman having been thrown off'. Expressed as it is, with the same pattern as the previous phrase, we may see the event from the point of view of Palinurus, who finds himself suddenly in the water, as if the ship 'has been struck away from under its helmsman'. In being dislodged, the steering oar provides Palinurus with something to clutch in his long journey to land, as Odysseus had part of his shattered raft to support him as he approached Phaeacia in *Odyssey* 5.

One effect of these lines is to reinforce in us the idea of Aeneas as a leader who inspires unconditional loyalty in his men.

355. **tres ... noctes:** 'for three wintry nights' – acc. of time 'how long'.

356 **violentus aqua:** to distinguish it from **aequora** (355), **aqua** (abl.) perhaps refers to rainwater, so 'blustery with rain', or 'with violent squalls of rain'.

357. **summa ... ab unda:** 'raised high on the crest of a wave'. The wave was a high one (**sublimis**), Palinurus was on the very top of it (**summa**), it was the fourth day (**quarto**), and even then he could only just (**vix**) see Italy by peering ahead (**prospexi**)!

358. **adnabam:** the imperfect has the idea of trying ('conative'): 'made the effort to swim'.

terrae: dat. for 'towards' (not *ad* + acc.) with the compound verb, as quite often.

tuta: acc. n. pl. 'safe things', i.e. 'safety'; 'I had safety within my grasp'.

359-61. Take it: **ni** (= *nisi*) **gens crudelis ferro invasisset** – 'if a cruel tribe had not attacked (me) with the sword'. Agreeing with the understood '*me*' are **gravatum** ... – 'weighed down with wet clothes', and **prensantem ...** – 'grasping with curved hands the rough top of a cliff'.

madida cum veste: one might expect simply **madida veste**: 'by wet clothes'. **cum** conveys the idea 'along with'; we are to think of all the other reasons why he was 'weighed down'.

capita ... montis: it seems that Palinurus was washed against a cliff, climbed it, and had his hands over the top when he was attacked. This makes good sense of his wet clothes, which are more noticeable as an encumbrance when he is out of the water. His body is flung back down to the foot of the cliff, where it remains (362). Otherwise **montis** refers simply to a rock rising out of the sea.

praedam ... putasset: '... and had ignorantly considered (me) as loot'.

The routine way of expressing the idea 'I would have been safe if they had not attacked me' is to use the pluperf. subj. in both parts of the sentence. (*tuta tenuissem ni me invasissent*). **putasset** is a short form of the pluperf. subj. *putavisset*. But Virgil uses the imperf. indic. **tenebam** here to make us feel more intensely how close Palinurus came to survival: 'I was actually gripping safety (and would have survived) if they had not attacked ...'.

363. **quod:** acc. n. sing. of rel. *qui,* acc. of respect*. 'And in respect of that'; 'and as for that'.

te: acc. with **oro** (364).

364. **Iuli:** Iulus was Aeneas' young son; he is also called Ascanius.

365. **invicte:** 'unconquered one'; not merely complimentary, but a passionate expression of Palinurus' hope and belief that, if he can come to the world below, Aeneas can achieve anything.

aut tu: this (grammatically unnecessary) **tu** has the force of a sudden idea, urgently expressed.

terram inice: Palinurus makes only a minimum demand, that Aeneas should give him the token funeral of a handful of earth placed on the body.

366. **require:** 'look for'. It just occurs to Palinurus that Aeneas could bury him; but he needs directions. Palinurus' ideas tumble over each other as he tries in his haste and misery to express them.

portus ... Velinos: Velia, a town a short distance north of Capo Palinuro.

367 **aut tu:** another new and sudden idea.

si qua via est: 'if there is any way'; **qua** (nom.) and also **quam** (understand *viam*) are from the indefinite pronoun.

diva creatrix: i.e. Venus.

368. **numine:** *numen* is 'divine authority', 'consent'. It is connected with *nuo* 'nod in agreement'. (For Jupiter's nod, cf. *Iliad* 1.524-30.)

divum: gen. pl.

370. **misero:** 'to an unhappy wretch'.

371. **saltem:** with **in morte**; 'so that in death at least I my rest in an untroubled place'. His life was one of defeat and wandering, at least death should bring him peace.

372. Read it **cum vates talia coepit.** The indic. after *cum* = 'when' is common when the *cum*-clause comes after the main sentence ('inverted cum-clause').

The Sibyl interrupts: it was Aeneas whom Palinurus was addressing. She gives him a blunt response, prepared for by the **talia ... talia** repetition: 'These were the words he uttered, and this was the answer he got' – a forceful reminder of the rigid laws governing the traffic of souls across the Styx.

373. 'From where did this shocking desire (occur) to you?'

374-5. **tu:** this use of **tu** marks the Sibyl's surprise. 'Are you going to gaze on ....'

amnem severum Eumenidum: severum 'stern' is transferred* to the river from the Furies* to whom, as agents of divine punishment, it is appropriate. The Furies' special river is traditionally Cocytus, the River of Wailing, which is here merged in the Styx.

The most heavily stressed words in these two lines are **inhumatus** 'unburied' and **iniussus** 'unbidden'.

376. Translate in the order **desine sperare fata deum** (= *deorum*) **flecti precando**. **sperare** has acc. and infin. following it. The bleak hopelessness of this line is emphasised by its heavy sound, which seems to arise from the repeated 'd's.

377. **cape dicta memor:** 'take (my) words mindfully', i.e. 'listen to what I have to say and remember it'.

duri solacia casus: solacia (plural for singular) is in apposition* to *dicta*; 'as a consolation'. **duri casus** is genitive after **solacia:** 'mitigation of your misfortune', 'comfort for your misfortune'.

378. **nam:** 'for' explains why what she says is a comfort.

tua agrees with **ossa** (379). The long separation means that Palinurus knows that something is in store for him, but has to wait some time before finding out what it is.

finitimi: 'the nearby peoples', i.e. those who live near the place where Palinurus was murdered (359-61).

379. **acti**: 'forced by signs from heaven' – a plague, according to Servius*.

380. **tumulum ... tumulo**: by the repetition of the word Virgil emphasises the formal status of Palinurus as a dead hero with a consecrated tomb.

   sollemnia: acc. n. pl. 'annual (offerings)'.

381. **aeternum**: adj. to be translated as adv.: 'for ever'.

   Palinuri: there is some comforting force in the Sibyl's emphasising the name instead of simply saying *tuum*. For the place see note on 337-83.

382. **emotae** (*sunt*), **pulsus** (*est*): main verbs with the auxiliary omitted, as often.

   parumper: the word, used by Virgil here only, is a compound of *per* + *parum*: 'for all too short a time'. For Palinurus the foreseeable future is grim and *nothing* can be done about it. (Pathos*.)

383. **corde ... tristi**: 'from' his gloomy heart; abl. without prep.

   gaudet ... terra: 'he rejoices in the land called-after-him'. **cognomine** is abl. of an adjective *cognominis* 'having the same name' agreeing with **terra** also abl.

384. The line serves as an unemphatic divider between two much more dramatic and descriptive passages – like 13 and 40-1.

385-6. **quos** is a connecting* relative. 'And as soon as (*ut*) the ferryman saw them ...'; **ire** in 386 follows as acc. + infin. '... that they were walking'. **iam inde:** 'from right out there'; take it with **adgreditur** more than with **prospexit**: Charon shouts at Aeneas from midstream. **tacitum** emphasises the shocking effect of his shout. The dactylic rhythm of 386 suggests that Aeneas and the Sibyl are moving rapidly down towards the river.

387. **adgreditur dictis** can be a neutral expression 'addresses (him) in words', but **prior** 'first', **ultro** 'unprovoked' and **increpat** 'scolds' all indicate Charon's alarm.

388. **armatus** is stressed, coming at the beginning of the clause before **qui**, and explains Charon's tone.

389. **fare**: imperative of *for fari*. **age** as in 343. **quid**: 'why', indirect question after **fare**, with **venias** subj. as normal. **iam istinc**: 'from right where you are'; effectively 'speak and don't come any nearer'. Charon is a decidedly nervous sentry.

391. **nefas** (*est*): 'it is forbidden' – on divine authority. **Stygia**: the 'a' is long and must agree with **carina** (abl). A carefully formed line: **corpora viva** forms a chiasmus* of meaning with **Stygia carina**; also of alliteration* with **vectare carina**.

392-3. **nec ... laetatus sum me ... accepisse**: 'I did not rejoice that I had accepted ...', 'I got no pleasure from having taken ...'. Charon speaks in the tones of a grumpy doorkeeper recollecting previous difficult visitors. For letting Hercules in, Charon was punished, according to Servius*, by sitting in chains for a year, so **nec sum laetatus** is an understatement. For the stories of Hercules (=Alcides), Theseus and Pirithous, see the note on 119-23.

    euntem: 'going', 'when he was on his way'.

393. **lacu:** 'on the lake' – abl. without preposition (as *toro* 220).

    Thesea is acc. sing.

394. **dis geniti**: 'born of gods' as in 131; **invicti viribus**: 'unconquered in strength'. Aeneas claims divine birth in 123 and he is described as *invictus* by Palinurus in 365. Charon does not know yet who Aeneas is, but he is giving notice that such qualities cut no ice with *him*.

      essent: **quamquam** normally takes the indic. Charon uses the subj. here as if the clause were part of an indirect statement – 'they (claimed that they) were born of gods ...' (Kennedy § 468).

395. **ille**: 'the former', i.e. Hercules. **Tartareum custodem**: 'Hell's sentry', i.e. Cerberus, the three-headed guard dog of Dis. **manu**: 'by physical force'. **in vincla**: associated with *peto*, *in* + acc. means 'with a view to', so here 'with a view to tying him up in chains' (*OLD* 12).

396. **ipsius ... regis**: take this with **petivit**. To get the dramatic force, we need some such translation as 'Chains at the ready, he went to get Cerberus from the king's own throne, and dragged him away as he cowered there.' As a good guard dog, Cerberus should have stayed by the gate. Charon observes with some contempt that he ran to seek the protection of his master. This contempt is noticeable in the brief alliterative* phrase **traxitque trementem**; and indeed one would not expect Cerberus to be seen shivering with fright.

397. **hi**: 'the latter', i.e. Theseus and Pirithous. **dominam**: 'the mistress': Charon speaks as a servant. Take **Ditis** with **thalamo**: 'from the bridal chamber of Dis'. **adorti** (*sunt*): 'they attempted'; *adorior* adds a note of violence not present in the neutral *conor*; it also

contributes to the striking d-alliteration* of the line, which no doubt represents Charon's angry grumbling.

Note the tense (perfect) of **petivit** and **adorti**. It is not so much that Charon is *explaining why* Hercules, Theseus and Pirithous. were in the underworld, which would be given by an imperfect tense. He is crossly stating what they *actually did* as soon as he had let them across the river.

398. Take **quae** (connecting* relative) with **contra** 'in response to'.

Amphrysia: the 'y' is scanned* long. A very obscure epithet. The Sibyl's connexion with the river Amphrysus is this: she is the priestess of Apollo; Apollo once served Admetus for a year; Admetus was king of Thessaly; the river Amphrysus flows through Thessaly. Such self-conscious displays of erudition were characteristic of the Greek tradition in which Virgil worked (see Intro. **3**). They no doubt satisfied an audience which was keen to feel itself part of a world-wide culture.

399. **insidiae**: it would not be entirely inconsistent with the Sibyl's sarcastic tone here to translate 'skulduggery'. Understand *sunt* as the verb.

400. **ingens ianitor**: 'the huge doorkeeper'. This is Cerberus, the three-headed monster dog who guards the house of Dis.

licet 'it is permitted' often has an infinitive with it – 'it is permitted to do something'. But often, as here, it is accompanied by a subjunctive with no conjunction – **licet terreat**. The subjunctive is jussive*: 'Let (Cerberus) frighten ...', and **licet** is effectively in parenthesis: 'Let him frighten (it is acceptable)'. Perhaps 'He can go on terrorizing the ghosts for all I care.'

400-1. The repeated 'a's in the phrase **antro ... latrans** may suggest Cerberus' wide-open barking mouth. **aeternum** acc. sing. neut. as adverb 'for ever'.

402. **servet ... limen**: When Virgil makes the Sibyl say 'Proserpina may keep the threshold', the meaning is: 'will not be forced by us to stir beyond it' (G&W). But there is also a reference to a wife's duty *domum servare* 'to look after the house'. Translate **casta** (which refers to Proserpina.) after the verb ('predicatively'): 'P. may keep the threshold *without being violated*'.

patrui: Jupiter was Proserpina's father and Pluto's brother; thus Proserpina was married to her uncle.

403. A very grand line, with the subject 'Aeneas' expanded to fill the whole of it, and summarising his ancestry, his nature and his

achievements. **pietate ... armis**: 'glorious because of his faithfulness and his deeds of arms'.

404. Both the *ad* phrases depend on **descendit**. English requires a slightly different approach: 'coming down *to* his father *in* the deepest darkness ...'.

The Sibyl speaks sarcastically indeed in lines 399-402. Cerberus is 'the gigantic doorkeeper', like the bouncer of a nightclub. He sits in his cave-hut, barking – but it is mere barking with no concern to defend the house in a more active way. The ghosts are bloodless anyway: they can offer no opposition. More remarkably, the Sibyl is insulting about the master and mistress of Dis' house: Proserpina may stay chaste – but what is the value of chastity when the marriage is an incestuous one already (**patrui**)? This is the authoritative tone the Sibyl adopted with Aeneas earlier on (37, 51, 151), but it is more striking here as spoken by a mortal to and about the immortals. Her two lines about Aeneas here (403-4) are, on the other hand, full of respect: Aeneas may hold his head high in the community of the underworld. As the armed representative of *pietas* boldly stepping out where few have stepped before, we can see him as the predecessor of Augustus as he appears in the statue at Prima Porta.

405. **pietatis imago**: **imago** is 'the visible representation' (Aeneas) of the abstract quality *pietas*. **nulla** is formally an adjective agreeing with **imago**, but must be translated with **movet** 'not at all'.

406. **at**: 'at least'. The parenthesis represents a dramatic pause before the Sibyl displays the branch; it also allows the two parts of the Sibyl's sentence to be uttered as abrupt and dismissive phrases – dismissive of any objection by Charon. **veste latebat**: think of this as meaning 'was concealed *by* her dress'. The Sibyl has deliberately concealed the Golden Bough in order to deceive Charon and make him reveal himself as aggressive to the weak and subservient to the powerful.

407. **tumida**: the 'a' is elided* so it is not possible to tell from the metre whether it is abl. or nom. Probably it agrees with **corda**, which would seem flat without an adjective. Then **ex** = 'after' (*OLD* 10), and a literal version is '(his) swelling heart subsides after (his) anger' – though it may sound better to translate 'the swelling anger in his heart subsides'.

408. **nec plura his**: understand *dicta sunt*. **his** is abl.; tr. 'no more than this was said' or 'that was the end of that': an abrupt stop was put to Charon's insolence.

409-10. **venerabile donum fatalis virgae**: 'the holy gift of the Branch of Destiny'. **fatalis virgae** is defining* genitive: 'the gift *consisting in* ...'.

> **longo ... visum**: 'seen a long time afterwards', 'not seen for a long time'. **post** is here an adverb, and the abl. suggests 'by': 'later by a long time'. Virgil makes no suggestion as to when Charon may have seen it or in whose possession.

410. **advertit**: 'turns his boat towards (Aeneas and the Sibyl)'.

411. **alias animas**: 'the others ones, the souls'. It has gradually become clear that Charon, when he saw Aeneas and the Sibyl, was half-way across with a load of dead souls. The sight of the branch has filled him with such a sense of urgency that he turns back without completing the crossing – too bad for his passengers!

> **longa**: the cross-benches are long; so at this moment we have to think of it as quite a large boat; and still it is small for Aeneas (413-14).

412. **deturbat**: 'pitches them out' – unceremoniously.

> **laxatque foros**: not only does Charon clear the boat for his distinguished passenger, but he makes sure that there is no crowding round the boarding-point.

> **alveo**: 'in the hull' – abl. without preposition (as *toro*, 220). Note that the word is scanned as two long syllables, the *eo* being pronounced as one syllable by synizesis*.

413. **ingentem Aenean**: a very heavy phrase. Aeneas is huge anyway, and his size is compounded by the fact that he is flesh and blood, by contrast with the insubstantial ghosts.

414. **sutilis**: 'stitched', because the planks are held together by thongs which now stretch or break – an ancient form of construction appropriate to Charon's image as a down-at-heel old ferryman.

> **rimosa**: '(being) leaky'. **paludem**: 'marsh-water'.

416. **in** governs both **limo** and **ulva**.

Apart from Charon's fiery eyes (300), there is nothing supernatural or grand about this part of the underworld. All is dingy and even scruffy.

417-18. **haec regna:** 'this part of the kingdom (of Dis)'; **regna** is object of **personat**.

>**latratu ... trifauci:** 'with three-mouthed barking'. Cerberus is huge, and barking from each of his three heads, it is not surprising that he fills the place with sound (**personat**).

418. **adverso:** 'facing' Aeneas and the Sibyl as they disembark.

419-21. The basic sentence is **cui vates offam obicit:** 'to him the priestess throws a morsel'. **colla:** acc., subject of **horrere**. Cerberus has snakes for fur on his neck; as hackles rise on threatened dogs, so do Cerberus' snakes.

>**soporatam ... offam:** 'food made sleepy with honey ...'. **soporatam** is transferred*.

422. **obiectam** agrees with *offam* understood.

>**atque** here is rather like *atque* in 162, where one thing happens instantly after another.

>**terga:** plural for singular; Cerberus has three necks but only one back.

423. **toto ... antro:** 'all over the cave' – a common idiom, where one might have expected *per totum antrum*.

424. **occupat:** as if this were a military manoeuvre of capturing a beachhead.

>**sepulto:** metaphorically 'buried' in sleep: 'overwhelmed'.

425. **evadit:** transitive – 'he gets clear of'. **celer:** adj. for adv.

The brief and brilliant paragraph about Cerberus proves to have been a bridge-passage, rather like the single line 384 but marking a more significant transition. We are now at last in the underworld proper. In this first part of it (416-547) reside those who die as infants, those who were unjustly condemned to death, suicides, victims of ill-starred love, and gallant warriors. The common element seems to be that they all died before their due time.

426-7. **auditae** (*sunt*): three things are heard: **voces, vagitus ingens, infantum animae flentes**. They increase in precision: human voices – a childish crying – the souls of infants weeping; and they increase in rhetorical emphasis: one, two and then three words.

427-9. The basic clause is **quos abstulit atra dies et funere mersit acerbo**: 'whom a black day has stolen away and overwhelmed in untimely death'. The rest of the sentence intensifies this idea:

'deprived of sweet life on (its) very threshold and torn from the breast'. Both **in limine primo** and **dulcis vitae** depend on **exsortes**. **exsortes** and **raptos** both agree with **quos**. *acerbus* = 'immature, untimely' and 'sour, bitter' of fruit which is immature. It carries both meanings here and, coming at the end of the sentence, is in sharp contrast with **dulcis** at the beginning.

430. **iuxta:** with **hos**. Understand *sunt* as the main verb, with **damnati** ('those condemned') as its subject.

    damnati ... mortis: 'condemned to death'. Latin puts the penalty in the genitive.

431-3. **datae** (*sunt*). **sorte, iudice, quaesitor, consilium:** the procedure is that of a Roman court. The **quaesitor**, the presiding judge, establishes his jury by lot (**sorte**), drawing their names out of an urn. **sine sorte, sine iudice** is thus a hendiadys* for 'without a jury established by lot'. The jury in session acts as a **consilium** (panel of advisers) for the judge.

    The point is that the dead receive a fair trial here when they did not on earth.

    Minos is the King of Crete referred to in 14ff. Legend had it that after death he became one of the judges of the underworld. This particular function, of re-trying those unjustly executed, is Virgil's invention.

    silentum: gen. of *silentes*, 'the silent ones' (pres. part. of *sileo*). *silentes* regularly refers to the dead. **consilium silentum** 'a jury consisting of the dead'.

    vitas ... discit: i.e. the lives of those of who have been falsely accused. A Roman court based its verdict on the career and character (*vita*) of the defendant as much as on the actual charge. Cicero's speech *Pro Caelio* makes this amusingly clear. That Minos' court should do the same shows that this did not seem unjust.

    (Two very important manuscripts read **concilium** for **consilium**. This would mean 'a meeting (of those who were unjustly killed)'. **silentum** would refer only to them and would then depend also on **vitas et crimina**. This would allow a more straightforward translation of **ille ... discit**, and adds the extra possibility that **silentum** would suggest 'even though they remain silent – (how unlike people in courts on earth!) – Minos is still able to find out all about them'.)

434. **maesti:** adj. as noun. 'The next region is occupied by those unhappy people who ...' (translating **tenent** as passive in order to preserve the order of the ideas).

435. **insontes:** 'though innocent'; i.e. they were not driven to suicide by an awareness of guilt. **peperere:** perf. of *pario*, 'bring about'. **manu:** 'by force' (395). **perosi:** perf. part. of *perodi*, translate as present (202).

436. **proiecere:** 3rd pl. perf. of *proicio*. Their lives were metaphorically* a piece of rubbish which they threw away.
     quam vellent: 'how much they would like ...!'
     aethere in alto: 'in the open air above'.

437. **pauperiem, labores.** In *Odyssey* 11, Odysseus meets in Hades the ghost of Achilles, who says he would rather be a hired labourer on earth than a king among the dead.

438. **tristis** is nom., **inamabilis** is gen. **undae** is gen. of description*: 'the gloomy marsh with its unlovely water'.

439. **interfusa:** 'flowing between' the departed spirits and the upper world. This suggests a topography different from what Virgil has so far described – but in the underworld topography is subordinate to ideas.
     As objects to **alligat** and **coercet**, understand *eos*, i.e. the *maesti*.

440-76. Aeneas arrives in the Plains of Mourning. In one sense, this episode corresponds to *Odyssey* 11.225-329, where Odysseus meets an array of women from legend. Of those who appear here Virgil says that they suffered as a result of unhappy love. But they do not all seem to fit under this heading (Eriphyle, Pasiphae, Caenis), nor is it clear how they prepare the way for Dido, the last and most important of them. See on 447-8; and on 483 for Virgil's use of names to build up to an important meeting.

(For more detailed information about all of them, see below, and for references to other authors who wrote of them, see March.)

440. **partem fusi in omnem:** 'spreading in every direction'.
     monstrantur: they are 'pointed out' by the Sibyl to Aeneas.

441. **Lugentes:** the adj. is transferred* to the plains from their occupants, cf. 639.

nomine dicunt = *nominant,* 'they call'. 'They' are not identified; Virgil seems to be attributing the name to a general and anonymous tradition.

443-4. Take the basic sentence thus: **calles celant et silva tegit** (*eos*) **quos amor peredit.**

444. **relinquunt** has the same object as **celant, tegit.**

445. All the first five names are acc., objects of **cernit**: (Aeneas) sees....

Phaedra, the daughter of Minos and wife of Theseus. She fell in love with her stepson Hippolytus, who rejected her. Fearing that he would betray her to Theseus, she hanged herself, leaving a letter which incriminated Hippolytus – an act which led to Hippolytus' death.

Procris, wife of Cephalus. Wrongly believing him unfaithful, she followed him when he went hunting in a wood; here he accidentally killed her.

Eriphyle, wife of the prophet Amphiaraus. She was bribed to persuade her husband to go to a war in which he knew he would die. For this she was murdered by her son Alcmaeon.

Eriphylen: the 'y' is scanned* long.

446. **nati ... vulnera:** 'her son's wounds', i.e. wounds inflicted by her son.

447. *Evadne*, wife of Capaneus, one of the heroes killed in the famous attack on Thebes (see on 479). She was so much in love with her husband that she flung herself onto his funeral pyre.

Pasiphae, wife of Minos; for her story see on 24. The other women here died by violence. We know of no such story for Pasiphae.

Laodamia, wife of Protesilaus, first of the Greeks to land on Trojan soil and the first casualty of the war. They were only just married, and Protesilaus was allowed to return from the underworld to his wife for three hours. Thereafter she killed herself rather than be without him.

447-8. **his ... it comes:** 'walks as companion for these' – 'keeps company with them'.

Caeneus began life as the girl Caenis. She was seduced by the god Neptune; when he offered her a gift she chose to be changed to a man, Caeneus, 'so that she should never have to suffer such offence again'. Caeneus was killed by Centaurs, who hammered him into the ground using whole trees as clubs. Now in the underworld, he changes back to his original sex.

Translate 'now a woman and changed back again ...'. Virgil makes mild fun of the gender-change by putting the masculine name Caeneus conspicuously at the end of the line and then having the feminine participle *revoluta* agree with it.

Two of the women Aeneas has seen (Evadne and Laodamia) were loving and devoted wives; Phaedra's love was incestuous, Pasiphae's unnatural, Procris' ruined by jealousy. Eriphyle preferred gold to love; Caeneus' story is one of womanhood abandoned but restored after death. There have been various suggestions as to the connection between their stories and Dido's. At its simplest, one can say this. Virgil has performed a *tour de force* in presenting a group which is deliberately Homeric (445 is close to being a quotation from the *Odyssey*), highly compressed, and theatrical in its variety. Now all of a sudden there is an abrupt change from sharply drawn characters from the distant past who have nothing to do with Aeneas to the dim vision of one from the present who is only too closely and tragically connected with him.

450 **recens a vulnere:** 'fresh from her wound'. The 'wound' is both that of love and of the sword with which Dido killed herself. Literally computed, her death was weeks or months ago. Here it is as if it has only just happened.

451. **quam** is acc. after **iuxta** and also obj. of **agnovit**. 'When the hero stood next to her and recognised her.'

453. **obscuram:** agreeing with **quam**; best translated as adv., 'dimly'. The darkness is such that Aeneas can only just recognise her, even though he is right next to her. But he has recognised Phaedra and the rest without difficulty. There is something else which comes between him and Dido – the impossibility of communication which is brought out in the following lines. The darkness stands for this, and is emphasised by the enjambement* **per umbras / obscuram.**

453-4. The basic clause is **qualem qui videt ...:** 'just as one who sees ....

Understand *se* as subj. of **vidisse** (indirect statement): 'thinks that he has seen'.

primo ... mense. Normally the new moon becomes first visible as it sets in the evening on the first day of the lunar month (**primo mense**). Often it is eagerly awaited and watched for. Very occasionally it may be visible as it rises (here **surgere**) in the morning, with difficulty and for a very few minutes before the sun rises. A watcher might gaze with special intensity, given the chance of seeing the new moon twelve hours earlier than normal, and for all his gazing still not be sure whether he had or had not seen it. So with Aeneas: he sees Dido ... is it Dido? ... can it be she? He is very anxious that it should be, and that he should have the chance of repairing the damage done at their parting. A brilliant simile, in total contrast with its subject: Dido disappears eventually into the gloom, the new moon into the sky's brightness.

456. **infelix**: 'unlucky', rather than 'sad'. 'Poor' will nearly do, except that it sounds a little patronising. If one remembers that that 'hap' in 'happy' is the same as in 'happen' and that 'happy' means 'the sort of person to whom (good) things happen', 'unhappy' or perhaps 'hapless' are just right.

456-7. Start the sentence **nuntius venerat** (*te*) **exstinctam** (*esse*): 'news had come that you were dead'; and take **ergo** closely with **verus**: 'the news which came was after all true'. The pluperfect combines the ideas of a sentence 'news <u>came</u> which <u>was true</u> all along'. In fact, Virgil does not mention any news about Dido reaching Aeneas after he left her, except for the unsettling sight of fire in Carthage which the Trojans saw as they sailed away (5, 3-7).

    extrema secutam (*esse*): 'Sought the last things' is a euphemism* for 'killed yourself'. **exstinctam** is also a euphemism, slightly less delicate. Aeneas is extremely uneasy in talking of Dido's death, though he forces himself to be direct in line 458.

458-9. Aeneas swears by three things: **'sidera'**, **'superos'** and 'if there is any trustworthiness in the world below' or 'whatever there is to trust ...'.

460. This line is very close to a direct quotation from a fanciful poem by Catullus (66.39 *invitus, regina, tuo de vertice cessi*), in which a lock of hair apologises to its royal owner for having abandoned her head. There has been much argument over what impression, if any, Virgil wishes to give by this reference, if it is a deliberate reference. I like to connect it with the language Aeneas uses to Dido when he abandons her in Book 4. There, in lines 332-61, he speaks the truth in a way which Virgil has artfully contrived will (a) seem hypocritical to Dido (b) allow the reader to entertain the suspicion that Dido may be justified. Line 460 is a simple statement of at least one side of the truth, but its frivolous origin

grates on the reader and contributes to our understanding of the reasons why Dido accepts no reconciliation with Aeneas. But this is a decidedly personal view, and not one which commands universal support.

461-3. The basic sentence is **iussa deum me imperiis egere suis**. **deum:** gen. pl. **egere:** for *egerunt*, perf. of *ago*. 'The instructions of the gods drove me by their commands (to leave Carthage).' *imperium* is more forceful than *iussum*, carrying the idea of legitimate and irresistible authority. But the repeated idea of 'orders', coming in the first and last phrases of the sentence, conveys Aeneas' anxiety to convince Dido that he left Carthage **invitus** (460). (Here too, true though Aeneas' words are, he is playing the unattractive part of the person who says 'I only did it because I was told to'.) There is a similar anxious repetition between **egere** and **cogunt** (462), and between **umbras** and **noctem**. **senta situ:** a conspicuous alliterative phrase – 'coarse with neglect'. *sentus* is a very rare adjective: English 'hoar' ('old and mouldy') might give the idea. The phrase describes, in particular, Charon's appearance (299-301) very aptly.

463. **quivi:** from *queo*.

464. **hunc tantum dolorem:** 'this pain so great', the regular Latin for 'such great pain'.

465. **siste gradum:** in 451, Dido was 'straying'; now we see that she is walking away.

    aspectu is dative; the *-u* ending is rare in the masc. but regular in the neut. of the 4th declension. For the dative meaning 'away from' see on 342.

    ne subtrahe: *ne* + imperative, as in 95.

466. **quem fugis?** implying 'I'm a friend; you can't be running away from *me*'. Dido had asked Aeneas a similar question in 4.314: *mene fugis?*

    extremum ... hoc est: 'This, by fate, is the last thing I say to you', 'I am doomed never to speak to you again after this'. For the quantity* of **hoc** see on 129.

467-8. **talibus:** with **dictis** 468. **lenibat:** for *leniebat*; the imperf. means 'tried to soothe' ('conative*', cf. 358). **torva:** acc. n. pl.; take closely with **tuentem** as adverb ('adverbial acc.*'), 'looking fiercely', 'with a fierce expression'. **ardentem** and **tuentem** both agree with **animum**, 'her heart', though 'with a fierce expression' refers more naturally to Dido herself than to Dido's heart. Dido's face is expressionless and she never looks at Aeneas (469-70), but in her heart all is tumult and it is with great difficulty that she stops herself looking straight at him with an expression of blazing anger.

lacrimasque ciebat: 'brought forth tears'. The normal meaning of *lacrimas ciere* is 'to rouse tears in oneself'. Here, then, the imperf. is then not conative, but inceptive*: 'began to bring forth'. But the previous imperfect **lenibat** is conative* and one expects this one to be so also. Virgil is perhaps stretching the meaning of **ciebat** to allow 'tried to make Dido weep'. It is very understandable that Aeneas should wish to break Dido's apparent apathy. Both meanings are apt. We should not have to choose.

469. **aversa:** 'facing away'. **tenebat:** a straightforward imperf. here, for what Dido 'was doing' while Aeneas was speaking. The repeated 'o's in this line create a doleful effect as in 314.

470-1. 'Nor is she more changed in expression ... than if she were standing there as a hard stone ....' **vultum:** 'as to her expression' – 'acc. of respect'*.

Marpesia cautes: Marpessus was a mountain on the island of Paros, famous for its marble quarries. One can think either of a marble statue with unchanged expression or of the cliff-face in the island, rough and gleaming white (as Dido's ghost perhaps glimmers faintly – 454).

The two monosyllables **aut stet**, especially the second, emphasise Dido's immobility.

472. **corripuit sese:** 'picked herself up'. She has been stunned with the shock of seeing Aeneas; she now returns to action with an abrupt gesture. **tandem**: it evidently took time and effort to do this.

473-4. Take the words **ubi Sychaeus, pristinus coniunx, respondet illi curis**; 'where her former husband Sychaeus answers her with troubles of his own', i.e. they comfort each other by sharing their griefs. Sychaeus was Dido's husband in her home city Tyre in Phoenicia. It was when he was murdered by Dido's brother that Dido fled from Tyre to found Carthage. Until now we have had no idea of his presence; Dido was 'astray in a great forest'. Seeing her now reunited with Sychaeus, we feel that Dido's fate has reached some sort of kindly resolution. The same is not true for Aeneas, tormented by guilt and anxiety.

475. **nec minus** with **percussus.** Understand *eam* as object of **prosequitur** and **miseratur**; and think of **euntem** as agreeing with *eam*.

477. **datum:** 'given', 'appointed'. **molitur:** *molior* means 'I do something with difficulty'. Thus 'he trudges along his appointed path'.

478. **ultima:** 'furthest', i.e. the last part of the area appointed for those who died before their time. **bello clari:** take together: 'those famous in war'. **secreta:** agreeing with the relative pronoun **quae.** English does not allow adjectives to go with relative pronouns, so it needs to be translated 'the secluded fields which ...', or taken as an adverb: 'the fields which famous warriors occupy apart'.

479-80. **Tydeus** (the 'y' is scanned* long), **Parthenopaeus** and **Adrastus** were among the seven commanders in the unsuccessful war against Thebes in the generation before the Trojan war.

    occurrit: singular, but each of the three names in these two lines, and also **Dardanidae** (482), must be taken separately as subject to it. The anaphora* **hic ... hic ... hic** makes it clear that the sentence goes thus.

    inclutus armis: translate together, like **bello clari** (478); also **bello caduci** (481)

481-2. **fleti** and **caduci** both agree with **Dardanidae.**

    multum ... superos: 'much lamented in the world above'. **ad superos,** 'among those above', involves an unusual meaning of *ad* (*OLD* 16b).

    quos ... ingemuit: the basic clause is **quos cernens ingemuit:** 'seeing whom he groaned'. **longo ordine** need mean not much more than 'in large numbers'.

483-4. The names are those of warriors whom Aeneas saw; they are acc. because in apposition* to **quos** (482). **Medonta, Polyboeten** are accusatives of Greek form (from *Medon, Polyboetes*). The three names in 483 are quoted in the same order and rhythm from *Iliad* 17.216, and to the same effect, that names coming in quick succession with little or no story attached to them are there to represent a huge and undifferentiated crowd. But they serve as a starting point to the sequence leading via Idaeus to Deiphobus, as 333-7 prepare for Palinurus and 442-50 for Dido.

    Cereri sacrum: 'sacred to Ceres' i.e. priest of Ceres. Polyboetes is not known from any other source.

485. Idaeus was Priam's charioteer. **currus** and **arma** are both obj. of
tenentem. Note the repeated **etiam**: Idaeus is *still* on duty! There is
pathos* in the absence of Priam, emphasised by the appearance of
his name and his son in 494.

    Notice how Virgil creates word-patterns with these names,
varying the amount he says about each and varying their
distribution within the line.

487. **vidisse semel**: 'just to have seen (him)'; take **nec** with **satis est.**

    iuvat usque morari: 'it pleases (them) to keep on dawdling
(with him)'.

488. **conferre gradum**: 'to bring (their) step together (with his)', i.e. 'to
walk with him'.

489. **Danaum**: gen. pl. **phalanges**: a Greek word referring to the close-
packed ranks of a Greek army – the ghosts of the Greeks who
fought at Troy. Virgil uses *phalanx* only here. Together with the
grandiose adj. **Agamemnoniae** ('belonging to Agamemnon, king
of Troy') it must be designed to create an impression of outlandish
splendour contrasting strongly with the feeble actions of those
described.

490-2. **ut** with indic. here = 'when'.

    videre = *viderunt*, as the long 1st syllable shows. **trepidare,
vertere, tollere**, however, are infinitives (historic*), giving the
sense of an imperf. indic. 'began to', as in 256.

    trepidare metu: cf. 290. This empty victory for Trojans over
Greeks is a poor consolation for their actual defeat, but it perhaps
prepares for the great victories which the Trojans' descendants will
really win against the later Greeks (foretold in 1.283-5).

492. **petiere rates: petiere** = *petiverunt*; **rates** refers to the ships of the
Greeks, drawn up on the shore at Troy and serving the Greeks as
camp and refuge in trouble. Occasionally in the *Iliad* the battle
goes in favour of the Trojans, and the Greeks run for the ships.

493. **exiguam**: they try to raise a battle-cry, but only a thin and weedy
sound emerges.

    inceptus ... hiantes: 'the attempted (i.e. failed) shout mocks
them-as-they-open-their-mouths-wide'; 'their failure to shout
makes a mockery of their gaping faces'.

    491-2 are full of activity; **exiguam** left over to the beginning of
493 (enjambement*) deflates it. Even the elision* of the last

syllable of **exiguam** cuts off the sound in the reader's throat to illustrate the failed cry.

494-7. Priamiden is acc. of Greek form.

laniatum: *lanius* = butcher; *laniare* = 'to cut up meat as a butcher would'.

Dēïphŏbūm: four syllables. See on 499, and for the metre of the passage, Intro. **8d**.

Virgil leaves telling us who it is until last: he is a son of Priam – he is horribly injured – he is Deiphobus. The next four phrases give very unpleasant detail to expand on **laniatum**.

lacerum ora: 'shredded as to his face'; **ora** (pl. with sing. meaning) is acc. of respect*, as are **manus, tempora** and **nares**. Note the repetition of **ora**, emphasising Aeneas' shocked reaction to the sight.

populata: 'ravaged' as if they were conquered territory; the idea is explained by **raptis auribus**.

inhonesto: a 'dishonourable' wound, because 'honourable' wounds are those given and received by enemies standing up to each other in battle – unlike this.

498. adeo: 'in fact'.

pavitantem, tegentem: 'cowering', 'hiding'. A hendiadys*. Deiphobus cowers away from Aeneas *in order to hide* his own hideous appearance.

499. supplicia: 'punishment'. In the last year of the Trojan War Helen's husband Paris was killed. She next married Deiphobus. When the Greeks captured Troy, Helen's original husband Menelaus tortured Deiphobus as a 'punishment' (**supplicia**) for Paris' seduction of her.

ultro: refusing to be discouraged by Deiphobus' appearance or his wish to hide, Aeneas speaks, taking the intiative (**ultro**) himself.

500. armipotens: a compound adjective 'mighty with arms'. Virgil is fond of such words; they are not native to Latin but very much a characteristic of Greek epic, and allow Virgil to be inventive and Homeric at the same time.

genus: a neuter noun, usually meaning 'kind, race', it comes to refer to an individual member of the race – 'son'. The context is always solemn. 'Offspring' might give the idea.

alto: 'high' in the sense of 'ancient' (*OLD* 8) and 'noble (*OLD* 11).

a sanguine Teucri: 'descended from the line of Teucer'. Teucer was the semi-divine founder of the Trojan royal line.

This grand and solemn address of Aeneas' contrasts starkly with Deiphobus' own pathetic self-effacement. Aeneas is restoring to Deiphobus his self-respect.

501. **optavit:** 'chose' but also with the suggestion that the person responsible finds pleasure in the choice. **sumere poenas:** to inflict punishment.

502-4. Think of **tantum** as if it were *tantas poenas sumere*. 'To whom was it permitted to inflict such punishment on you (**de te**).'

fama ... tulit: understand *nuntium*. 'Rumour brought (the report) that ...'; an acc. and infin. follows: **te ... procubuisse.** **suprema:** abl. with **nocte**, i.e. Troy's last night. **fessum:** with **te. vasta caede:** take closely with **fessum** – 'exhausted by ...'. **Pelasgum:** gen. pl., after **caede**, 'killing of Greeks'.

confusae stragis acervum: think of **stragis** as a collective noun referring to many dead bodies. Aeneas hoped that because they were all 'mingled', Deiphobus would have escaped notice and mutilation.

505. **Rhoeteo in litore:** 'on the Rhoetean shore'. Rhoeteum was a short way northward along the coast from Troy.

506. **magna ... vocavi:** the mourner summons the spirit to enter the tomb. The double alliteration* **magna manes** and **voce vocavi** gives a ritual quality to the sentence.

507. **nomen ... servant:** 'Your name and your arms keep watch over the place', i.e. keep it as a sacred place. How did Aeneas get hold of Deiphobus' arms? Servius* thought Aeneas was merely referring to a painting of the arms on Deiphobus' tomb.

507-8. **te, amice: te** is not elided against **amice**, but it becomes a short syllable ('correption*'). It represents colloquial speech, and, with the affectionate **amice**, is another side of Aeneas' attempt to restore Deiphobus' dignity (500). **te** is object of both **conspicere** and **ponere**.

509. **Priamides:** understand *respondit*.

nihil tibi relictum (*est*): The dative **tibi** gives 'by you' – such a dative is not uncommon in verse. ('dative of agent'*.)

Two points call attention to the close friendship between these two: (a) **o ... amice:** the separation of these words adding to the emotional intensity; (b) **tibi, amice** answering **te, amice** in the same position in line 507.

510. **solvisti:** 'paid' as if obligation to bury were a financial debt.

funeris umbris: 'for the ghost of his/my body'. **funus** here = corpse; **umbris** is plural for singular.

511. **Lacaenae:** 'the Spartan woman' (a deliberately offensive expression) is Helen (see on 499). Her 'murderous crime' is explained in the following lines.

512. **monimenta:** 'things to remember her by' – his wounds.

513-14. **ut ... egerimus: ut** = 'how'; **egerimus** is perf. subj. in indirect question; **ago** = 'pass (time)'. **nosti** = *novisti (nosco)*.

falsa ... gaudia: there was joy because the Greeks had sailed away. The joy was false because their departure was only a trick to lure the Trojans into taking the wooden horse into Troy. Book 2 tells the story (Intro. **5**).

514. **nimium ... necesse est:** 'one cannot help remembering only too well'. **necesse** refers not to what one is obliged to do but to what inevitably happens.

515-18. **cum ... venit, ... ducebat ... tenebat: cum** taking the indicative 'at the moment when'. Deiphobus compresses the time-sequence, with vivid effect: 'just when the horse arrived, there was Helen, leading the Trojans and brandishing a torch'.

fatalis equus: 'the Horse of Destiny'. The wooden horse is imagined here, terrifyingly, as a live horse of monstrous size jumping lightly over the great fortifications of Troy and landing in the citadel.

saltu ... venit: 'came at a leap', 'came leaping over'.

516. **Pergama** n. pl., the citadel at the very heart of Troy.

peditem: sing. for pl. **gravis:** 'pregnant', agreeing with **equus**.

517. **chorum simulans:** 'pretending (to arrange) a ritual dance'. In 2.238-9, Virgil tells how the Trojans celebrated the entry of the horse into Troy with songs and dances. This serves as a cover for Helen's actions. (In fact, the story as told here is rather different from Book 2, perhaps because of Deiphobus' selective memory.)

euhantes: a participle in form, though there is no indicative, meaning 'crying *euhoe*'. *euhoe* is the ritual cry of the women worshippers of Bacchus, often in ecstatic night-time dances. **euhantes** agrees with **Phrygias**.

> **orgia:** 'the secret rites'; internal accusative* after **euhantes**: 'crying the ritual (cries)'.

In *Odyssey* 4.274-89 there is a totally different account of a visit by Helen to the wooden horse. But the Helen of the *Odyssey* is a sorceress, ageless and subtle. In the *Aeneid* she is the woman with no conscience, determined to save herself by any means from the consequences of her own misdeeds.

> **circum:** the verb is **circumducebat**, the two parts separated (tmesis*) – 'was leading the Trojan women around'. Interestingly, *circumduco* is common in comedy with the meaning 'deceive', 'make a fool of'.

518-19. **media:** 'in the middle'. It was standard practice for Bacchic dancers to have torches, so Helen has an excuse for the one she carries, but of course it is a huge one – **ingentem** is bitterly stressed by Deiphobus (separated widely from **flammam** and placed at the beginning of the line).

519. **Danaos ... vocabat:** 'she was inviting the Greeks', with her torch as a fire signal, to attack from outside the city. Meanwhile Sinon, the Greek agent who had been accepted by the Trojans as a deserter, opened the horse itself (2.258-9).

520-2. Basic sentence **me habuit thalamus, (*me*) pressit quies:** 'the marriage-chamber held me (I was in the marriage-chamber), sleep overpowered me'; **confectum, gravatum** and **iacentem** all agree with **me. tum ... gravatum** seems to describe his state before lying down – the reasons why he went to sleep; **dulcis ... morti** describes the consequent sleep.

523. **egregia:** 'splendid', used sarcastically, as often.

524. **capiti:** 'away from my head'. Deiphobus evidently kept his sword by his pillow. The dative is 'disadvantage', as in 342, 465.

> **subduxerat:** pluperf. She removed (historic present) the weapons and *had already* taken my sword (as a preliminary precaution).

526. **scilicet** with **sperans:** 'obviously hoping that ...' – sarcastic. The acc. + infin. (**id ... fore** and **famam ... posse**) follows **sperans. 'id'** refers to her betrayal of Deiphobus.

> **amanti:** refers to Menelaus, again sarcastically, as if Menelaus is visiting Helen as a young lover his girlfriend. 'Menelaus meets

Helen after the war' is a standard topic in ancient art and literature, and Menelaus is represented as being overcome by love when the 'manly' thing would have been to take revenge on her. Here it is even worse: Menelaus tortures Deiphobus as a substitute for the anger he would more legitimately feel against Helen, whom he dare not punish, or Paris, whom he cannot.

527. **famam veterum malorum:** 'the disgrace of her previous misdeeds'.

528. **quid moror:** 'why am I delaying?' i.e. 'to put it in a few words'.

    additus (*est*): 'was added (to them)', i.e. 'joined them'. 'Aeolides joined together (with them) as a companion.'

529. **Aeolides:** 'descendant of Aeolus' i.e. Odysseus. Aeolus was father of Sisyphus the great trickster. It was sometimes alleged that Odysseus was born of an illegitimate relationship between his mother and Sisyphus, so to refer to Odysseus as 'descendant of Aeolus' is equivalent to calling him a bastard.

    hortator scelerum: 'instigator of wickedness'. In literature after Homer Odysseus is often a clever and unscrupulous villain (March pp. 277 & 282).

    talia: 'such things' as have been done to Deiphobus. We know what they are (494-7); no further description is needed.

530. **instaurate:** *instauro* means 'to start something all over again' – only this time, it is to be done against the Greeks.

    pio ... ore: 'justly' (*pius* with a general meaning of 'morally good').

531-2. **sed te:** corresponding to *sed me* (511). Deiphobus, aware that he has gone on too long about himself, breaks off to start a new subject.

    qui casus: 'what events?' (nom.); **qui** is the interrogative adjective.

    fare: imper. of *for fari*. **attulerint:** perf. subj. (indirect question introduced by **fare**).

    pelagi-ne: ne is the interrogative suffix. **pelagi ... erroribus actus:** 'driven by the unpredictability of the sea'. Deiphobus wonders if it is mere accident which has brought Aeneas to the underworld.

533. **fatigat:** 'what misfortune dogs you?'

534. **adires:** it is odd to find an imperf. subj. following a present tense; but think of **fatigat** as referring to misfortunes which have began in

the distant past and are still continuing, so that the present tense embraces the past too. (**ut ... adires** is a result clause.)

535. **hac vice sermonum:** 'during this exchange of speeches'. The abl. is that of 'time during which'. Note the odd noun **vice** which has no nom.; it occurs in the English expression 'vice versa'.

    roseis ... quadrigis: the sun-god rides across the sky every day in his chariot; Dawn accompanies him. This brief reminder of the bright world above reminds us forcibly of the darkness below.

536. **medium ... traiecerat axem:** 'had crossed the middle of the sky'.

537. **traherent:** *traho* often means 'extend' 'drag out'. They are actually extending their conversations rather than the time; the idea is transferred*. The imperf. subj. puts us alongside them: 'they would be dragging out the time ...'; the abrupt perf. **admonuit** cuts them off and distances us.

    omne datum tempus: 'all the permitted time'. We have not been told before that Aeneas' time in the underworld is limited. To hear of it now lends pathos* to Deiphobus' farewell and reminds us of the Sibyl's personality.

538. **comes Sibylla** is the subject of both verbs.

539. **ruit:** 'is falling on us fast'. An exaggeration, and spoken sharply, as appears from 544 (**ne saevi**). The Sibyl does not want to waste time in sentimentality.

    flendo: abl. of gerund, 'in weeping'.

540. **partes:** with **ambas**. 'In both directions'. 'Both' rather than 'two' suggests that these two routes – to heaven and hell, effectively – have been discussed before. In the *Aeneid* they have not, but a right-hand upward route for the just and a left-hand downward route for the wicked appear in Plato's *Republic* (Intro. **6.iii.d**).

541-2. **dextera quae ... tendit:** '(the road – **via** in the previous line) which, on the right, heads for ... and, on the left, (**laeva**) ...'. **dextera** and **laeva** are adjectives agreeing with **quae** which need to be translated adverbially.

    iter Elysium: '(our) way to Elysium'. Acc. of motion without preposition, and even more unusual because depending on a noun not a verb. Elysium is the part of the underworld reserved for the spirits of the good.

543. **exercet poenas:** the road 'sets the punishment in motion' by conveying the wicked to Tartarus. Tartarus is the deep pit in the underworld where the wicked are punished. Virgil sometimes uses

the sing. *Tartarus*, which is masc., sometimes (as here) the pl. *Tartara*, which is neut. **impia** is transferred* from the occupants to the place.

544. **ne saevi:** *ne* + pres. imper. as in 74, 95.

545. **explebo numerum:** 'I will fill out the number'. *Numerus* here perhaps as in *OLD* 8b 'a confused mass', 'a group which has nothing but quantity'; an expression of despair as Deiphobus looks on a living person for the last time.

    reddar: fut. pass. of *reddo*, 'give back', as if Darkness were an owner claiming him as a runaway slave.

    Deiphobus' three sentences in one line express his pathetic anxiety not to give offence to the Sibyl.

546. **i decus, i, nostrum: decus** with **nostrum**: 'our glory', 'glory of the Trojan people'; the command becomes more urgent for being repeated and for being placed between noun and adjective.

    utere: imper. of *utor*, here = 'experience', 'enjoy'.

547. **effatus:** understand *effatus est.* **in verbo:** 'as he spoke'.

548-624. The passage is in two parts: (i) 548-79, a description of the place where sinners go, their trial and sentence (ii) 580-627, a selective account of those here confined. The list alternates between named or recognisable characters from legend (580-607 and 616-20) and unnamed sinners who have committed crimes familiar in Roman moral discussion (608-15 and 621-4). Virgil tells the stories from legend in a form which shows that he knows the traditions well and is prepared to be faithful to them in some cases, while in others he makes his own modifications. The more general crimes are perhaps there to bring the ideas nearer home. (Compare 8.667-70, where Aeneas briefly sees Tartarus pictured on the shield made for him by Vulcan: Catiline the terrorist of 63 BCE is the only sinner presented.)

548. **respicit:** Aeneas gazes at the departing Deiphobus, then makes a sudden movement (**subito**) to look round. To the left he sees what the Sibyl had told him about in 542-3.

    sub rupe sinistra: 'under a cliff on the left'.

549. **moenia** refers to the buildings of a city or fortress, **muro** to the wall around it.

550. **flammis:** abl. Translate either with **ambit**: 'surrounds with fire', or with **rapidus**: 'greedy with scorching fire', like *ramus aureus foliis* (137).

551. **torquetque:** the force of the current twists the rocks against each other, so that there is a grinding sound. Hard to pronounce, the word reflects the events (onomatopoeia*).

552. Supply *est*. 'Facing him *there is* a huge gate ....'

   solidoque adamante: abl. of description* – 'columns of solid adamant'. *adamas* is a Greek word meaning 'unconquerable'; it is used of a legendary substance of unique hardness.

553-4. Take the sentence **ut nulla vis virum** (*valeat*) **exscindere** (*eas*). **ut** introduces a result clause: 'such that no force ...'. **virum** is gen. pl. (= *virorum*). **caelicolae** is another subject of **valeant**.

   ad auras: as if the verb had been 'rises'. **stat** suggests the static solidity of the iron tower.

555. **Tisiphone** is one of the three Furies (Eumenides), spirits with particular responsibility for avenging murder.

   palla: a dress worn by women out of doors. **succincta** (nom.): 'dressed ready for action'. The dress was pulled up so as to fall in a fold over the girdle and leave the legs unencumbered.

556. **exsomnis:** translate as adv. 'sleeplessly'.

557. **exaudiri, sonare:** historic* infinitives; 'could be heard', 'were resounding'.

558. **stridor** and **catenae** are both nom., subjects of **sonare**. 'The noise of iron and dragged chains' is a hendiadys* for 'the grating sound of dragging iron chains'. The many 'r's suggest the dragging of chains and are sufficient proof in themselves that Latin 'r's were rolled (onomatopoeia*). The flurry of anxious questions recalls 318-20.

560. **quae scelerum facies?** 'what kind of crimes' (are represented here)?'

   effare: imper. **-ve:** 'or' (cf. 104).

561. **quis** (*est*). **plangor ad auras:** 'cries (rising) to the air above'.

562. **orsa** (*est*). **Teucrum** is gen. pl.

563. **nulli:** dat., **casto** agrees with it. **fas** (*est*).

564. **cum** + indic.: 'at the time when'. **Hecate:** see 247.

565. **deum** is gen. pl. 'The gods' punishments' are the punishments *imposed by* the gods.

omnia: everything in Tartarus. The presence of Hecate as guide protects the Sibyl from the pollution she would otherwise incur (563).

566. **Rhadamanthus** was brother of Minos, another judge in the underworld (432). **haec ... habet durissima regna:** 'has these very harsh kingdoms', i.e. 'reigns very sternly here'.

567. **castigatque auditque dolos:** first he reprimands them (in general terms, for having done something deserving trial in his court), then he hears (the details of) their trickery.

567-9. Take the sentence thus: **subigitque** (*eos*) **fateri piacula quae, commissa apud superos, distulit quis, laetatus furto inani, in mortem seram.** 'He forces them to confess the crimes which, having been committed in the world above, any of them (**quis**) has postponed, delighting in empty deceit, until death – too late.' By 'postponed the crimes' Virgil means 'postponed paying for the crimes'. The word **piaculum** means 'a crime needing atonement'; the idea 'crime' comes early in the sentence, 'atonement' later. The thought is clear, though the syntax is a little strained.

570-1. Take the sentence **continuo sontes Tisiphone quatit**. Tisiphone is described by **ultrix** and **accincta flagello. quatit** = 'makes them writhe' with her scourge. Take **continuo** with both **sontes** (because the sinners confess, they are 'immediately' found 'guilty') and with **quatit** (punishment follows instantly upon verdict).

    insultans: like **intentans** 572 a pres. part., suggesting that all these things happen simultaneously – she leaps on them, she scourges them (with her right hand), she directs her snakes at them with her left, all the while shouting for her companions to join her.

    sinistra: understand *manu*.

572. **agmina ... sororum:** 'the companies of her sisters'. One tradition stated that there were three Furies, the sisters Tisiphone, Megaera and Allecto. In another they existed in unknown number. They appear as the chorus in Aeschylus' play *Eumenides*. See March under 'Furies', where there are some interesting ancient illustrations.

572-3. **sacrae ... portae.** *sacer* means 'dedicated to a god' in the sense either that the god protects ('sacred, holy') or punishes ('cursed'). Here the word, applied to the gates, makes them more frightening. Notice how slowly the gates open: the phrase covers the end of a line and consists of seven successive long syllables, with the end of a line intervening and the p-alliteration* adding a note of finality.

574-5. **custodia qualis ... facies quae:** 'what sort of sentry ... what sort of shape'. The Sibyl contrasts Tisiphone, the visible horror outside the gates, with the far worse ones to be imagined within.

576. **Hydra:** 'clearly not the *belua Lernae* (287) but a relative' (Austin).

Read **immanis quinquaginta hiatibus:** 'frightful with its fifty yawning (mouths)'. For the effect of the five long 'a's, compare 237.

577. **tum:** 'next' after the gateway, for one walking in.

578. **bis tantum:** 'twice as much'. **patet in praeceps,** 'opens up straight downwards' and **tendit sub umbras,** 'heads for the darkness' both give the same general idea of a deep pit, with different emphasis.

579. 'As much as is (understand *est*) the upward view of the sky towards heavenly Olympus.'

For the whole sentence, perhaps 'Then there is Tartarus itself, a yawning pit which stretches sheer downward into the darkness twice as far as one looks up to the sky towards heavenly Olympus.' Olympus is the sky and the home of the gods more than any particular mountain. This idea of Tartarus probably comes to Virgil from Hesiod*, who speaks in his poem *Theogony* ('Tales of the Birth of the Gods') of a bronze wall surrounding a pit so deep that it would take an anvil of bronze nine days to fall from ground level to its bottom.

580. **hic** (*erat*).

Titania pubes: 'the Titanic brood', i.e. the race of the Titans. The Titans were children of Earth (**genus Terrae**), older than Jupiter and the other gods, on whom they made war. Defeated, they were flung into Tartarus.

581. **fulmine:** the thunderbolt was the characteristic weapon of Jupiter.

582. **Aloidas:** Otus and Ephialtes were nominally sons of Aloeus, but really of the sea-god. At nine years old they were 16 metres tall (**immania corpora**). By piling mountains one on top of another they too attempted unsuccessfully to reach heaven and cast down the gods.

584. **adgressi** (*sunt*): 'made a move to ...'. It is the context rather than the word which gives the note of aggression.

585. **Salmonea:** this is the acc. (Gk.) of the name *Salmoneus*. Salmoneus founded a city near Olympia in southern Greece, where he

represented himself as Jupiter, riding in a chariot and imitating thunder and lightning as described in the following lines. For this arrogance he was struck with a real thunderbolt. What his later punishment in the underworld was, we are not told. (Though see on 586.)

dantem poenas: *poenas dare* = 'to pay a penalty', 'to be punished'.

586. '... while he mimicked Jupiter's fire and the noises of the sky.'

This is a disputed passage. A convincing version is 'I saw S. paying the penalty (*which he had incurred*) while he mimicked Jupiter's fire etc ...'.

587. **invectus:** 'riding'.

lampada is acc. sing. (Gk.).

588. **Graium** is gen. pl. **mediae ... urbem:** 'a city of mid-Elis', 'a city in the heart of Elis'. Elis is a region in southern Greece. The city is the one founded by Salmoneus. Elis is mentioned probably because within its boundaries lay Olympia, Jupiter's most important shrine, close to which Salmoneus' activities were especially blasphemous.

589. **ibat ovans:** 'used to go in glory' (West). For a Roman general, an *ovatio* is a lesser form of triumph, celebrated by a procession on foot. But *ovare* is occasionally used of a full triumphal procession, and we are perhaps reminded of the procedure on such occasions: the victorious general rides in a chariot wearing an embroidered toga of a type otherwise worn only by Jupiter himself in his temple on the Capitol. This is so close to 'claiming the honour due to the gods' (589) that the general was accompanied by a slave constantly reminding him of his mortality. In 29 BCE Augustus had celebrated a triple triumph, which cannot have been far from Virgil's mind as he was writing this – indeed he refers to it directly in 8.714-28. He may have wished us to think of the modest behaviour of the Roman ruler by contrast with Salmoneus' folly, and this would account for the presence of a relatively unfamiliar story in a conspicuous place among the punishments in the underworld.

590-1. **demens, qui nimbos ... simularet:** *qui* followed by a subjunctive very often gives a reason: 'fool, (in being one) who imitated the storm-cloud ...'; 'what folly to imitate ...'.

aere: there are different versions of how Salmoneus used bronze to imitate thunder. One says that he drove over a bridge made of bronze.

593-4. ille: '(Jupiter cast his thunderbolt), not torches or pinewood, not he! ...'.

fumea taedis lumina: 'lights smoky with pine-brands' is a striking expression for 'the smoky light of torches'.

594. Understand *eum* (= Salmoneus) as obj. for **adegit**.

595. nec non et: 'and also' (the repeated negatives cancel each other out).

Tityon (acc.): Tityos was a son of Earth, punished for attempting to rape Apollo's mother Latona. A vulture tears for ever at his ever-restored liver (see 600).

596-7. cernere erat: 'it was (possible) to see'.

per tota ... porrigitur: 'whose body is spread over nine whole acres'. (**cui** is dat. of reference*.) The vulture must be of correspondingly monstrous size.

598-9. iecur and **viscera** are both objects of **tondens**.

fecunda poenis viscera is a peculiarly grisly phrase, each word a surprise in relation to the others: *entrails* which are *fertile*; *fertile* for *agony* – **poenis** is probably dat. rather than abl.

rimaturque ... habitatque: the '**que**'s mean 'both ... and'. **epulis:** dat. – 'ferrets around for his feast'.

600. fibris: *fibra* is the medical term for a lobe of the liver. **renatis:** perf. part. of *renascor*.

The long and rambling sentence 595-600, with its horrid ideas, is no doubt meant to convey the size of Tityos, and the endlessness and horror of his punishment.

601. quid memorem: deliberative* subj., as in 122-3.

Lapithas, Ixiona, Pirithoum: Ixion, king of the Lapiths, a tribe in Thessaly, attempted to rape Hera (for the story, see March). His son (or Zeus' son by Ixion's wife, cf. 393-4) was Pirithous, who came with Theseus to the underworld to seize Proserpina. The account of their punishment most usually given is that Ixion was bound to an ever-spinning wheel and Pirithous held fast for ever in a chair where he had sat on Dis' invitation. In this passage (in addition to the terror of a rock about to fall on them), they both suffer perpetual hunger and thirst, tormented by the sight of food which they cannot reach. This is the punishment usually assigned to another sinner, Tantalus, who tested the gods by serving them a stew made from the body of his own son. This and some other passages suggest that these traditions were not hard and fast. But in varying them, Virgil is also continuing to create the atmosphere of an underworld where nothing can quite be pinned down.

602. **quos super ... silex ... imminet:** 'above whom a rock hangs threateningly.' **iam iam lapsura** and **cadenti adsimilis** ('just like one actually falling') both describe the rock. The second phrase increases the terror of the first. The doubled **iam** intensifies the single word: 'at any moment now'.

    cadentique: unusually, the final vowel is elided against the vowel beginning the next line. The line falls over into the next line – as the rock seems to be about to fall on the sinners. Lines with such an extra syllable are called 'hypermetric*'.

603. One can think of the sinners as facing, from the open side, the three-couch arrangement (*triclinium*, see *OCD*) of a Roman dining room. They get a good view of the furniture: *geniales tori* which are, in grand fashion, high off the ground and, also grandly, equipped with head and back-rests (**fulcra**). Closer to them (**ante ora**) is the food on the little tables on which each course was served, so that **mensas** refers either to the table or to the dishes on it. The Fury is reclining on one of these couches (**accubat** is a word particularly used of presence at table) as if she were a guest. She brandishes her torch as a weapon like the one illustrated in March p. 205.

604. **genialibus ... toris** is dat. of reference*. 'The golden **fulcra** on the festal couches gleam ....'

604. **paratae** (*sunt*).

605. **Furiarum maxima:** see on 571. It is not clear who 'the greatest of the Furies' is.

    iuxta: adv.

606. Understand *eos* as obj. for **prohibet**. Take **manibus** with **prohibet**: she makes a threatening gesture.

607. **ore:** her last and most frightening action is to make a thunderous shout.

608-14. Start by translating **hic** (608) **inclusi poenam exspectant** (614): 'imprisoned here they are awaiting punishment ....' Then, to tell us who 'they' are, there follow the four relative clauses **quibus ...** (608), **qui ...** (610), **quique ... quique ...** (612).

    hic, occurring three times (580, 582, 608), referring to different places in Tartarus, forms a very extended anaphora*.

    quibus invisi (*sunt*) **fratres pulsatusve** (*est*) **parens:** lit. 'those by whom their brothers were hated or a parent struck'. **quibus** is dat. of agent*. Translate as active: 'those who hated their brothers ...'.

dum vita manebat: 'for as long as life lasted': i.e. they never sought reconciliation.

609. **... fraus innexa (*est*) clienti:** lit. 'deceit was contrived against a dependant'. For the disadvantaged in Roman society, almost the only hope of security lay in attaching oneself as a dependant (*cliens*) to a member of the upper classes. The loyalty owed to clients by their upper-class patrons and vice versa was one of the most loudly-stated principles of Roman social ethics.

610-11. 'Those who found treasure and then hoarded it on their own.' **incubuere** and **posuere** are perf. indic.

611. **quae maxima turba est:** 'a number (**turba**) which is particularly large' (i.e. the misers).

612-13. **caesi, secuti** ('took up'), **veriti:** understand *sunt* with each of these.

adulterium: An old custom had it that adulterers could in certain circumstances be killed out of hand by offended parties. But Augustus was the first to bring adultery under a formal law. Virgil is perhaps acknowledging Augustus' evident sense that it was a crime, and a serious one.

nec veriti ... dextras. The master shows his confidence in his slave by offering him his right hand to clasp. Thus the right hand is a symbol of trust and confidence, which the slaves betray. They have betrayed it in taking up **arma impia**, i.e. joining in an armed rebellion. The reference is almost certainly to Octavian's (Augustus') war (38-36 BCE) against Sextus Pompeius, who encouraged slaves to run away and join him. It was for this war that the engineering works in the area of Cumae were undertaken (Intro. **6.i.d**).

614. **expectant:** the pit of Tartarus suddenly becomes a place of detention before execution. Is Virgil thinking of the place for such detention in Rome – the Tullianum, itself a pit inside a fortification – the prison on the edge of the forum? It was, according to Sallust*, a place of 'darkness, desolation and stench, foul and terrifying to behold' (*Catiline* 55.4).

615. **quam poenam:** understand *exspectant*, indic. because **mersit** is also indic. The clause is relative: 'Do not seek to be taught the punishment which they are expecting, or the form or fortune which has overwhelmed them.' There is dispute as to what is meant by

'form or fortune'. (i) Perhaps 'type or luck (of punishment)', i.e. a sort of hendiadys* 'the type of punishment which it has been their luck to receive'. (ii) Servius* took *forma* as 'rule of law'; thus 'the (broken) law or unlucky circumstances which have brought them to Tartarus' – i.e. it is about the crime rather than the punishment. Recent editions rather prefer (i). But possibly (iii) the phrase is a throw-away generalisation by the Sibyl, where *forma* covers anything that happens according to rule, i.e. predictably, and *fortuna* anything that happens by chance, i.e. unpredictably. 'Do not trouble yourself about what has been their ruin – design or chance.'

616. To roll a stone is traditionally the punishment of Sisyphus (see March); to be stretched on a wheel that of Ixion. Virgil varies the stories as discussed above 601ff.

618. For **Theseus** and his punishment, see on 119-23. **aeternum** seems inconsistent with the version there. **Phlegyas** was said to have set fire to Apollo's temple at Delphi. We are not told what his punishment was: it must have given force to his warning (620).

619. **testatur:** 'bears witness'. i.e. to the validity of the command he is about to give.

620. **discite** has two objects: (i) **iustitiam**, (ii) **non temnere divos**.

    moniti: 'being warned' i.e. 'by what has happened to me'.

    Consideration of punishments has brought the Sibyl back to figures from mythology, and ended the main part of the section (ring composition*) with Phlegyas' stern line echoing through the darkness. The following seven lines thus form a summary of and conclusion to the section.

621-3. **hic ... hic:** 'one ... another', referring to unnamed sinners; the lines read like the objections of Virgil and his contemporaries to moral standards in their own times.

    pretio, auro: abl. of price. **leges pretio, auro patriam:** striking parallel juxtapositions emphasising the shameful character of such corruption.

    dominum: 'a tyrant' in that he treats the citizens as a master would his slaves. **potentem:** 'overbearing'.

    fixit ... refixit: laws and decrees at Rome were passed by the senate or the appropriate assembly, but published in the form of bronze tablets fixed to walls on the Capitol*. *refigo* = 'unfix', i.e. cancel. The reference is probably not to any single individual, but

fixit ... refixit is language strikingly similar to some passages written about Mark Antony (Intro. **1c**) by his enemy Cicero*.

623. **invasit:** 'forced his way into' both **thalamum** and **hymenaeos**.

624. **ausi** and **potiti:** understand *sunt*. **ausi:** 'dared (to commit) ...'.

 auso potiti: 'achieved what they had dared'. *potior* = 'achieve'; what you achieve is abl. *ausum,* neut. of the perf. part. of *audeo,* has here a pass. meaning 'that which has been dared'.

625. **non:** take this with **possim** (627), 'I would not be able' (potential* subj., cf. 841).

 mihi si ... sint: 'if there were to me...', 'if I had ...'; **mihi** is possessive* dat.

628-36. a bridge passage which eases the transition from the dark horror of Tartarus to the bright joy of Elysium. It also brings to a conclusion the account of the Golden Bough.

630-1. **acceleremus:** jussive* subjunctive, 'let us hurry'.

 Cyclopum ducta caminis: 'forged in the foundries of the Cyclopes'. The Cyclopes are the giant smiths of the gods, making thunderbolts for Zeus and arms for Aeneas in Book 8. Their forge was under the volcano Etna in Sicily. (Sicily was also the traditional home of Polyphemus, the rather different Cyclops encountered by Odysseus in *Odyssey* 9.) The walls here mark the boundary of Elysium and the home of Proserpina and are likely to be magnificent rather than gloomy and terrifying, so perhaps they are like the splendid brazen walls in the mythical palace of King Alcinous in *Odyssey* 8.

 duco here means 'to beat out', as in metalwork.

 adverso fornice portas: 'the gates in the arch which faces us'.

632. **praecepta** ('instructions') is the subject. **haec** with **dona** (acc.).The instructions are Proserpina's, in particular (see 142-3).

633. **opaca viarum:** opaca is n. pl. 'dark things / parts', but the phrase is equivalent to *per opacas vias*, except in that it invites more emphasis on the darkness – which is so soon to be dispelled (640).

634. **corripiunt:** 'they take up quickly' **spatium medium:** 'the space between (themselves and the gate)', i.e. they hurry across it.

635-6. **occupat ... aditum:** just as in 424.

 corpus ... aqua: a ritual of purification as he passes into the special realm of the blessed.

adverso as in 631.

628-76. The entry to Elysium forms a strange passage. The Sibyl sees gates in the arch ahead. Are they closed, so that Aeneas opens them by properly placing the branch? Or are they already open, so that placing the branch ensures that the two of them are not stopped by some other means? It is not even entirely clear whether the gates *are* the entrance to Elysium or whether the '*moenia Ditis*' constitute a fortress placed *beside* the entrance. There is no one to welcome them or question their right of access – a conspicuous contrast with Charon and Cerberus, and even with the phantoms which seem to threaten Aeneas at Orcus' gateway (273ff.). In fact the welcome comes from Anchises in 687-94. This suggests that the space between is to be seen as transitional, and that another boundary of equal importance is crossed in 677-8 (see the note there).

In fact the following passage, 637-76, relates as closely to what precedes as to what follows. The occupants of this stage of Elysium are like all whom Aeneas has so far met, in that they are involved in activities and experiences determined by their life on earth, the difference being that up to this point life on earth has led to misery in death, while from here on it leads to bliss in death. This change is also signalled by a sudden change from oppressive darkness (633) to brilliant open air and light (640). But in another sense happiness based on the past prepares us for hope in the future. It is the prospect of life yet to come and specifically the lives of Romans yet to come which are the main focus of attention in Elysium. The passage contrives to be both conclusion and introduction.

637-9. It is worth thinking about this sentence as an example of Virgil's careful choice and ordering of words. **demum** 'at last' tells us to expect a change – but how different a change from when it was last used (573)! 637 consists of two abl. abs. phrases in chiasmus*; the effect is to put the participles **exactis, perfecto** together and thus emphasise the sense of a task achieved. *devenere,* with its initial 'd', picks up the 'd's of **demum** and **divae** and forms a climax. The three long syllables at the beginning of the word break off into the shorts of the second foot, thus the slow effort of preparatory work yields to quick and easy movement on arrival in Elysium (note the l-alliteration). There follow four phrases with chiasmus much in evidence: noun-adj., adj.-noun; adj.-noun, noun-adj., calling our attention to the adjectives especially. The words **amoena** ...

nemorum should be seen as a single phrase whose climax is **fortunatorum**, a striking word taking up the whole of the first half of the line, with effective clash of ictus* and accent*. The final phrase forms a relaxing coda to the sentence with the stress falling lightly, as is only proper in heaven, on **beatas.**

637. **divae:** i.e. Proserpina. It is dative: 'when they have carried out their duty to the goddess'.

638. **devenere:** is perf. indic.; 'reached'.

   locos, virecta: understand *ad locos, ad virecta.* Omission of *ad* is rather less frequent than of *in* + abl.

638-9. **laetos, fortunatorum, beatas:** the adjectives. are transferred* to the places from their occupants, as with *Lugentes Campi* (441). 'The place of joy, the woodland of prosperity, the home of bliss.'

640-1. The sentence is abbreviated: 'a wider sky here clothes the plains, and (clothes them) in radiant light.'

   purpureo: the adjective was used of Misenus' clothes in 221, meaning 'bright red'. Here the idea is little more than 'bright'.

   norunt = *noverunt*, 'they – i.e. the inhabitants of Elysium – know' (*nosco*).

642. **pars ... pars** (644) = *alii ... alii,* 'some ... others' (see on 218-22).

644. **pedibus plaudunt choreas:** in English one can say 'they dance the waltz', where 'waltz' looks like a direct object. Think of **pedibus plaudunt** as equivalent to 'they dance', and **choreas** as 'the waltz'. (**choreas** is internal* acc.) Note the alliteration* and the onomatopoeic* effect of **pars pedibus plaudunt**: 'they stamp their feet to the dance'. (On the line, see Intro. **8c**)

645. **Thrēĭcĭŭs ... sacerdos:** the 'Thracian priest' is Orpheus, the legendary singer and player of the lyre. (See Intro. **6.iii.e** for reasons why he is mentioned here, also March for legends about him.) He appears **longa cum veste** as is proper for a musician.

646. **discrimina:** literally 'an interval' in music, e.g. the difference between the pitch sounded by two different strings. *voces* is a metaphor* for the strings of the lyre. So here **septem ... vocum** ('the seven intervals of the strings') means 'a lyre with its seven strings all sounding at different pitches and creating harmony by the intervals between them'! Orpheus 'makes them speak' (**obloquitur**) 'in accompaniment to the rhythm' (**numeris** – dat.). **discrimina** is internal* acc. A difficult line for its compressed ideas and inventive grammar.

647. **eadem pulsat:** 'he strikes the same (sounds, i.e. **discrimina vocum**)'. He is clearly a very accomplished player.

648. **hic** (*erat*). Compare 580, deliberately similar, in contrast.

    Teucri: see on 500 for Teucer.

650. Members of the Trojan royal line. Dardanus married the daughter of Teucer. Ilus and Assaracus were Dardanus' great-grandsons; Assaracus was Aeneas' great-grandfather.

651ff. This is a scene of warriors off duty: their weapons are not ready to hand; their chariots are empty (no charioteer); the horses are not yoked to the chariots. Compare 485, where Idaeus is still at his post.

    virum: gen. pl.; as in 615.

652. **soluti:** 'out of harness'.

653-5. Take the sentence **eadem gratia currum armorumque quae fuit** (*eis*) **vivis,** (*eadem*) **cura quae** (*fuit eis*) **pascere nitentes equos, sequitur** (*eos*) **repostos tellure.**

    currum: a very rare form of the gen. pl.

    gratia currum: 'delight in (their) chariots'.

    vivis is dat. (possessive*), agreeing with *eis* understood, but one can translate 'was in them while they were alive'.

    nitentes: 'sleek', 'well-groomed'.

    The subjects of **sequitur** are **gratia** and **cura**.

    repostos: short for *repositos* (*repono*). **tellure repostos** = buried.

656. **ecce:** 'suddenly' – from Aeneas' point of view.

657. **paeana:** acc. (Gk.) of *paean*, a hymn to Apollo.

658-9. **lauris** with **odoratum:** 'scented with bay'; 'a grove full of the scent of bay-trees'. The bay was sacred to Apollo.

    plurimus Eridani amnis: *plurimus* of something of which there is a great quantity, so 'the mighty river Eridanus'. *Eridani* gen., not, as one might expect, nom. (see on 84). It is a defining* gen. The Eridanus was originally a legendary river. By Virgil's time it was identified with the Po, the great river of his home country in the north of Italy.

    superne: this may mean (a) 'from above', i.e. downhill, as one would expect a river to flow, or (b) 'upwards'; part of the course of the Po is underground, so it could be thought to flow from the underworld to the upper world. Both meanings are found elsewhere. If 'upwards', the idea contributes to the dream-like quality of much of Virgil's description.

660. The sentence is compressed: 'Here the company (consists of) ...', then **passi** = 'those who suffered'; or one can say that the masc. pl. **passi** agrees with the plural idea contained in **manus**.

>**pugnando:** abl. of gerund, 'in fighting'.

>It is left to our imagination to decide what the difference is between these and the *bello clari* of 478.

661-2. **quique:** 'and those who were ...'. Understand *fuerunt* in both these lines and **locuti** (*sunt*) in 662.

>**dum vita manebat** as in 608.

>**Phoebo**: abl., with **digna**, as is usual: 'worthy of Phoebus'.

663. **inventas** with **artes:** 'improved life by means of the crafts/skills which they discovered'.

664. **merendo**: *mereri* very often means 'to do good service' (thereby deserving appreciation). So here 'who have made some people remember them by their good service / kindness.' The line carries the optimistic implication that everyone can do *someone* (**aliquos**) a kindness and so merit a place in heaven.

665. **omnibus his:** dat. of reference*. 'All their heads (*tempora*) ....'

>**nivea ... vitta:** on earth, bands of white wool are a mark of the priest or prophet, the servant of a god (*OLD* 2a); here all are consecrated and so all are entitled to wear them.

666. **quos:** connecting* relative, 'these folk', obj. of **adfata est**.

>**circumfusos:** perf. part. *circumfundo,* 'crowding round'.

667-8. **Musaeum:** Musaeus was a legendary poet, the pupil of Orpheus and the father of Eumolpus who founded the cult of Proserpina at Eleusis (see Intro. **6.iii.e**, and note on 136); hence his importance here.

>**plurima turba:** 'the crowd at its thickest' (cf. 659); **medium hunc habet:** 'has him in the middle', i.e. 'he is in the centre'.

>**umeris altis:** 'with his shoulders high (above them)'.

669. The Sibyl asks Musaeus for directions. This is her last contribution. In the early part of Hades she was sure of herself. In this transitional zone (628-76) she takes the lead to the extent of asking the question. In Elysium proper Anchises is the guide. When Dante wrote *The Divine Comedy* he made a similar distinction. Dante's guide through Hell is Virgil himself. When he comes to Paradise, he is guided by Beatrice.

optime: the word suggests 'kindest' as well as 'most accomplished'.

670. **Anchisen:** is acc. (Gk.) of *Anchises.*

    illius ergo: 'for his sake', **ergo** is here a preposition governing **illius** (gen.).

671. **amnes** plural; only one in the narrative, but see on 439 for Virgil's deliberate vagueness on this point.

672. **paucis:** understand *verbis.* **heros** is nom. Note that '*ui*' in *huius, huic* forms a single long syllable.

673. **nulli certa domus:** understand *est.* **nulli** is dat. (possessive*): 'none (of us) has ...'

674. **riparum toros:** 'couches which are the river banks', i.e. the banks which are soft and curved like the cushions on couches. **riparum** is defining* gen.

    rivis goes closely with **recentia:** 'made fresh by streams'.

675. **vos:** nom., subject of **superate**, so not necessary for the grammar. Such redundant pronouns are colloquial. **si ... voluntas:** 'if the wish in your heart carries (you) thus', i.e. 'if this is your heartfelt wish' . This is a formal expression. Musaeus is simultaneously friendly and courteous.

676. **hoc iugum:** it appears that they are high up in a mountain pasture.

    sistam: understand *vos* as object.

677-723. Musaeus directs Aeneas and the Sibyl over a mountain ridge into a valley where Anchises is found contemplating the souls which are to be reborn as his descendants, in due course Romans. The ridge marks an important division, between the underworld as a place which reflects on life past and as a place which prepares for life to come. It also marks a turning point for the *Aeneid* as a whole, where Aeneas the struggling exile from ruined Troy becomes Aeneas the founder of a future kingdom in Italy. He makes the transition under the guidance of the musicians and poets of mythology. Is this a proud claim on Virgil's part for the importance of poetry in building Augustus' new world? There may be the further point that Musaeus was especially associated through his son with the foundation of the Mysteries at Eleusis. Augustus had been initiated into this cult (see on 136).

677. **ante ... gressum:** 'walked on ahead'; **ante** is adv.

678. **dehinc** is scanned as one syllable ('synizesis'*).

679-81. Read the sentence thus: **Anchises lustrabat animas, penitus inclusas convalle virenti, ituras (*que*) ad lumen superum.**

    ituras: fut. part. of *eo*.

    superum ad lumen: 'to the light of the world above'.

    studio: 'with enthusiasm', or as adv. 'intensely'.

681-3. **omnemque suorum numerum** ('the whole company of his people'), **caros nepotes** ('his dear descendants') and **virum** (gen. pl.): these three expressions all refer to the same men, of whom Anchises is thinking in three different ways: how many they are, how affectionately he regards them, and how they are going to fare in life. **numerum, nepotes** and all the accusatives in 683 are objects of **recensebat**. By piling up the three verbs *lustro, recolo, recenseo* ('review', 'consider', 'survey') Virgil is emphasising the intensity of Anchises' involvement with the *animae*. *lustro* is also the word for a formal review of an army or of the citizen body by a Roman magistrate. Anchises, acting as a Roman, is preparing to address Aeneas as *Romane* in 851.

    fataque ... manusque: this line with its alliterative pairs is clearly meant to sound proverbial and to be comprehensive: 'what will happen to them by fate, what by chance; what their characters will be, what their achievements'. **manus** of 'the works of one's hands', *OLD* 20b, though it is straining the word a little to make it refer to every sort of achievement.

684. **tendentem adversum:** 'coming to meet him'.

685. **alacris:** rare form of the nom. masc. sing.; the usual form is *alacer*. Translate as adv., 'eagerly'.

    tetendit: perf. of *tendo*, transitive here though intrans. in 684. The same verb used both of Aeneas and Anchises emphasises their common eagerness.

686. **effusae** understand *sunt*. **genis:** 'over his cheeks' or 'from his eyelids'. The word usually means 'cheeks' but sometimes must mean 'eyelids', and Servius* takes it so here.

687-8. **tandem:** 'at last'. Anchises has been expecting Aeneas.

    tua ... pietas: literally 'has your goodness, longed for (**exspectata**) by your parent, overcome the difficult journey?'

    parenti: dat. of agent*.

    datur: 'is it permitted?' (by the powers of the underworld).

689. **tua** with **ora** (688); **ora** is pl. for sing.

notas ... voces: 'to hear and give back the well-known voice' means 'enjoy the familiar pleasure of conversation'.

690. **sic ... ducebam:** 'this is in fact just how I worked it out'.

rebar from *reor*. **futurum:** understand *esse*.

691. **tempora dinumerans:** as if crossing off dates on a calendar (Austin).

692-3. Take it so: **vectum** (*per*) **quas terras et per quanta aequora accipio te:** lit: 'carried (i.e. travelling) through what lands ... do I welcome you!', 'What lands, what vast seas you have passed through for me to welcome you!' The line recalls Catullus 101.1 and makes a moving contrast with it.

iactatum agrees with **te** (692), continuing the sentence in the same form.

694. **quam metui:** the **quam** is exclamatory, 'how frightened I was!'

quid: 'in any way' – adverbial* acc.

nocerent: Anchises was afraid for Aeneas in two ways. He might suffer physical harm; he might also be damaged if he gave in when Dido tried to persuade him to stay in Carthage, thus failing in his divine mission.

695. **ille autem:** understand *respondit.*

tua is stressed by its position at the beginning of the sentence and by its repetition. The effect is roughly 'It was *your* image, father, which₂ coming often before me ....' Virgil mentions appearances by Anchises' ghost on two occasions (4.351 and 5.722-3).

tristis: conveys not only the idea 'mournful' but also 'stern, severe'.

696. **haec limina:** understand *ad haec limina.*

697-8. **stant sale Tyrrheno:** 'are moored on the Tyrrhenian sea.' 'Tyrrhenian' refers to the sea which washes the west coast of Italy. Aeneas may say this with some pride: he has done all that his father could ask of him so far.

da (*mihi*): 'permit (me)'. Again, the repetition of **da**, and of **genitor** from 695, indicates Aeneas' urgent grief.

ne subtrahe: *ne* + imper., as 74, 195 etc., and esp. 465 (to Dido) *teque aspectu ne subtrahe nostro.*

amplexu: dat. as in 465.

700. **conatus** (*est*).

collo ... circum: read it **circumdare bracchia collo**: 'to put (his) arms around (his, i.e. Anchises') neck. (Tmesis* as in 254.)

701. Take **frustra** closely with **comprensa**. 'The ghost, having been embraced in vain ...' – but much better 'The embrace failed and the ghost escaped his hands'.

    manus: acc. pl., as the quantity* indicates.

702. **somno:** *somnus* is 'sleep', not 'dream', but Virgil is here using a passage in Homer where Odysseus tries with equal lack of success to embrace his mother's ghost (*Odyssey** 11.207); the word there is 'dream', so perhaps Virgil intends us to understand it, loosely, thus here.

    Aeneas' failure to embrace his father points to one uncrossable barrier between the dead and the living – the difference between material and immaterial. But notice that Anchises gave all the signs of welcome, including arms outstretched, *except* an embrace: i.e. he *knew*. Knowledge / ignorance is another barrier, and will characterise the ensuing exchanges between father and son.

705. **Lethaeum amnem:** 'the river of Lethe' – one of the seven waters (132). *Lethe* in Gk = 'forgetfulness'; those who drank the waters of Lethe forgot everything. We see why Lethe is relevant in 714-15.

    domos placidas: Musaeus has explained in 673-5 what sort of *domus* are lived in by the inhabitants of Elysium.

    praenatat: *nato* = 'swim'. Here, in an engaging metaphor*, it refers to the water moving in its own channel, lazily, like a swimmer on a summer day.

706. **circum** governs **hunc.**

    volabant: not 'flying' but 'moving rapidly about'; nonetheless the root idea 'fly' prepares us for the following bee-simile, so perhaps 'swarming'.

707-9. **ac veluti ... ubi:** 'and as when ...' The verbs following **ubi** are **insidunt** and **funduntur**; the main sentence begins with **strepit:** '(just so) the whole space is abuzz'.

710. **horrescit ... subito:** 'shudders at the sudden sight'; but his reaction is not fear. 'Feels a thrill of surprise'.

711. **causasque ... inscius:** '(being) unaware, asks the reason', or 'unaware of the reason, asks ...'.

712. **qui-ve:** 'and who are those men who have filled ...'.

    complerint = *compleverint*, perf. subj. in the indirect question.

713-14. **animae ... debentur:** 'souls to whom a second body is owed by fate', i.e. 'who are due to have a second life'.

    ad: 'at' (*OLD* 13).

715. **securos ... oblivia. latices et oblivia** forms a hendiadys* ('waters and forgetfulness' = 'waters from which comes forgetfulness'). The waters are *securi* not because they *are* carefree but because they make one so.

716-17. Start with **iampridem cupio** – 'for a long time now I have been wanting'; the three infinitives depend on **cupio.**

    hanc prolem meorum: 'this line of my (descendants)'.

718. **quo** introduces a purpose clause; it is regularly used instead of *ut* when the clause contains a comparative (**magis**). **laetere** is short for *laeteris* pres. subj.

719. **anne** introduces a question with a tone of surprise; it is here nearly equivalent to *num*. So with **putandum est** (gerundive): 'must one really think ...?'

    ad caelum: not 'to heaven' but 'to the open sky of the world above'.

720. **sublimes** agrees with **animas**, trans. as adv. with **ire** 'go aloft'.

721. Understand *est* as verb; **miseris** is dat. (possessive*). 'What desire for light, so ill-fated, is there in the poor creatures?' 'Why do the poor creatures suffer from so ill-fated a desire for light?'

724-51. Anchises gives Aeneas a mystical and philosophical explanation of purification and rebirth. (Intro. **6.iii.c-g**)

724-6. **Principio:** the appropriate word with which to begin a philosophical lecture – 'to start with'. But there also a suggestion that he is talking of a first principle of Nature. Perhaps 'First of all ...'.

    caelum ... astra: all these words make up the object of **alit**; the subject is **spiritus.**

    campos liquentes: i.e. the sea.

    Titania astra: astra is plural for singular. 'The Titan's star' is the sun. The Titans were the generation of gods before Jupiter. One of them was the sun-god Hyperion.

726-7. Read **mens, infusa per artus, agitat totam molem. molem** refers to the great mass of the universe, which is treated as if it were animate, having limbs (**artus**) and a body (**corpore**).

    The paragraph 724-9 is carefully built up: at the start two lines listing the apparently inanimate components of the universe, at the end two lines listing the animate components; between these pairs a further pair whose lines are almost identical to each other in substance and metrical pattern.

spiritus and **mens** refer to two aspects of the Stoic* world-spirit: it is mind, reason and also breath which give life, so they are the elements which form the link between animate and inanimate.

728. **inde ... genus:** 'from it' (i.e. the union of the world spirit with the material of the universe) '(are born – understand *gignuntur*) the races of men and beasts'. The union is seen as a sexual one, in which the spirit represents the male and the material the female. (This was a common view in antiquity, that the female is simply the ground or field in which the male plants his seed.)

vitae volantum: 'lives of flying creatures', a periphrasis*in the manner of Lucretius* for 'birds'. (**volantum** is a poetic alternative for the standard gen. pl. *volantium*.)

729. read **et monstra quae pontus fert sub marmoreo aequore.** (*fero* = 'bring forth'.) **monstra:** 'strange creatures' – not necessarily large.

730-2. read **est igneus vigor ollis seminibus et caelestis origo** – 'there is a fiery vigour ...'. *ollis* is an archaic* form of *illis* appropriate (a) because of the solemn universal truth uttered (as in English, religious and therefore solemn language tended to be old-fashioned); (b) because it recalls Lucretius' archaic diction. It is dative (possessive*). *semina* are the particles of the divine fire which are also the 'seeds' of *mens* or *spiritus* planted in matter, from which living creatures grow. The word is also used to refer to the 'atoms' of the philosophy of Epicurus*. (Compare line 6 and Intro. **6.iii.g.**)

quantum ... tardant: '(The particles come from heaven and have a fiery origin) in so far as harmful bodies do not slow (them) down ...'. Understand *ea* as object of **tardant** and **hebetant**. The idea is compressed: bodies do not alter the *nature* or *origin* of the particles, only their *effect*. Note that 732 is almost unnecessary for the sense (there is barely any difference in meaning between *corpora, membra* and *artus*); so the suggestion is that the three adjectives 'damaging', 'earthly' and 'mortal' are effectively equivalent.

733. **hinc:** 'as a result' (of the body which dulls the effectiveness of the spirit).

metuunt ... gaudentque: to be governed by emotion is the sign of someone who has not yet aligned himself with reason and the divine fire.

auras: 'the open air of heaven'.

734. **clausae:** the understood subject of the verbs in 734 is *homines*. But **clausae** is fem. as if the subject had been *animae*.

clausae ... caeco: the body is the prison of the soul. Plato attributes this idea to the followers of Orpheus, who had existed as a sort of cult for some hundred years in his day. They appear also to have originated some of the ideas of an after-life of blessedness for the specially good (Intro. **6.iii.e**).

735-8. 'What is more (**quin et**), when life has left them along with their last day, still not all the evil nor all the bodily ills depart entirely from the poor (creatures) (**miseris**), and it is inevitable that many things, long stuck fast together (**concreta**), become remarkably (**modis miris**) deep (**penitus**) ingrained.'

Note that **penitus** (adv.) goes with **inolescere**.

The point is that the soul-elements become clogged in life with body-elements and some sort of detergent is required.

739. **exercentur.** *exerceo* = 'activate' 'set going' (cf. 543). Perhaps 'they are put to it'.

malorum: 'their misdeeds'.

740. **aliae:** 'some (souls) ...'.

inanes: is probably acc., agreeing with **ventos**, not nom., agreeing with the subject.

741-2. **aliis ...:** 'for others their ingrown crime ...'.

Note that there is nothing striking or pictorial about these ordeals of air, fire and water. One of the functions of the punishments of Tartarus was that the victims should be *seen* to be in agony and thus constitute a striking warning (620 *discite iustitiam moniti*). Illogical this may be – who, after all, could ever have seen Phlegyas until it was too late anyway? But it reflects the practice of society: crucified slaves, criminals flung from the Tarpeian rock. The punishments here have no purpose except to cure those who suffer them. (It is also true that dramatic individualised details would jar with this context of universal truths.)

743. **quisque suos patimur manes:** 'each of us suffers his own *manes*' – one of the strangest and most striking sentences in Virgil, puzzling

ancient commentators as well as new. As punctuated here, it sums up the previous four lines and continues their thought. Virgil's point is that in each person the soul is contaminated with earthly elements in a different way and to a different extent, and it is this which determines the process of purification. Thus the soul can be seen as a prescription for its own punishment, or in Virgil's expression, equated with the punishment itself. It is as if one might blame one's misfortunes thus 'I am suffering from my genes' – it is not so much the genes, as their inevitable effects. Perhaps 'We each suffer our own spirits.' This is consistent with *manes* as used in lines 119 and 506.

    suos: strict grammar might lead one to expect *nostros* after a 1st person pl. subject. But we understand 'all people' as the subject , and this imports a sense of 'they' which accommodates **suos**.

744. **pauci ... tenemus:** 'a few of us occupy (i.e. remain in) the blessed fields'. Anchises is so good that he does not need the rebirth which is the fate of others (*has omnes*, line 748). But even Elysium is a place of purification (745-6) – this was a doctrine of the Orphics*.

745-7. 'Until a long age, when the cycle of time has been completed, has removed the ingrown defect, and leaves pure the heavenly mind and the fire which is spirit alone.'

    longa dies: *dies* in the sense of 'passing time' is normally fem., as here (*OLD* 10).

    perfecto ... orbe. In Plato, it is said to take 10,000 years for a soul to return to its original purity; for a philosopher the time is shorter. Anchises appears to have attained philosopher status in avoiding rebirth.

    aurai simplicis ignem: aurai (three long syllables) is an archaic genitive. The gen. is one of definition*. *simplex* means 'consisting of one thing only'. **aura** is sometimes used of 'breath', and is here identical with *spiritus* (736).

748. **has omnes:** i.e. the *animae* which Aeneas saw in 705, contrasted with the *pauci* of 744. Read **deus evocat omnes has** etc.

    ubi ... annos: 'when they have turned the wheel for a thousand years'. The wheel of birth and rebirth is an Orphic* image. **volvere:** note long 1st 'e', making the word perf. indic. not infin.

749. **deus:** with no suggestion of any particular god; the context is impersonal (cf. on 741-2).

750-1. 'Obviously in order that they should return to the world above without-remembering-anything (**immemores**), and that they should begin ....' **supera convexa:** 'the upper vault (of heaven)', i.e. the world above.

752-5 forms a brief and simple bridge-passage between the high points of the philosophical account of the afterlife and the parade of Roman heroes.

752. **unaque:** 'along with him' – **una** is adv.
753. **trahit:** 'made (them) hurry behind him'; the word stresses Anchises' eagerness.
754. **capit:** 'occupies', 'takes his place on'.
    posset: the subj. makes it a purpose clause.
755. **venientum** for the more usual *venientium* (cf. 728).

756-886. Anchises shows his son the long line of those who are to come after, creating and extending the Roman state and its empire. On this, see Intro. **6.iv**. It falls into three sections:

(i) 756-807. The kings of Alba Longa (see on 766) – Romulus – the city and goddess Roma – the Emperor Augustus – an exhortation to Aeneas.

756-9. **nunc age:** 'come now'.
    Start now with **expediam dictis** (759). ('I will set out in words'); then there are three things which he sets out: (i) **quae gloria sequatur Dardaniam prolem**; (ii) **qui nepotes Itala de gente** (*te*) **maneant**; (iii) **inlustres animas ... ituras**.
    quae gloria, qui nepotes: almost exclamation, 'what glory, what descendants!' **Itala de gente**: 'Italian-born'; **maneant**: 'await'; deinde: 'in the future'.
760. Read **ille iuvenis, qui nititur pura hasta, tenet proxima loca ....**
    The **hasta pura** is a spear with no metal tip; it was a Roman military award.
761. **proxima ... loca:** 'holds by lot the next place of light', i.e. is the one next due for rebirth, as the next clause makes clear.
762. **Italo ... sanguine:** 'mingled with Italian blood', 'of part-Italian stock'. Aeneas' first son, Ascanius, was wholly Trojan.

763. **Silvius:** the name is loosely tagged on to the sentence, and **Albanum nomen** is in apposition* to it. Translate 'He will be called Silvius, an Alban name'. (For 'Alban', see on 766.)

764-5. **quem ... educet ... :** 'whom your wife Lavinia will bear to you after a long time (**serum**), in your old age (**longaevo**) ...' For Lavinia see Intro. **5**, Book 7. As for 'old age', Jupiter foretells in Book 1 (261-96) that Aeneas will reign in Italy for only three years; perhaps **longaevo** should be thought of as 'at the end of your life' and carry the implication of a long three years of childlessness.

   silvis: 'in the woods'. The name Silvius was recognised in Rome as a genuine Alban name; the story that Lavinia gave birth 'in the woods' is designed to explain the origin of the name.

   regem, parentem: these are in apposition* to **quem.**

766. **unde:** '(descended) from whom'.

   Jupiter's prophecy (see on 764) was of three years' rule for Aeneas, followed by 30 years after which Ascanius would found Alba Longa (or simply 'Alba'), followed by 300 years in which Aeneas' descendants would rule there before the foundation of Rome. There was a tradition at Rome that Alba, on the hills just south of Rome, had been there first; the first duty of a consul* when he took up office on 1 January was to sacrifice to Jupiter on the mountain at Alba.

767. **proximus:** understand *est.* 'That one nearest (to Silvius) is Procas.'

   The four names in 767-9 are more kings of Alba, not in order of ruling. Capys was also the name of Anchises' father: this is another tie between Alba and its Trojan ancestors.

768. **qui ... reddet:** 'one who will recall you by his name'.

769-70. **pariter** with **egregius:** 'equally distinguished'.

   si: there was a tradition that Silvius was kept out of his kingdom until he was 53; hence the doubt expressed in **si.**

   regnandam (gerundive): 'to be ruled over', 'as his kingdom'. The gerundive here gives the same idea as a purpose clause.

   acceperit is fut. perf.; English requires a present tense here.

771. **qui iuvenes:** what (fine) young men!

772. 'and they have their temples shaded with the Citizen's Oak'. The 'Citizen's Wreath' (*civica corona*) was the highest award for bravery in the army, a wreath of oak-leaves awarded for saving the life of another Roman citizen in battle. Virgil gives it antiquity by

suggesting it is of Trojan origin. Augustus took great pride in the award, hanging the wreath over his doorposts.

773-5: All the names in this sentence are in the accusative; **Collatinas arces** is the object of **imponent**; for the rest, understand a verb 'they will build' to take them as its objects.

The names are those of members of the Latin League, an alliance formed perhaps in the sixth century BCE under the leadership of Alba Longa for protection against Etruscan domination. They are all towns near Rome which in Virgil's day were tiny or even deserted, but Virgil's concern is (a) with the beginning of empire: the first early steps reveal the same national resolve as later much greater ones, (b) with the idea of these tiny villages having been long ago places of great importance – a touch of nostalgic humour.

777-9. 'Yes, Romulus too, son of Mars, will add himself to his grandfather as a companion.' This probably means 'will join his grandfather and support him'. His grandfather was Numitor (768), king of Alba, whose daughter Ilia (778) bore Romulus and Remus to the god Mars. Numitor was driven from his kingdom, but when Romulus grew up, he returned to Alba and restored Numitor.

Mavortius: an adjective formed from *Mavors*, an archaic* form of *Mars.*

Assaraci sanguinis: 'of the blood of Assaracus' is a descriptive* gen. attached to **quem** 'him'. 'His mother Ilia will bear him (a young man) of the line of Assaracus.' Assaracus was Anchises' grandfather (650).

779. viden: a shortened colloquial form of *vides-ne*. Both syllables are short. 'Do you see how ....' **ut** the indicative is regular when the indirect question constitutes an exclamation (*OLD* 2b).

geminae ... cristae: 'twin crests'. There is some reason to believe that a twin-crested helmet was a characteristic of Mars.

780. 'And the father of the gods himself (i.e. Jupiter) is distinguishing him with his own mark of honour.' **superum**: gen. pl. Anchises' speech here moves up to a level of greater exaltation, and it is proper that Romulus should appear with the helmet of Mars and the majesty of Jupiter.

781. auspiciis: *auspicium* is the process of finding out the gods' will by studying the activity of birds. At the foundation of Rome this had played an important part, when Remus saw six vultures over the Aventine Hill and Romulus twelve over the Palatine. To 'take the auspices' is the right of a commanding officer; so *auspicia* can be weakly translated as 'leadership'.

illa: 'she, the glorious one, Rome'. This is the first mention of the name of Rome in this book, so it deserves something of a fanfare.

782. 'will make her empire equal with the lands, her spirit equal with Olympus', i.e. 'will extend her empire over the whole earth and raise her spirit to heaven'.

783. **una:** '(though a) single (city)'.

arces: these are the summits of the seven hills of Rome.

784-5. **felix prole virum:** 'blessed in her offspring of men' (*virum* is gen. pl.). *felix* suggests 'fertile' – there will be many men; *virum* carries the idea 'real men', i.e. heroes. So perhaps 'blessed for her many hero-sons'.

qualis ... curru: 'just so does the Mother of Berecyntus ride in her chariot ...'.

The 'Mother of Berecyntus' is the goddess Cybele whose home is on Mount Berecyntus in Phrygia not far from Troy. She is equated with Rhea the mother of Jupiter and with the Earth; hence she is mother of the gods and, as the earth has its cities whose walls stand up like crowns, so the Mother Goddess traditionally wears a crown in the form of a ring of towers (**turrita**). Virgil looks on her as a guardian-goddess of Troy. She was brought to Rome in 204 BCE to secure victory in the war against Carthage. Her temple is on the Palatine Hill. Augustus' house is sandwiched between it and his own temple of Apollo. Representations of the goddess Roma show her too wearing a turreted crown. This simile* is unlike others in the book, whose subject matter has no importance except in giving vivid life to the ideas which are the subject of the comparison. Here the content of the simile is itself important for Trojan and Roman history.

curru: it was drawn by two lions.

786. **laeta deum partu:** 'exulting in her bearing of gods' (i.e. having given birth to them); **deum** is gen. pl. The phrase matches **felix prole virum** (784) of Rome.

787. 'all of them dwellers in heaven, all of them occupying the heights above'. The phrases refer to **nepotes**; both make the same point. Anchises is offering an exalted view of Rome, embracing her human children as the Mother Goddess does her divine ones.

788. **gentem:** 'family, clan'. In the next line we see the names of Caesar and Iulus close together, and are reminded that the family *Iulius Caesar* is descended from and named after Aeneas' son Iulus. Of the three names generally carried by Roman citizens, it is the second, ending in *-ius*, which indicates the wider family, the *gens*. Hence also **Romanosque tuos:** 'your very own Romans'.

789. **hic Caesar** (*est*). This reference is almost certainly to Augustus, not Julius Caesar, as it expressly is in 792.

791. **quem ... audis:** 'whom you very often hear promised to you', i.e. whose coming is often foretold. (**promitti** is pres. infin. pass.) No such prophecy is mentioned, but there have been several references (345, 456, 503) to prophecies or events as having taken place in the past although there is no corresponding mention in the appropriate place. Virgil does not expect to be treated as a witness in a trial.

792. **Augustus Caesar:** on Augustus, see Intro.**1c-e**.

   divi genus: 'offspring of a god'. Augustus' adoptive father was Julius Caesar. Julius Caesar was made an official god of the Roman state in 42 BCE, with the title *divus Iulius*.

792-3. read **qui condet aurea saecula rursus Latio ...**; the **qui** is confusingly delayed. Virgil probably does so in order to create the assonance **Augustus ... aurea** by putting **aurea** at the beginning of its clause.

   aurea saecula: it was commonly told how the early period of human existence had been a 'golden age' of simplicity and innocence. (The golden age was identified for Romans with the reign of Jupiter's father Saturn.) This had been followed by successive deteriorating ages until the iron age, a time of immorality, ambition and violence which is 'the present day'. The story also told how, once the ages had run their course, the sequence would be repeated and a new golden age begin. Romans did not find it difficult to represent their own times as 'the last days' and to see Augustus as the ruler who would re-institute the Golden Age (see Intro. **1d-e**). Virgil had used this idea as the basis of a much earlier poem – *Eclogue* 4.

   Latio: 'in Latium' (cf. 89).

793-4. **regnata per arva Saturno quondam:** 'over the territory once ruled by Saturn'. **Saturno** is dat. of agent*.

The first of the two **et**'s connects the verbs **condet** and **proferet**, the second connects **Garamantas** and **Indos**. **Garamantas** is a Gk.-type acc. pl., with short 'a'.

The Garamantes were an African tribe, representing the extreme south of the known world, as the Indians represent the extreme east, confirming line 782.

795. **tellus:** the land which Augustus will bring under his rule.

extra sidera: this is explained by **extra ... vias** (theme and variation). 'The paths of the year and the sun' is a hendiadys* for 'the paths of the sun during the year'. The sun passes through the constellations (**sidera**) of the Zodiac. Augustus' conquests will be so fantastically remote as to be beyond even these.

796. **Atlas:** one of the Titans* who, according to legend, for his part in rebelling against Jupiter, was condemned to hold up the sky.

798. **in:** 'in expectation of'.

799. **responsis:** abl. 'because of oracles'. **divum:** gen. pl.

Maeotia tellus: the land round the Sea of Azov, at the north of the Black Sea.

800. **turbant:** a rare intransitive use: 'are in turmoil'.

These are distant romantic-sounding places, emphasising again Augustus' universal authority. The Nile stands for Egypt, which was conquered by him in 30 BCE.

trepida ostia Nili: the elision* of the 'a' of **trepida** creates a bump in the rhythm which illustrates the idea.

801-5. In these lines Virgil compares Augustus' achievements to those of the hero Hercules (**Alcides**) and the god Liber, Dionysus to the Greeks. He refers to Hercules' Third, Fourth and Second Labours, with the Hind of Ceryneia, the Boar of Erymanthus and the Hydra of Lerna (March 193-4). Of Dionysus the story went that, as Jupiter's child by a mortal woman, he was subject to the jealousy of Juno. To evade this he was hidden on the far-distant Mount Nysa and brought up by the nymphs. When grown up, he returned in triumph to Greece in his tiger-drawn chariot (March 136) with its reins made of vine-tendrils in celebration of his discovery of wine. Both Hercules and Dionysus were great travellers – but not as great as Augustus. They were also, like Augustus, bringers of peace and its delights.

801. **telluris:** 'partitive' genitive. As in phrases like *plus vini* 'more wine', tr. without 'of': 'so much territory'.

802. Read **licet cervum fixerit. licet** here = 'although'; it requires a subjunctive. **fixerit, pacarit** (= *pacaverit*), **tremefecerit**: all perf. subj; *figo* here = 'shoot'. The point is that Hercules spent a year chasing the hind, so covered a good deal of ground.

804. Read **nec Liber (tantum telluris obivit), qui ....**
    victor: 'in triumph'.

805. **Nysa** (the 'y' is scanned* long) is Dionysus' Indian mountain – see on 801-5.

806. **dubitamus:** Anchises really means 'are *you* hesitating?', but he puts it more gently by including himself.
    virtutem extendere factis: 'to stretch excellence by achievement'. The idea covers 'testing' and 'displaying' excellence as much as increasing it.

807. **aut metus:** understand *nos*. 'Does fear prevent us ....'
    Ausonia: adj., with **terra.**

(ii) 808-53. Anchises breaks off and casts his eyes over a fresh crowd of his descendants, which reaches a second climax in 847-53 in the exhortation to Aeneas and through him the Roman nation.

808. **quis ... autem** (*est*)? It is Numa, the second king of Rome, said to have established Rome's religious and legal systems. The olive spray is a sign of priesthood. The 'holy things' which he carries are perhaps an image of the god to whom he is sacrificing. He was invited to come to Rome from his home in the Sabine town of Cures (811).
    ramis ... olivae: 'conspicuous with a spray of olive' twined in his hair. **ramis** is pl. for sing.

810. **primam:** the adjective is transferred* from Numa to the city. Translate 'who first established the city with law' (as Romulus had with military force).

811. **Curibus:** 'from Cures'.

812. 'Tullus will next succeed him, (Tullus) who will shatter his country's idleness ...'. The subject is delayed until 814. **cui** ('him') is the connecting* relative and is dative following **subibit.**
    Tullus was traditionally the second great warrior-king, and captured Rome's parent-city Alba Longa.

815. **quem:** connecting relative, referring to Tullus.
    iactantior: the comparative gives the idea 'rather over-confident'.

popularibus auris: abl. 'because of'. The *populares aurae* are the fickle winds of popular support, which statesmen cultivate at their peril. We know nothing about Ancus Marcius, fourth king of Rome, to suggest that he was so disposed during his reign. But the later Marcii, one of whom was Augustus' stepfather, claimed descent from the king, and there is evidence to suggest that this family took pride in a tradition of bringing help to the oppressed masses.

817-23. Tarquinius Priscus and Tarquinius Superbus were the fifth and seventh kings of Rome. Virgil omits the sixth, Servius Tullius. Tarquinius Superbus was expelled in 510 BCE by a conspiracy headed by L. Brutus. A republican form of government was set up, of which the chief officials were two consuls elected annually. The symbols of their authority were the **fasces**, bundles of rods and axes carried before them by special bearers. Shortly after the revolution Brutus' sons conspired to re-establish the monarchy. Brutus, as consul, had the responsibility for their punishment. He had them executed.

817. **vis:** 'do you wish?'

 videre is the following infinitive.

 superbam: the word can carry a favourable idea – 'splendidly proud' – or unfavourable – 'dominating, arrogant'.

818. **ultoris:** Brutus was 'avenger' on two counts. He avenged Tarquin's tyranny by expelling him and his sons' treachery by killing them.

 fasces: see on 817-23 above.

 receptos: 'received' or 'recovered'. The first meaning will do if we think of Brutus taking power from Tarquin. For 'recovered', see note on 823 below.

819. **consulis imperium:** see on 817-23 above.

 secures: the axes which were part of the **fasces** – and also the instrument of execution, hence **saevas**.

820. **natosque pater ...:** 'and he, their father, will summon his sons ...'.

821. There is tension here between the splendour of liberty and the horror of executing one's children. The alliteration* and juxtaposition* **poenam – pulchra** contributes to it.

822. He is 'unlucky however later generations receive his deed', i.e. even if they glorify him and it, they will be failing to understand his distress.

823. understand *eum* as obj. of **vincet**.

 Brutus' story is a troubling one. The king driven out by him was Tarquinius Superbus. In 817 Virgil leads one to expect that

animam superbam will refer to Tarquinius – and then surprises us in 818 by connecting it to Brutus. Line 819 gives us the greatness and the harshness of the authority imposed on Brutus (described by the historian Livy as 'hardly different from that of the kings'). Line 820 **pater**, put right next to **natos**, suggests 'they ought to be so close, but are so deeply separated' – by the seriousness of the boys' crime. Line 821 offers a glorious political interpretation to be put on Brutus' action. Line 822 rejects that from a human point of view. Line 823 sums up Brutus' *superbia* in all its ambivalence: *patriotism*, driven by a desire for *glory* – fine things, but a desire which sticks at nothing (**immensa**). The painful dilemma is presented and not resolved.

Romans would also think of the other Brutus, their contemporary, who murdered his friend Julius Caesar in 44 BCE under the watchword *libertas* (821), aiming to recover a republican form of government (*fasces receptos* 818) from the 'tyranny' of Caesar. Augustus has a problem with this event: on the one hand Caesar was his adoptive father and he had taken vigorous and violent action to avenge his death; on the other hand he claimed, as one of his finest achievements, to have restored the republic – as Brutus had hoped to do!

824. **quin:** take closely with **aspice**, and trans. as 'come and look at ...'.

Decios. The elder Decius in 340 BCE and the younger in 295 were consuls commanding armies which were in danger of defeat. They averted this by formally sacrificing themselves to the gods below, thus losing their own lives and enabling their troops to win.

Drusos. The Drusi were a branch of the family whose middle name (see on 788) was Livius, one of whose members had won a crucial victory in the war against Hannibal (207 BCE). The most distinguished living member of the Drusi was Augustus' wife Livia.

saevumque securi: 'cruel with the axe' – **securi** abl. The phrase describes Torquatus (825), who had his son beheaded when he disobeyed his orders in battle (340 BCE). The phrase recalls line 819 and the similarity between Brutus and Torquatus.

825. **Camillum.** Camillus defeated the Gauls who captured Rome in 390 BCE, and subsequently recaptured the gold which had been used in an attempt to buy them off. Virgil (or Virgil's source) has changed this gold bullion into captured gold military standards, thus

reminding Romans of Augustus' much-publicised determination to bring back Roman legionary standards lost to a victorious Parthian* army in 53 BCE.

826-7. Start the sentence with **illae animae, quas ....**

    concordes ... premuntur: 'at unity (with each other) now and for as long as they are sunk in night' – i.e. as long as they remain in the underworld before being reborn. A surprising expression, given that Virgil has stressed the brightness of this part of the underworld (637ff.).

    The two souls are those of Julius Caesar and of Pompeius Magnus (see Intro. **1b-c**). In speaking of them as at unity now, Virgil alludes to the fact that they were friends and allies for much of their lives, and encourages us to think of their quarrel as unnatural.

828-9. The basic sentence is **quantum bellum, quantas acies ciebunt**, 'what war, what battles they will set going!' **si attigerint** (fut. perf.) 'if they reach ...' rather than 'when ...' because Anchises does not wish to think that it is certain that they will (an anxiety comparable with, but different from 770).

830. **socer** and **gener** are in apposition* to **animae** (827). The 'father-in-law' is Caesar, whose daughter was married to Pompey, the 'son-in-law'.

    'The father-in-law swooping down from the Alpine ramparts and the castle of Hercules, the son-in-law drawn up (for battle) with the peoples of the East opposing (Caesar).' Virgil is referring to events of 49 BCE, when Caesar invaded Italy from Gaul which he had conquered over the previous nine years, while Pompey withdrew from Italy to the Roman provinces in the east in order to gather strength to fight him. *Arx Monoeci* is the ancient name for Monaco, on the Mediterranean coast of France.

832. **pueri:** 'my children'.

    ne ... bella: 'do not make such wars habitual to your natures' – 'do not become hardened to such conflict'. The words are formally addressed to Caesar and Pompeius, but to be understood as including all Anchises' children, all the Romans.

833. The *v*-alliteration* heightens the urgency of Anchises' tone.

834-5. These two lines are addressed to Caesar, who 'traces his line from Olympus' as the descendant of Iulus and Aeneas and so Venus; and is also **sanguis meus** – descended from Anchises.

parce: 'restrain yourself.'

meus: nom. used for voc.

The short phrases, the repeated **tu**, the p-alliteration, the fact that the two lines mean the same in different words, and most conspicuously the abrupt ending of 835, breaking off after the 4th foot, all give the impression of great anxiety, as if Anchises were ineffectually trying to control a violent brawl already begun – in contrast to 827. But see on 94 for incomplete lines and whether Virgil intended them to remain so, and compare 884-7 for the idea that strong emotion prompts Anchises to break the barrier between past and present.

Virgil is in two minds about Caesar as he was in two minds about Brutus (see on 823).

836. Anchises breaks hastily away and points out a less controversial figure.

ille: Mummius the conqueror of Corinth in 146 BCE.

triumphata Corintho: abl. abs. (*Corinthus* is fem., like most city-names) 'Corinth having been triumphed over' like *regnata* = 'ruled over' (793).

Capitolia ad alta: the hill is called *Capitolium*; Virgil uses pl. to aid the metre. The hill was the sacred centre of Rome; to the temple of Jupiter on its summit generals led their triumphal processions after victory.

837. **insignis:** nom., agreeing with **ille**. 'Glorious because of the Greeks he has slaughtered.'

838. **ille:** another Roman. It is said that he will destroy Argos, Mycenae, and the descendant of Achilles. 'The descendant of Achilles' is almost certainly Perseus king of Macedonia, who claimed this relationship. He was defeated by Lucius Aemilius Paullus in 168 BCE. Paullus did not conquer Argos and Mycenae specifically, but Argos and Mycenae can stand for 'Greece' as the leading cities in the Trojan War, and in Roman eyes Macedonia and Greece are for many purposes the same.

Argōs: acc. of *Argi* masc. pl., which is a common Latin alternative for the Gk. neut. sing. *Argŏs*.

Agamemnonias: Mycenae is so described because Agamemnon was its king.

839. **Aeaciden:** 'descendant of Aeacus'. Aeacus was Achilles' grandfather. Perseus claimed descent from an earlier conqueror, Pyrrhus of Epirus, and Pyrrhus from Achilles.

> **genus:** 'descendant' here; 'family' in 842; 'son' in 792.

> **Achilli:** gen., as if from a noun ending in -*us*.

840. **ultus:** 'avenging'

> **avos Troiae:** 'his (i.e. Paullus') Trojan forefathers'. Paullus would be a descendant of one of Aeneas' company.

> Read **et temerata templa**. The Trojan princess Cassandra was raped in Minerva's temple by Ajax son of Oileus (see March).

841. **Cato:** a leading figure of the early second century BCE, famous for his uprightness and his uncompromising stand for old-fashioned Roman values.

> **Cosse:** Cossus won the *spolia opima*, awarded to a commander who killed an enemy commander in single combat, at the capture of the city of Veii in 426 BCE.

> **tacitum:** not 'unspeaking' but 'unspoken of'.

> **relinquat:** potential subjunctive – 'could leave'.

842-3. Understand **quis (tacitum relinquat) Gracchi genus**. But one can translate 'or the family of Gracchus'. Gracchus was the name of (i) a conqueror in Spain and Sardinia and (ii) of his two sons, reforming statesmen, in the mid-second century BCE.

> **geminos ... Libyae:** 'the two Scipios, thunderbolts of war, the ruin of Africa'; the two latter phrases are in apposition* with the first. **Scipiadas** is a Greek version of the name; *Scipiones* would not scan. The elder Scipio defeated Hannibal in 202 BCE, the younger destroyed Carthage in 146 BCE.

> (Carthage, a city in North Africa, was Rome's greatest and most persistent enemy in the third and second centuries BCE. Hannibal, her greatest general, defeated the Romans in Italy on several occasions.)

843-4. **parvo potentem:** 'mighty with a little'; 'poor but powerful'.

> **Fabricium:** Fabricius, famously incorruptible, led the Romans when Italy was invaded by Pyrrhus (839) in the early third century BCE.

> **Serrane:** Serranus was commander of a Roman invasion of Africa in 256 BCE during the first war against Carthage. A legend told that he was sowing his fields when summoned to become consul*, thus confirming the austerity and unpretentiousness which

the Romans attributed to their ancestors. Another of his names was Regulus, under which he is very famous as the hero of the grim story told by Horace (*Odes* 3.5). Virgil suggests that his name derives from the verb *sero*, 'I sow'. The participle **serentem** suggests that Serranus is sowing as Anchises sees him.

845. 'Where are you hurrying that weary one on to, you Fabii?' Anchises identifies the Fabii, a large family of great antiquity and many achievements. He addresses all of them, and then singles out one – the 'weary one'. He is Q. Fabius Maximus who, in the war against Hannibal, pursued a policy of wearing the enemy down by refusing to confront him in a pitched battle. He acquired the name *Cunctator* – 'Delayer'. Evidently he is 'going slow' even before he reaches the upper world.

The last two in this list, Serranus and Fabius, are performing actions related to their future glory. It may be that others in the list are doing so too. See above for Caesar and Pompey. Fabricius may be dressed as a *faber* (workman). The Scipios may be carrying thunderbolts (they claimed to derive their name from *skeptos*, Gk. for 'thunderbolt').

846. A near-quotation from Ennius (see on 179-82). A remarkable effect is created by the monosyllabic ending, which breaks the rhythm (holds it up – 'delays' it) in a way which Virgil almost everywhere else takes care to avoid.

Read **qui unus restituis ...:** 'you who single-handedly (or 'on your own') restore ...'. The adverbial use of **unus** is quite common.

rem: short for *rem publicam* – 'commonwealth' or 'nation'. The little word *res* shifts between referring to almost nothing and almost everything.

847-53. These lines contain Virgil's view of a shared culture for the world, in which 'others' will have their function and the Romans theirs. By 'others' he is referring to the Greeks. The first four of these lines are a generous acknowledgement of Greek superiority in the plastic arts, rhetoric and astronomy, with the implication that it extends to all intellectual activity – though the omission of epic poetry is perhaps the nearest thing to a boast which Virgil makes. The last three lines assign to the Romans their sphere: war and government.

847-8. **mollius:** 'with greater delicacy and precision'.

spirantia aera: 'breathing bronzes', i.e. bronze statues so fine that they seem alive – the same point made of marble in **vivos vultus.**

excudent ('beat out') is an inappropriate word for the modelling involved in casting bronze; **ducent** ('draw' – also properly of metal work) is inappropriate for chiselling marble. Odd.

849-50. Take **melius** with all three verbs in these lines.

causas orabunt: 'will plead cases'.

caeli meatus: 'movements *in* the sky'. An astronomer is imagined giving a lecture, pointing to diagrams in sand.

surgentia ... dicent: 'will name the stars as they rise'.

851. **tu** is very heavily stressed at the beginning of the line (compare **alii** in 847 2nd word) and reinforced by **memento** ('be sure to') solidly at the end. The words are addressed to Aeneas, with the suggestion (a) that he has become what is fated for his descendants – a Roman, and (b) that the fulfilment of all that he has seen now depends on him. It is a heavy burden. Anchises speaks not as an affectionate old man, but with the *gravitas* of a Roman father. For their fabled sternness, see on 820 and 825. (Of course it is also right to see **Romane** as addressed to Virgil's readers too.)

852. **hae ... artes:** *(bonae) artes* means nearly 'education'. Anchises is saying 'success in war and government firm but kindly will be your way of showing that you are educated'.

paci ... morem: *mos* carries the idea of 'civilised good order'. *pax* is an absence of armed conflict; *mos* must be imposed on it before an acceptable society can be formed.

853. A favourite line of Winston Churchill: 'to spare the conquered and war down the proud'.

(iii) 854-92. Lament for the young Marcellus.

854. **sic** *(dixit)*.

(eis) **mirantibus addit,** 'and added for them as they marvelled'. 'Them' refers to Aeneas and the Sibyl. Anchises thus becomes the guide, and the Sibyl is, with Aeneas, the visitor. Like Aeneas, she has glory to gain from the Augustan future (Intro. **6.i**).

855-6. **aspice ut ... ingreditur:** like *viden ut* + indic. (779).

insignis spoliis opimis: 'conspicuous for the *spolia opima*'. *spolia opima*, literally 'rich spoils', but see on 841 for the technical

179

meaning. Marcus Marcellus won them in 222 BCE, killing the Gallic chief Viridomarus at the cavalry battle of Clastidium. The Greek writer Plutarch has a description of Marcellus' triumph which suggests that **insignis** and **supereminet** may not be simply Virgil's decorative words but actually recall traditions of the occasion. (Plutarch *Marcellus* 8)

    victor: 'as victor'.

857. **rem Romanam** ('the Roman nation', see on 846) is obj. of both **turbante** and **sistet**.

    tumultu: *tumultus* is the proper word for 'a national emergency' particularly one cause by an invasion by the Gauls.

858. **eques:** 'as a cavalryman'. The word is emphasised at the end of its clause. It was a rarity for Roman supreme commanders to fight on horseback.

    sternet Poenos: Marcellus defended Nola against Hannibal in 216 BCE and defeated his attacking forces. It was the first significant Roman success against Hannibal.

    rebellem: the Gauls are said to have made peace and then provoked Marcellus by renewed attacks.

859. **suspendet:** 'will hang up' as an offering in a temple.

    patri Quirino: the tradition was that *spolia opima* be offered to Jupiter Feretrius not Quirinus. But Quirinus is regularly identified with Romulus, and it was Romulus who built the temple of Jupiter Feretrius and established the rules for *spolia opima*. So to honour Jupiter Feretrius is also to honour Quirinus.

    tertia arma: 'the third lot of arms'. The *spolia opima* take the form of the enemy general's armour. The award had only been won twice before (by Cossus (841) and Romulus himself), and were never won again.

860. **atque hic Aeneas:** understand 'said'.

    Read **namque videbat iuvenem una ire:** 'for he saw a young man walking together (with Marcellus)'.

861. **egregium** agrees with **iuvenem**; **forma** and **armis** (abl.) explain in what the young man is *egregius*.

    The young man is another Marcus Marcellus, a descendant of the hero of Clastidium, and Augustus' nephew. He married Augustus' daughter Julia, and Augustus seemed to be thinking of him as a successor, but he fell ill and died in 23 BCE. Augustus was much shaken. He had Marcellus buried in the great tomb which he was building for himself (873-4) and spoke the funeral oration. It is likely that Anchises' words of mourning bear a close relation to what Augustus actually said.

862. Understand *erat* with **frons** as subject, and *erant* with **lumina** as subject. The two halves of this line mean the same – theme and variation*. Just as the Scipios and Fabius showed signs of their future triumph, so Marcellus now shows signs of his own tragic destiny.

> **laeta parum:** 'too little happy', i.e. 'not happy at all' (litotes*).

863. **quis** (*est*)?

> **virum:** i.e. Marcellus.

864. Suggested answers to the question of 863. **anne:** 'or'.

865. 'What a noise of companions (there is) around him! What a presence in himself!' For a Roman aristocrat, the size of the throng accompanying him in a public place is an indication of his standing.

> **instar:** a noun usually accompanied by a genitive: 'the effect' of something. Here there is no word to indicate the effect.

866. **umbra:** abl.

867. **ingressus** (*est*) – 'began'.

> **lacrimis obortis:** abl. abs.; the *ob-* compound suggests 'getting in the way of speech'. For the whole phrase perhaps 'tried to speak through his tears'.

868-9. Heavy lines. The exclamatory 'o' occurs ten times in this book, always conveying some special grief or urgency. The lines also have the largest possible number of long syllables. Anchises' grief is such that it is not until line 883 that he can bear to mention Marcellus' name.

> **tantum:** closely with **ostendent.** 'The fates will give the world only a glimpse of this man.'

869-70. **ultra esse:** 'to exist any longer'.

870-1. **nimium** with **potens. visa** (*esset*). 'The Roman race would have seemed too powerful ....'

> **propria:** 'its own to keep'.

> **haec dona:** i.e. the presence of the younger Marcellus.

872. Read **quantos gemitus** (acc.) **virum** (gen.) **ille campus aget ad magnam urbem Mavortis.**

> **ille campus:** to a Roman talking about Rome **campus** will mean the Campus Martius, the flat ground enclosed by the bend in the

river Tiber just west of the city. It was used for parades, exercise and public assembly, and later became almost completely covered with splendid public buildings. Here it is the scene of Marcellus' funeral. In saying **ille campus** Anchises distances himself from it: neither he nor Aeneas is familiar with it.

Mavortis ad urbem: Rome is Mars' city because the god was Romulus' father.

873-4. **quae funera:** 'what a funeral' (pl. for sing.).

Tiberine: voc., the river Tiber.

praeterlabēre: short for *praeterlabēris*, 2nd sing. future.

The grief of Rome is heard and seen, not by people, but by the city itself and the river. The centre of the city is cut off from the Campus by the ridge of the Capitol and the Quirinal hills. Virgil imagines the city lying silent with all its people gone to the funeral, the sound of which comes as a distant clamour over the hills between. On the far side, the river sees, as it well can, the *tumulus*, the huge mausoleum on the river bank at the north end of the Campus, which Augustus was even then building (**recentem**) – see on 861.

875-6. 'No young boy of Trojan blood will ever raise the glory of his Latin ancestors so much by his own promise.'

nec quisquam: 'and not any'. **quisquam** for 'any' when the context is emphatically negative.

in tantum: 'to such an extent'. The preposition is not grammatically necessary.

spe tollet avos: 'will exalt his ancestors by his promise'. The achievements of a descendant can reflect glory on his ancestors. Marcellus is too young to have achievements, but so great is his promise (*spes*) that even this can reflect glory.

Latinos avos: think esp. of the elder Marcellus, whose glory (857-9) is very great anyway.

876-7. **Romula:** with **tellus.**

quondam: 'at any time in the future'.

tantum: with **se iactabit.**

ullo alumno: 'because of any son of hers'.

878. Marcellus' virtues: **pietas**, through which he will do right by his family and by the gods; **fides**, through which he will stand by others – friends, clients, even enemies, to whom he has made a commitment; and **invicta dextera**: skill and courage in battle.

heu: 'alas for'; what follows is nom., as an exclamation.

bello: 'in war', closely with **invicta**.

879. Read **non quisquam tulisset se obvius illi armato impune**: 'no one would have put himself in the way of Marcellus under arms without suffering for it'.

pedes: as adv., 'on foot'.

equi: the younger Marcellus is imagined as emulating his ancestor's equestrian excellence.

tulisset, iret, foderet: there is pathos* in these subjunctives. The obituary notice of an adult speaks of things which did happen; of a very young person, it can say no more than what might have.

882. **si rumpas** is a wish, as *ostendat* in 188.

883. 'Give (me) lilies in handfuls, (so that) I may scatter (their) bright blooms and load the spirit of my descendant with these gifts at least, and fulfil an empty duty.'

But Marcellus is not yet dead – he is walking gloomily past Aeneas, Anchises and the Sibyl as they gaze down from a hill at the long line of Aeneas' descendants. Evidently at this moment of strong emotion, 'then' and 'now' have become confused: Anchises is imagined as forcing his way forward in time and being himself present at Marcellus' funeral. **date** is then addressed to the attendants on the Campus Martius. (There was perhaps a similar confusion of times in 834-5, when Anchises addressed Julius Caesar with urgent anxiety.)

884-5. **spargam** is subjunctive, as **accumulem** (885) must be. The verbs seem to form a purpose clause following **date**. But it is odd to have no word to introduce the clause (*ut* or *quibus*).

purpureos: in 221 *purpureus* meant 'purple', in 641 'bright'. If lilies must be white, we must translate 'bright'. But there is some evidence for a 'lily' which was purple.

885. **inani:** see 213 for the idea that offerings to the dead are empty, futile.

There is a tradition that, when Virgil read these lines for the first time to Augustus, Marcellus' mother Octavia was present, and fainted at the reading.

886-901. Departure from the underworld. For a note on the Gates of Ivory and Horn, see Intro. **6.v.**

886-7. 'They roam everywhere, throughout that region, in the broad fields of air, and survey it all.' **aëris in campis:** *aer* refers perhaps (i) to the misty, gloomy air throughout the underworld (an idea in the Greek original of the word); (ii) to the bright air of Elysium (640); (iii) to the space between earth and moon, which was called *aer* by some and said to be the region of departed spirits. All of them seem difficult for one reason or another. Whatever Virgil intended by the word, the sentence describes a region altogether less precise and substantial than anything which Aeneas has so far experienced. It is the beginning of the mysterious passage in which he returns to the upper world.

888. Take **quae** (connecting* relative) closely with **per singula** and translate 'through these things one by one'.

889. **venientis:** pres. part.; 'glory which was already on its way'.

890. **quae ... gerenda** (*sunt*). **deinde:** 'later'.

891. **docet:** 'explains about'.

'The Laurentine peoples and the city of (king) Latinus': Aeneas will find these occupying the coastal area south of the Tiber estuary where he lands at the beginning of Book 7. For the story of books 7-12, see Intro. **5**.

892. Read **et quo modo fugiatque feratque quemque laborem.** The two *que*'s mean 'both ... and'. The subjunctives are both indirect question and deliberative* ('how he is to avoid, how to bear ...').

893. **sunt:** 'there are'.

fertur: understand **esse** – 'is said to be ...'.

895. 'the other gleaming, made all through with bright white ivory'.

elephanto: except for line 11, all the four-syllable words which end lines in this book are Greek. The Greek association is especially appropriate here, since the idea of the Gates is taken from the *Odyssey** and the word occurs in its Greek form twice at the end of successive lines in that passage.

896. **manes**, here 'the spirits of the world below', is the subject.

897-8. **his** with **dictis**. 'Anchises accompanies (them) with these words', i.e. what he has been saying in 889-92.

899. **viam secat:** 'cuts his way'. Probably no more than 'makes straight for', though it has been suggested that he has come up in mid-forest and has to hack his way back to the shore. The point is that he is firmly back in the real world, as is reinforced in the last two

lines of the book, which in completely undramatic narrative bring us down from the imaginative heights of what has gone before.

Note that the Sibyl disappears from the narrative without any remark at all.

900. Read **ad portum Caietae**. Caieta lies on a conspicuous headland some 40 miles up the coast from Cumae.

recto litore: 'straight along the shore'.

901. **stant litore puppes:** the last picture in the book reflects the first (lines 3-4) (ring composition*).

Appendix
Virgil, Ennius, Lucretius

Virgil often invites us to compare him with his Latin predecessors. In *Aeneid* 6 there are two passages where this is most conspicuously so. (a) 179-82, which is a close adaptation of some lines of Ennius which, fortunately for us, an ancient reader thought it worth quoting. (b) 724-51, which do not recall particular lines of Lucretius but are very much in his style. The following two notes aim to illustrate the relation between these two authors and Virgil.

(a) Ennius' lines (*Annals* 187-91) for comparison with 179-82

incedunt arbusta per alta, securibus caedunt,
percellunt magnas quercus, exciditur ilex,
fraxinus frangitur atque abies consternitur alta,
pinus proceras pervortunt. omne sonabat
arbustum fremitu silvai frondosai.

(On they go through the high groves; they cut them with axes, they strike down great oaks, the ilex is cut down, the ash is broken and the high fir-tree laid low. They bring down lofty pines. The whole grove of the leafy wood resounds with the hubbub.)

(i) In old Latin a final s was evidently pronounced so lightly that it could be disregarded where it occurs at the end of a word before a following consonant. This occurs twice in Ennius (*securibus, fraxinus*), but by Virgil's time had come to seem old fashioned.

(ii) The lines are heavily spondaic: in each of 2, 4 and 5 there is no more than one dactyl; line 5 ends with the double spondee *frondosai* (archaic genitive) in cumbersome rhyme with *silvai*. The poet intends to emphasise the heavy rhythmic blows of the axe.

(iii) Alliteration and assonance are conspicuous: (*exciditur ilex, fraxinus frangitur, pinus proceras*, etc.).

(iv) The first seven verbs are all pres. indic., 3rd pl. or 3rd sing; there are five verbs which are virtually synonyms meaning 'cut down'.

(v) There are five different types of tree, each presented in a slightly different form of expression.

Virgil hints at these features (spondees: 182 especially; alliteration: 180). But it is noticeable that only one of his main verbs means 'cut down' (*scinditur*), the others all refer to different events or activities. His alliteration is more sparing and more subtle (note the double *sonat icta securibus ilex*). He also offers five trees, four of the same as Ennius', one different (the *ornus*). He is acknowledging Ennius' excellence and contributes his own: a much more varied activity, with less emphasis on the constant axe-blows of the woodcutters. He avoids Ennius' sonorous concluding line, wishing to make Aeneas and his activities the idea towards which the passage is working.

(b) Lucretius 2, 1048-66, for consideration in the context of 724-51

Principio nobis in cunctas undique partes	
et latere ex utroque supra subterque per omne	
nulla est finis; uti docui, res ipsaque per se	1050
vociferatur, et elucet natura profundi.	
nullo iam pacto veri simile esse putandum est,	
undique cum versum spatium vacet infinitum	
seminaque innumero numero summaque profunda	
multimodis volitent aeterno percita motu,	1055
hunc unum terrarum orbem caelumque creatum,	
nil agere illa foris tot corpora materiai;	
cum praesertim hic sit natura factus, ut ipsa	
sponte sua forte offensando semina rerum	
multimodis temere incassum frustraque coacta	1060
tandem coluerunt ea quae coniecta repente	
magnarum rerum fierent exordia semper,	
terrai maris et caeli generisque animantum.	
quare etiam atque etiam tales fateare necesse est	
esse alios alibi congressus materiai,	1065
qualis hic est, avido quem complexu tenet aether.	

(To start with, in every direction from us, on both sides, above and below, (1050) there is no end, as I have explained, as the facts themselves cry out, and as the character of deep space reveals itself. Now in no way can one think it probable, when an endless distance opens up in every direction, and atoms numberless in number and boundless in total (1060) are moving about under the influence of a perpetual motion, that this is the only earth and sky created, that outside it all those particles of matter are up to nothing; especially when this (world) has been made by Nature in such a way that the very atoms, bumping into each other under the influence of their own movement in many ways, haphazardly, by accident, pointlessly and without any effect, have finally coalesced as things which, coming together all of a sudden, turn perpetually into the basis of mighty things: the earth, the sea and sky, and the race of living creatures. Consequently one has to admit over and over again (1065) that there are other comings-together of matter such as this one which the outer air holds together in its possessive embrace.)

The argument is: 'Space is infinite; beyond our universe there are innumerable atoms in accidental collision as they are here; accidental collision has led to the formation of this universe; therefore it is hardly likely that it has not led to the formation of other universes too.'

Lucretius' expression is repetitive (1048-9), rambling (1058-63), prosaic (1052), cumbersome (the *-um* sounds in 1052), colloquially emphatic (1064), humorous (*nil agere* 1052: 'achieving nothing' but also 'hanging around doing nothing' (*OLD* 22a)), archaic (*materiai* 1065), grand (1063), imaginative (1066: the heavens rapturously embracing the earth). The general impression is of a speaker urgently concerned to catch the attention of his audience and press home an important point. The majority of these features can be found as deliberate stylistic elements in *Aeneid* 6.724-51.

Index

1. Literary, grammatical and metrical terms

accent: *see* ictus.

accusative (i) adverbial: the Hydra is described (287) as *horrendum stridens* – 'hissing a dreadful (hiss)', or 'hissing dreadfully'. The acc. *horrendum* is translated by the adverb. 50, 201, 205, 287, 467, 694 **(ii) internal.** The acc. can depend (as in (i)) on an intransitive verb, as in expressions like *ludum ludere*: to play a game. Five times in *Aen.* 6: 122, 313, 517, 644, 646. **(iii) of respect**: parts of the body are regularly referred to in the acc. to indicate the part described. 470: *nec magis vultum movetur* – 'nor is she changed as to her face ...', or 'nor does her expression change'. Also 243, 495 and, slightly different, 363. **(iv) retained**: 156, 281: see note on 156.

aetiology: use of a mythological story to provide an explanation of a current practice: 212, 337, (764).

alliteration: creating a word-pattern by beginning adjacent or nearly-adjacent words with the same letter. 79-80, 180, 296, 316, 396, 397 (Intro. **8c**).

anaphora: connecting a sentence or phrase to its predecessor by using the same first word: 32-3, 110-12, 479-81, 580-608.

antecedent: the word to which a relative pronoun refers. 'The prophecy which Aeneas heard was true.' 'Prophecy' is the antecedent. In Latin antecedents are often separated quite widely from the relative pronoun.

apostrophe: when an author addresses one of his own characters: 18, 30, 251.

apposition: 'Take this money, a small reward for your efforts.' 'A small reward' is said to be in 'apposition' to 'money', and would be in the same case as it in Latin. 7, 22, 26, 221, 215, 378, etc. Apposition to the sentence: (Shakespeare *King Lear* 4.6.15: 'Half way down / Hangs one that gathers samphire, *dreadful trade*'; 'dreadful trade' is in apposition not to 'samphire' but to 'gathers samphire'). 223, 245-6.

archaic: term for the deliberate use of obsolete linguistic features: 321, 730, 747, 777.

arsis: metrical term; another word for 'ictus' – the stress imposed on a syllable by the metre. Very occasionally, a short vowel occurring in such a position is lengthened for this reason alone: 254.

assonance: creating an effect by placing words with identical or

191

similar sounds close to each other: 165, 314 (Intro. **8c**).

caesura: metrical term. A word-break which in a line of verse occurs in the middle of a foot; more particularly, in a hexameter, one occurring after the first syllable of the third foot (Intro. **7d** & **8d**).

chiasmus: at its simplest, chiasmus occurs when there are two successive pairs of words, each pair consisting of, say, adjective and noun, and the order is reversed: adjective noun, noun adjective: *incertam lunam, luce maligna* (270). 269, 391, 637-9.

compound adjective: an adjective formed from more than one root: *auricomus*, 'golden-haired' from *aurum* and *coma*. 141, 500, 839.

conative: *see* imperfect.

connecting relative: the relative pronoun *qui* may have as its antecedent a word in a previous sentence. In such instances it is helpful to think of it as meaning 'and he', 'and she / it / they etc'. 46, 158-9, 385-6 etc.

correption: metrical term. A long final syllable, when the following syllable begins with a vowel, is occasionally not elided but reduced to a short syllable: 507.

dactyl: metrical term for a foot of one long followed by two short syllables (Intro. **7b**).

dative (i) of agent: the person by whom something is done is sometimes indicated by the dative in poetry: 509 *nihil tibi relictum*: 'nothing has been left out by you'. Also 608, 687, 793.
(ii) of reference: the person for

whose advantage or disadvantage something is done, or in reference to whom something happens, is indicated by the dative case: 1, 46, 54 etc.
(iii) possessive: ownership is indicated by the dative. *mi genus est* (123): 'there is a family for me', 'I have a family'. 264, 627, 655 etc.

description, ablative and genitive of: in Latin, phrases in the abl. or gen. are attached to nouns to provide a description: *ingenti mole sepulcrum* (232, abl) 'a massive tomb'; *atri velleris agnam* (249, gen) 'a black-fleeced lamb'. Also 438, 778 (gen); 296, 299 (abl).

diaeresis: metrical term. A break between words which corresponds to the end of a foot.

diphthong: a syllable consisting of two vowels pronounced together as one.

ecphrasis: a descriptive passage, setting a scene or separating sections of narrative: 20ff., 237-41.

elision: term for when a vowel sound at the end of a word is obliterated by or assimilated to a vowel sound at the beginning of a following word. (Intro. **7.c**(iv) & **8c**).

ellipse: omission of a word which would make the syntax complete. Much the most common ellipse is of parts of *sum*.

enjambement: when the sense runs on from one line to another without allowing a pause, the two lines are said to be in enjambement. When there is a sense break, the line is said to be 'end-stopped' (Intro. **8d**).

euphemism: an inoffensive expression substituted for a an offensive or hurtful one: 457.

genitive: **(i) defining**: attached to nouns and making the idea in the noun more precise. 674 *riparum toros*: 'couches which are actually river-banks'. Also 84, 285, 409, 659. **(ii) of description**: *see under* description. **(iii) partitive**: see on 801.

hendiadys. A single idea is presented as if it were two. 298: *aquas et flumina* meaning 'the waters of the river'. 29, 114, 120, 218, 230, 271, 298, 431 etc.

hexameter: metrical term for the six-foot line of verse of the rhythmic pattern used by all epic poets including Homer and Virgil (Intro. **7b**).

historic infinitive: use of a present infinitive as the main verb of a sentence. It is normally a metrically useful alternative to an imperfect tense. 199, 256, 491, 492, 557.

historic present: use of the present tense to refer to events in the past. It is designed to bring those events into sharper focus. 1, 2, 3 and often.

hypermetric: term for a line whose last foot has more than the normal two syllables; the extra syllable is elided against the following line: 602.

hysteron proteron: reversing chronological sequence. *Aeneid* 1 and 2 are hysteron proteron on a grand scale (see summary in the Intro. **5**). 'They arrange hot

water and seething kettles' (218-19) is one on a small scale.

ictus: metrical term for the stress which falls on a syllable where it is imposed by the verse pattern, as opposed to accent, the stress of normal speech (Intro. **8b**).

imperfect: the imperfect tense conveys a number of ideas other then 'was doing' or 'used to do', of which the commonest are 'tried to do' ('conative') and 'began to do' ('inceptive'): 4, 468.

impersonal passive: the 3rd person singular of the passive voice is regularly used to suggest the action conveyed by the verb without specifying a particular subject: 45, 179.

inceptive: *see* imperfect.

intransitive: see transitive

juxtaposition: putting two words or ideas immediately next to each other for emphasis or contrast: 821.

litotes: saying much less than one means: 263.

metaphor: making one idea stand for another: 1-4, 424, 436, 705 etc.

metonymy: where a word is replaced by another which is related to it: 26, 165.

onomatopoeia: using words which by their sound illustrate the events they describe: 78-9, 165, 182, 209, 237, 551, 644.

oxymoron: an apparent self-contradiction, designed to make a point. 135, 280.

parenthesis: an expression grammatically unrelated to the words around it – in brackets, as it were: 177.

pathos: words so used as to invite a reaction of pity or sorrow: 30, 32, 314, 880-1.

periphrasis: putting an idea in another way, usually longer and more complicated: *vitae volantum* for *aves* – 'birds' (728).

personification: treating things or ideas as if they were people: 146.

quantity: metrical term distinguishing syllables whose 'quantity' is long from those whose 'quantity' is short (Intro. **7b**).

ring composition: returning at the end of a passage to the opening idea, thus framing the passage and making a unity of it: 77-100, 580-620.

simile: comparing one thing with another, a feature of epic style and frequently extended over several lines: 205-9, 309-12, 453-4, 707-9, 784-7.

spondee: metrical term for a foot with two syllables, both long (Intro. **7b**).

subjunctive (i) deliberative: *quid faciam?* 'What am I to do?' *quid faceremus?* 'What were we to do? 123, 601. **(ii) jussive:**: when the main verb of a sentence is in the subjunctive, it very often is virtually a command: *moriatur,* 'let him die'. The subjunctive is called 'jussive'; this word is derived from *iubeo.* 62, 76, 400 etc. **(iii) potential**: adds the idea 'could'. 625, 841.

synizesis: metrical term for an occasion when two vowels normally pronounced separately are pronounced as a single syllable: 33, 280, 412, 678.

theme and variation: repetition of an idea in different words, for emphasis: 68, 93-4, 229-31, 331, 387, 795-6, 862.

tmesis: in a compound verb, separating the verb from its compounding preposition: 254, 517, 700.

transferred epithet: *Dardana tela Paridis* (57): 'the Trojan weapons of Paris' meaning 'the weapons of Trojan Paris'. *Dardana* is transferred from *Paridis* to *tela.* 2, 57, 214, 374, 420, 537, 543, 810.

transitive / intransitive: verbs are said to be transitive when they take a direct object ('we take breakfast'); intransitive when they do not ('we hurried to school'). Most English verbs can be either: ('we hurried to school' / 'we hurried the latecomers to school'). Very few Latin verbs can be both.

trochee: metrical term for a foot with two syllables, long followed by short (Intro. **7b**).

2. Names in the text

References are to the lines of the Latin text. A line-number in brackets indicates a reference which does not include a name. Thus the Hydra is referred to but not named in 286-7.

Achātēs -ae *m.* Achates, Aeneas' most constant and loyal companion: 34, 158-9

Acherōn Acherontis *m.* Acheron, one of the rivers of the underworld: 295

Palinūrus -ī *m.* (i) Palinurus, helmsman of Aeneas' ship (ii) a headland called after him: 357-83

Paris Paridis *m.* Paris, son of Priam, who seized Helen and started the Trojan war: 57

Parthenopaeus -ī *m.* Parthenopaeus, a Greek hero: 480

Pāsiphaē -ēs *f.* Pasiphae, wife of Minos: 447

Pelasgī *gen.* **-um** *m.* the Pelasgi, another name for the Greeks: 503

Pergama -ōrum *n.pl.* Pergamum, the citadel of Troy: 516

Pergameus -a -um *adj.* Trojan: 63

Phaedra -ae *f.* Phaedra, daughter of Minos and Pasiphae: 445

Phlegethōn -ontis *m.* Phlegethon, the fiery river of the underworld: 265, 551

Phlegyās -ae *m.* Phlegyas, a Greek king, punished in the underworld: 618ff.

Phoebus -ī *m.* Phoebus, another name for the god Apollo: 18, 35, 56, 69 etc.

Phoenissa -ae *fem. adj.* Phoenician: 450

Phrygius -a -um *adj.* Phrygian, from Phrygia in NW Turkey: 785; also = Trojan: 518

Pīrithoüs -ī *m.* Pirithous, king of the Lapiths, friend of Theseus: 397, 601

Poenī -ōrum *m.pl.* the Carthaginians: 858

Pollūx Pollūcis *m.* Pollux, a Greek hero, brother of Helen of Troy: 121

Polyboetēs -ae *m.* Polyboetes, a Trojan priest and warrior: 484

Pōmetiī -ōrum *m. pl.* Pometii, a town near Rome, also Pometia: 775

Prīamidēs -ae *m. adj.* son of Priam, i.e. Deiphobus: 494

Procās -ae *m.* Procas, a king of Alba Longa: 767

Procris -is *f. acc.* **Procrim** Procris, wife and victim of Cephalus: 445

Prōserpina -ae *f.* Proserpina (Gk: Persephone), wife of Dis (Gk: Pluto), the lord of the underworld: (138), 142, 251, 402

Quirīnus -ī *m.* Quirinus, a Roman god sometimes identified with Romulus: 849

Rhadamanthus -ī *m.* Rhadamanthus, brother of Minos, a judge in the underworld: 566

Rhoetēus -a -um *adj.* of Rhoeteum, a place near Troy: 505

Rōma -ae *f.* Rome, the city and the goddess of the city: 781

Rōmānus -a -um *adj.* Roman: 789, 810, 851, 857, 870

Rōmulus -a -um *adj.* of Romulus: 876

Rōmulus -ī *m.* Romulus, founder of Rome: 778

Salmōneus *acc.* **Salmōnea** Salmoneus, a Greek king, punished in the underworld: 585-94

Sāturnus -ī *m.* Saturn, Jupiter's father: 794

Scīpiadae -ārum *m. pl.* members of the family of Scipio; Roman nobles: 843

Scylla -ae *f.* Scylla; a legendary monster: 286

3. Other names

Vocabulary

The Vocabulary is set out indicating:

- for verbs: as many principal parts as seem to be necessary or useful.
- for nouns: genitive singular and gender.
- for adjectives: nom. sing. f. and n.; if masc. = fem., the nom. neuter alone is given; if all nominatives the same, the gen. sing. is given.
- for all other words, part of speech and meaning.

Numbers in brackets refer to special meanings in particular lines.

ā, ab *prep.* + *abl.* by, from
absistō -ere abstitī withdraw, stand back, cease (399) + *infin.*
abstrūdō -trūdere -trūsī -trūsum hide
abstulī *see* **auferō**
absum abesse āfuī am absent
ac *conj.* and
accelerō -āre -āvī -ātum hasten
accendō -ere -cendī -cēnsum ignite, inspire
accersō -ere summon
accingō -ere -cīnxī -cīnctum gird, equip
accipiō -ere -cēpī -ceptum receive, welcome
accubō -āre recline (at one's place at table)
accumulō -āre -āvī -ātum heap up

acerbus -a -um *adj.* bitter, unripe, untimely
acervus -ī *m.* heap
aciēs -ēī *f.* edge, sight (200), battle (831); *pl.* eyes (798)
ad *prep.* + *acc.* to, towards; (with places) at, near; among (481)
adamās adamantis *m.* adamant, an unbreakable substance
addō -ere addidī additum add
adeō adīre adiī aditum approach
adeō *adv.* in fact, really
adferō adferre attulī adlātum bring
adflō -āre -āvī -ātum breathe on, inspire
adfor -fārī -fātus *dep.* address
adforet = adesset *imperf. subj. of* **adsum** be present, arrive
adgredior -gredī -gressus *dep.* approach, address (387), try (584)
adhūc *adv.* still, even now
adigō -ere adēgī adāctum drive, force
aditus -ūs *m.* approach, entrance
adlābor -ī -lāpsus *dep.* glide up to
adloquor -loquī -locūtus *dep.* address
admīror -ārī -mīrātus *dep.* marvel at
admittō -ere -mīsī -missum admit
admoneō -ēre -monuī -monitum advise, warn
adnō -āre -nāvī swim towards
adorior -orīrī -ortus *dep.* attempt
adsimilis -e *adj.* like

adsuēscō -ere -suēvī -suētum
make x (*acc.*) habitual to y
(*dat.*)
adsum -esse -fuī be present
adulterium -ī *n.* adultery
adventō -āre approach
adventus -ūs *m.* arrival
adversus -a -um *adj.* opposite,
facing
advertō -ere -vertī -versum turn x
(*acc.*) towards y (*dat.*)
advolvō -ere -volvī -volūtum roll
down
adytum -ī *n.* inner shrine, sanctum
aemulus -a -um *adj.* jealous
äēnus -a -um *adj.* made of bronze,
brazen
aequō -āre -āvī -ātum make equal,
keep up with (263)
aequor -is *n.* sea, level surface
aequus -a -um *adj.* fair
āēr āěris *m.* air
aeripēs -pedis *adj.* brazen-footed
āěrius -a -um *adj.* airy, sky-high
aes aeris *n.* bronze
aestās -ātis *f.* summer
aestuō -āre seethe
aeternus -a -um *adj.* everlasting
aethēr -is (*acc. sing.* **aethera**) sky,
heaven
aetherius -a -um *adj.* heavenly
age! come on!
agger -is *m.* rampart
agitō -āre -āvī -ātum drive, chase,
harass, set in motion (727)
agmen agminis *n.* troop, company
agna -ae *f.* ewe-lamb
agnōscō -ere agnōvī agnitum
recognise
agō agere ēgī āctum do, perform,
drive; **se agere** = **īre** to go (337)
age come on now (343, 389)
aiō (*no other tenses*) say
āla -ae *f.* wing
alacer alacris alacre *adj.* (*masc.*
alacris 685) eager
aliquī aliqua aliquod *adj.* some

aliquis aliquid *pron.* someone,
something
aliter *adv.* otherwise, if not
alius ... alius, aliī ... aliī one ...
another, some ... others
alius alia aliud *adj.* other
alligō -āre -āvī -ātum bind in
almus -a -um *adj.* kindly
alō alere aluī nourish, feed
alter altera alterum *pron.* and *adj.*
second, other
alternus -a -um *adj.* alternating
altus -a -um *adj.*; *adv.* **altē** high,
deep; open (of the sea 310);
noble (500)
alumnus -ī *m.* son, foster-son
alveus -ī *m.* hull (of ship)
alvus -ī *f.* belly
amāns amantis *m.* lover
ambāges -um *f. pl.* winding ways,
confusion, riddles
ambiō -īre surround
ambō ambae ambō *adj.* both
amictus -ūs *m.* cloak
amīcus -ī *m.* friend
amnis -is *m.* river
amō -āre -āvī -ātum love
amoenus -a -um *adj.* pleasant
amor -ōris *m.* love
amplexus -ūs *m.* embrace
amplus -a -um *adj.* large, spacious
an *conj.* (1) introduces an urgent
question (2) or
ancora -ae *f.* anchor
anguis -is *m.* snake
anhēlus -a -um *adj.* panting
anima -ae *f.* soul, spirit, life (436)
animus -ī *m* . mind, spirit, courage
(often as **animī** *pl.*)
anne = **an** (1)
annōsus -a -um *adj.* full of years,
aged
annus -ī *m.* year, season (311)
ante *adv.* sooner, before, in front
ante *prep.* + *acc.* before, in front of
antequam *conj.* before, until
antīquus -a -um *adj.* ancient
antrum -ī *n.* cave

aperiō -īre aperuī apertum reveal
apertus -a -um *adj.* open
apis -is *f.* bee
aprīcus -a -um *adj.* sunny
aptus -a -um *adj.* fitted, adorned
apud *prep.* + *acc.* among
aqua -ae *f.* water
āra -ae *f.* altar
arbor -is *f.* (*nom.* **arbos** 206) tree
arcānus -a -um *adj.* secret
arceō -ēre arcuī hold off
arcus -ūs *m.* bow
ardeō ardēre arsī blaze, burn
  (literally and metaphorically)
arduus -a -um *adj.* steep, high
arma -ōrum *n. pl.* arms, tools,
  equipment
armātus -a -um *adj.* armed
armipotēns -entis *adj.* mighty in
  arms
armus -ī *m.* forequarter of a horse
ars artis *f.* skill, art, craft
artus -ūs *m.* limb
arvum -ī *n.* field; in *pl.* territory
arx arcis *f.* citadel, high place
aspectō -āre -āvī gaze at
aspectus -ūs *m.* sight
asper -a -um *adj.* rough, harsh
aspiciō -ere aspexī aspectum see,
  set eyes on
ast = at *conj.* but
astō astāre astitī come to a stop
astrum -ī *n.* star
at *conj.* but, at least (406)
āter ātra ātrum *adj.* dark, black
atque *conj.* and
attingō -ere attigī reach, attain
attollō -ere pick up, lift
attonitus -a -um *adj.* dumbstruck
auctor -ōris *m.* founder, originator
audēns audentis *adj.* bold, daring
audeō audēre ausus *semi-dep.*
  dare
audiō -īre -īvī -ītum hear
auferō auferre abstulī ablātum
  take away, remove

aura -ae *f.* (*gen.* **aurāī** 747) air,
  breeze; (for 204 and 733 see
  notes); spirit (747)
aureus -a -um *adj.* golden
auricomus -a -um *adj.* golden-
  haired, with golden leaves
auris -is *f.* ear
aurum -ī *n.* gold
auspicium -ī *n.* auspice (see on
  781)
ausus -a -um *perf. part.* **audeō**
aut *conj.* or
aut ... aut: either ... or
autem *conj.* but
autumnus -ī *m.* autumn
āvellō -ere -vellī / -vulsī -vulsum
  tear away
āvertō -ere -vertī -versum turn
  away (transitive)
avidus -a -um *adj.* eager, impatient
avis -is *f.* bird
avus -ī *m.* grandfather, ancestor
axis -is *m.* pole (north or south),
  sky, vault

bacchor -ārī -ātus *dep.* rave, rage
beātus -a -um *adj.* blessed
bellum -ī *n.* war
bēlua -ae *f.* beast, monster
bibulus -a -um *adj.* thirsty
bidēns bidentis *f.* sheep
bifōrmis -e *adj.* two-shaped
bonus -a -um *adj.* good
bis *adv.* twice
bis tantum twice as much
brācchium -ī *n.* arm
brattea -ae *f.* (gold) foil
brevis -e *adj.* short, brief
brūmālis -e *adj.* wintry

cacūmen -inis *n.* summit
cadō -ere cecidī fall, fail
cadūcus -a -um *adj.* fallen
cadus -ī *m.* jar, casket
caecus -a -um *adj.* blind, unseeing,
  dark
caedēs -is *f.* slaughter
caedō -ere cecīdī caesum kill, beat

caelestis -e *adj.* heaven-sent (379)
caelicola -ae *m.* dweller in heaven, god
caelifer -a -um *adj.* heaven-bearing
caelum -ī *n.* sky
caenum -ī *n.* mud, slime
caeruleus -a -um *adj.* dark-coloured
calcar calcāris *n.* spur
calidus -a -um *adj.* warm
cālīgō cālīginis *f.* darkness, gloom, murk
callis -is *m.* pathway
camīnus -ī *m.* foundry
campus -ī *m.* plain
candēns -ntis *adj.* bright white
candidus -a -um *adj.* white
canis -is *m.* dog
cānitiēs -ēī *f.* white or grey hair
canō -ere cecinī sing, prophesy
canōrus -a -um *adj.* tuneful
cantus -ūs *m.* singing, playing
capiō -ere cēpī captum take, catch, suffer (fear) (352), occupy (754)
caput capitis *n.* head
carcer -is *m.* prison
cardō -cardinis *m.* hinge
careō -ēre caruī + *abl.* lack
carīna -ae *f.* keel, boat
carmen carminis *n.* poem
carpō -ere carpsī carptum pluck, take up (journey) (629)
cārus -a -um *adj.* dear
castīgō -āre -āvī -ātum scold, punish
castra -ōrum *n. pl.* camp
castus -a -um *adj.* chaste, pure
cāsus -ūs *m.* fall, misfortune
catēna -ae *f.* chain
causa -ae *f.* cause, reason
cautēs -is *f.* crag, stone
cavus -a -um *adj.* hollow
cēdō -ere cessī cessum give way, abate (102), depart (460)
celer -is -e *adj.* swift
cēlō -āre -āvī -ātum hide

celsus -a -um *adj.* lofty
centum *adj.* a hundred
centumgeminus -a -um *adj.* hundredfold
cernō -ere crēvī crētum (fore)see, notice
certāmen certāminis *n.* competition
certō -āre -āvī -ātum compete
certus -a -um *adj.* certain, sure, fixed
cerva -ae *f.* hind, deer
cessit see **cēdō**
cessō -āre -āvī -ātum hesitate, dawdle
ceu *adv.* just as
chorea -ae *f.* dance
chorus -ī *m.* dance, chorus
cieō ciēre arouse
cingō -ere cīnxī cīnctum surround
cinis cineris *m.* ash
circā *adv. & prep.* + *acc.* around
circum *prep.* + *acc., also adv.* around
circumdō -dare -dedī -datum surround, put x (*acc.*) round y (*dat.*)
circumferō -ferre -tulī -lātum carry round, purify (229, note)
circumfundor -ī fūsus (*pass. of* **-fundo**) come crowding round
circumstō -stāre -stetī stand round
circumveniō -īre -vēnī -ventum surround
circumvolō -āre -āvī hover around
cithara -ae *f.* lyre
cīvīlis -e *adj.* belonging to (appropriate for) a citizen
clādēs -is *f.* disaster, ruin
clāmor -ōris *m.* shouting
clārus -a -um *adj.* bright, famous
classis -is *f.* fleet
claudō -ere clausī clausum close, enclose
cliēns clientis *m.* client, dependant
coepī coepisse coeptus began
coerceō -ēre coercuī keep in, restrain

cognōminis -e *adj.* having the same name

cognōscō -ere cognōvī cognitum recognise

cōgō -ere coēgī coāctum drive, compel

collum -ī *n.* neck

color -ōris *m.* colour

coluber -brī *m.* snake

columba -ae *f.* dove

columna -ae *f.* column

coma -ae *f. ha*ir

comes comitis *m. or f.* companion

comitor -ārī comitātus *dep.* accompany

committō -ere -mīsī -missum commit (crime)

commixtus -a -um *perf. part. of* **commisceo** mingled, mixed

compellō -āre -āvī -ātum address

complector -ī complexus *dep.* embrace

compleō -ēre -plēvī -plētum fill

comprendō *short form of* **comprehendō -ere -prehendī - prehēnsum** embrace, include

comprimō -ere -pressī -pressum restrain, check

cōmptus -a -um *adj.* neat

concha -ae *f.* conch-shell

conclāmō -āre -āvī -ātum cry, shout

concors concordis *adj.* harmonious, in agreement

concrētus -a -um *adj.* set, coagulated

concursus -ūs *m.* gathering

concutiō -ere -cussī -cussum shake, shake out

condō -ere condidī conditum lay, hide (271), establish, set up

cōnfectus -a -um *perf. part.* **cōnficio** exhausted, worn out

cōnferō -ferre -tulī collātum bring together

cōnfūsus -a -um *perf. part.* **cōnfundo** mingled

congerō -ere -gessī -gestum heap up

coniciō -ere coniēcī coniectum throw

coniūnx coniugis *m. or f.* husband, wife

conlābor -lābī -lāpsus *dep.* fall in, collapse

cōnor -ārī -ātus *dep.* try

cōnsanguineus -a -um *adj.* kin, relation

cōnsīdō -ere -sēdī -sessum settle

cōnsilium -ī *n.* panel of advisors, jury

cōnsistō -ere cōnstitī stop, stand

cōnspectus -ūs *m.* sight

cōnspiciō -ere -spexī -spectum catch sight of, see

cōnstituō -ere -stituī -stitūtum set up, make to stand

cōnsul -is *m.* consul (see note on 819)

cōnsultum -ī *n.* decision, response

contendō -ere -tendī -tentum compete

conticēscō -ere -ticuī fall silent

contingit -ere -tigit *impersonal* it happens (of pleasant things)

contingō -ere -tigī -tāctum touch

continuō *adv.* immediately

contorqueō -ēre -torsī -tortum hurl

contrā *prep. + acc., and adv.* opposite, facing, in response (to)

contus -ī *m.* pole

convallis -is *f.* glen, deep valley

convellō -ere -vellī -vulsum tear off, uproot

conventus -ūs *m.* assembly

convexa *n. pl.* arches, vaults

convexus -a -um *adj.* arching

cor cordis *n .*heart

cōram *adv.* face to face

corneus -a -um *adj.* made of horn

cornipēs cornipedis *adj.* horny-hoofed

cornū -ūs *n.* horn

corporeus -a -um *adj.* bodily
corpus corporis *n.* body
corripiō -ere -ripuī -reptum seize, grasp, take a grip on (472), cover quickly (634)
cortīna -ae *f.* oracle (347)
crātēr -is *m.* bowl
creātrīx -īcis *f.* mother
crēdō -ere crēdidī crēditum believe, commit, trust
cremō -āre -āvī -ātum burn, cremate
crepitō -āre rustle
crīmen crīminis *n.* charge
crīnis -is *m.* hair
crista -ae *f.* crest
croceus -a -um *adj.* yellow
crūdēlis -e *adj.* brutal, cruel
crūdus -a -um *adj.* fresh, vigorous
cruentus -a -um *adj.* bloody
cruor -ōris *m.* blood
cubīle -is *n.* lair
culter cultrī *m.* knife
cum *conj.* when, since
cum *prep.* + *abl.* with (*often following a pronoun:* **mēcum, quibuscum**)
cumba -ae *f.* small boat
cunctor -ārī cunctātus *dep.* hesitate, delay, resist (211)
cuneus -ī *m.* wedge
cupīdō cupīdinis *f.* desire
cupiō cupere cupīvī / cupiī cupitum desire
cupressus -ī *f.* cypress-tree
cūra -ae *f.* anxiety
currō -ere cucurrī run
currus -ūs *m., gen. pl.* **currum** (653) chariot
cursus -ūs *m.* course, voyage (313)
curvus -a -um *adj.* curved
custōdia -ae *f.* guard, sentry
custōs custōdis *m.* guardian

damnō -āre -āvī -ātum condemn
daps dapis *f.* feast, meal

dē *prep.* + *abl.* from, according to, made of (69), derived from (70), down from (805)
dea -ae *f.* goddess
dēbellō -āre -āvī -ātum defeat in war
dēbeō -ēre dēbuī dēbitum owe
dēcēdō -ere -cessī depart
dēcerpō -ere -cerpsī -cerptum pluck
decorō -āre -āvī -ātum adorn
decus -oris *n.* glory
dēdūcō -ere -dūxī -ductum lead away, take away
dēficiō -ere -fēcī -fectum fail
dēfīgō -ere -fīxī -fīxum fix down
dēfīxus lūmina (156) with lowered eyes
dēfleō -flēre -flēvī -flētum weep over (220, note)
dēfungor -ī -fūnctus *dep.* come to the end of (+ *abl.*)
dehinc *adv.* next, then
dehīscō -ere -hīvī gape, open
dēiciō -ere -iēcī -iectum fling down
dēiectus -a -um *adj.* downcast
deinde *adv.* then, in the future (756, 890)
dēlūdō -ere -lūsī -lūsum mock, deceive
dēmēns dēmentis *adj.* mad
dēmittō -ere -mīsī -missum let down, let flow (455)
dēmum *adv.* finally
dēns dentis *m.* tooth
dēnsus -a -um *adj.* thick
dēpendeō -ēre hang down
dēpōnō -ere -posuī -positum lay down
dērigō -ere -rēxī -rēctum guide
dēscendō -ere -scendī descend
dēscēnsus -ūs *m.* descent
dēscrībō -ere -scrīpsī -scrīptum mark out
dēsinō -ere cease
dēsuētus -a -um *perf. part.* **dēsuēscō** unaccustomed

dēsum deesse dēfuī be missing;
hoc mihi dēest: this is missing
for me; I lack this

dēsuper *adv.* from above

dētrūdō -ere -trūsī -trūsum force
off

dēturbō -āre -āvī -ātum push out,
eject

deus -ī *m.; pl. nom.* **dī,** *gen.* **deum,**
dat. & abl. **dīs** god

dēveniō -īre dēvēnī arrive at, reach

dexter -a -um *and* **dextra,**
dextrum *adj.* right-hand, on the
right

dextrā *adv.* on the right

dextra -ae *f. or* **dextera** right hand

dī, dīs: *see* **deus**

dīcō -ere dīxī dictum say, speak,
utter, call (234)

dictum -i *n.* saying, word

diēs diēī *m., sometimes f.* day

differō differre distulī dīlātum
postpone, put off

digitus -ī *m.* finger

dignus -a -um *adj* worth,worthy

dīnumerō -āre -āvī count

dīrus -a -um *adj.* shocking

discēdō -ere -cessī depart, go away

discessus -ūs *m.* departure

discō -ere didicī learn, find out
about

discolor -ōris *adj.* different in
colour

discordia -ae *f.* discord, quarrelling

discrīmen -inis *n.* distinction,
difference; a musical interval
(646)

dispiciō -ere -spexī -spectum
espy, perceive

distringō -ere -strīnxī -strictum
stretch apart

distulī *see* **differō**

diū *adv.* for a long time

dīva -ae *f.* goddess

dīverberō -āre -āvī strike apart

dīves dīvitis *adj.* rich, precious
(195), wealthy

dīvitiae -ārum *f. pl.* riches, wealth

dīvus -ī *m., gen. pl. often* **dīvum**
god

dō dare dedī datum give, grant,
permit; **datur** (327, 688) it is
permitted; **datus** (350)
appointed

doceō -ēre docuī doctum teach,
explain

doctus -a -um *adj.* learned

doleō -ēre doluī suffer pain or grief

dolor -ōris *m.* grief, pain

dolus -ī *m.* trick

domina -ae *f.* mistress

dominor -ārī -ātus *dep.* rule over
(+ *abl.*)

dominus -ī *m.* master

domō -āre domuī domitum tame

domus -ūs *f.* house

dōnec *conj.* until

dōnum -ī *n.* gift, offering

dubitō -āre -āvī hesitate

dubius -a -um *adj.* doubtful,
difficult

dūcō -ere dūxī ductum lead,
bring, draw (lots) (22); draw
out, prolong (539); calculate
(690)

ductor -ōris *m.* leader

dulcis -e *adj.* sweet, pleasant

dum *conj.* while

duo duae duo *adj.* two

dūrus -a -um *adj.* hard, long-
suffering, hard to bear (377)

dux ducis *m.* guide, leader

ē *or* **ex** *prep.* + *abl.* out of, from,
after (407)

eburnus -a -um *adj.* made of ivory

ecce! *interjection* see!

ēdūcō -ere ēdūxī ēductum bring
up, build high, bear (764, 779)

effingō -ere -fīnxī -fīctum
represent

effor -fārī -fātus *dep.* speak out

effugiō -ere -fūgī escape

effundō -ere -fūdī -fūsum pour out

effūsus -a -um *adj.* poured out, streaming (305), tumbling out (339)

egēnus -a -um *adj.* needy

egestās -ātis *f.* poverty, need

ēgī *see* **agō**

ego mē meī mihi *or* **mī mē** *pron.* I, me

egomet *pron.* I myself

ēgregius -a -um *adj.* excellent, outstanding

ēlātus -a -um *perf. part.* **efferō** rising

elephantus -ī *m.* ivory

ēluō -ere ēluī ēlūtum wash away

ēmicō -āre -uī come out like a flash (5)

ēmittō -ere -mīsī -missum send out

ēmoveō -ēre -mōvī -mōtum remove

ēn *interj.* see!

enim *conj.* (*2nd word*) for, indeed (317)

ēnō -nāre -nāvī swim away

ēnsis -is *m.* sword

ēnumerō -āre -āvī -ātum count out

eō īre iī / īvī ītum go

epulae -ārum *f. pl.* feast

eques -itis *m.* horseman

equidem *adv.* for my part

equus -ī *m.* horse

ergō *adv.* therefore; *prep. + gen.* for the sake of

ēripiō -ere -ripuī -reptum snatch away, steal, rescue, draw (sword) (260)

errō -āre -āvī wander

error -ōris *m.* uncertainty, straying

ēructō -āre -āvī belch, vomit

ēruō -ere ēruī ērutum overthrow

este *imperative of* **sum**

et *conj.* and, even, in fact

etiam *adv.* still

euhāns -antis *participle with no verb* crying 'euhoe', a sacred ritual cry

euntem *from* **iēns euntis**, *pres. part. of* **eō**

ēvādō -ere -vāsī -vāsum emerge, come out, get away from (425)

ēvehō -ere -vēxī -vectum carry aloft

ēventus -ūs *m.* outcome

ēvocō -āre -āvī -ātum summon

ex *see* **ē**

exanimus -a -um *adj.* (*also* **exanimis -e**) lifeless

exaudiō -īre -īvī -ītum hear clearly

excēdō -ere -cessī -cessum depart

excīdō -ere -cīdī -cīsum, *compound of* **caedō** carve out

excidō -ere -cidī, *compound of* **cadō** fall

excipiō -ere -cēpī -ceptum take on, receive, welcome

excolō -ere -coluī -cultum improve, develop

excūdō -ere -cūdī -cūsum beat out, forge

excussus -a -um *perf. part.* **excutiō**

excutiō -cutere -cussī -cussum shake off

exerceō -ēre exercuī activate

exigō -ere -ēgī -āctum achieve, complete

exiguus -a -um *adj.* thin, insubstantial

exim *adv.* next

eximō -ere -ēmī -ēmptum remove

exinde *adv.* then, next

exitiālis -e *adj.* deadly, murderous

exitus -ūs *m.* way out

exoptō -āre -āvī -ātum long for

expediō -īre -īvī -ītum make ready, set forth (759)

expendō -ere -pendī -pēnsum pay

expleō -plēre -plēvī fill out

expōnō -ere -posuī -positum unload, disembark (trans.)

exsanguis -e *adj.* bloodless

exscindō -ere -scidī -scissum tear down

exsequor -ī -secūtus *dep.* carry out

exsomnis -e *adj.* sleepless

exsors exsortis *adj.* deprived of (genitive)
exspectō -āre -āvī -ātum await; long for (687)
exstinguō -ere -stīnxī -stīnctum put out, kill
exstō -āre exstitī stand out
exsurgō -ere -surrēxī -surrēctum stand up, rise
exta -ōrum *n. pl.* entrails
extemplō *adv.* immediately
extendō -ere stretch (*trans.*)
externus -a -um *adj.* external, alien
exterreō -ēre -terruī -territum terrify
extrā *prep.* + *acc.* outside, beyond
extrēmus -a -um *adj.* furthest, last, final
exūrō -ere -ussī -ustum burn away

faciēs -ēī *f.* appearance, form, shape
facilis -e *adj.* easy
faciō -ere fēcī factum make, do
fallāx fallācis *adj.* deceitful
fallō -ere fefellī falsum deceive, break an oath
falsus -a -um *adj.* false
fāma -ae *f.* story, rumour
famēs -is *f.* hunger
fās *indeclinable noun* morally right
fascēs -ium *m.* fasces (see note on 818)
fātālis -e *adj.* destined
fateor fatērī fassus *dep.* confess
fatīgō -āre -āvī -ātus weary, tire out
fātum -ī *n.* utterance, oracle, fate, destiny
faucēs -ium *f. pl.* jaws
favilla -ae *f.* ash
fax facis *f.* torch
fēcundus -a -um *adj.* fertile
fēlīx fēlīcis *adj.* lucky, fruitful
fēmina -ae *f.* woman
fera -ae *f.* wild beast
fērālis -e *adj.* funereal

feretrum -ī *n.* bier
feriō -īre strike
ferō ferre tulī lātum carry, bear; (of a road) lead (295); *ferunt* (284): they say; take (well or badly)
ferreus -a -um *adj.* made of iron
ferrūgineus -a -um *adj.* dark-coloured
ferrum -ī *n.* iron, sword
ferus -a -um *adj.* wild, savage
fessus -a -um *adj.* tired, weary
festīnō -āre -āvī hurry, perform quickly
fēstus -a -um *adj.* festival
fētus -ūs *m.* offspring
fibra -ae *f.* tissue, lobe (of the liver)
fidēs -ēī *f.* trustworthiness, faith, guarantee, pledge, sense of honour
fidēs -ium *f. pl.* the strings of a lyre
fīdus -a -um *adj.* faithful, trustworthy
fīgō -ere fīxī fīxum fix, fasten, plant (159), shoot (802)
figūra -ae *f.* form, shape
fīlius -ī *m.* son
fīlum -ī *n.* thread
findō -ere fīdī fissum split, divide
fīnēs -ium *m. pl.* boundaries, territory
fingō -ere fīnxī fīctum mould, shape
fīnis -is *m.* end
fīnitimus -a -um *adj.* living nearby
fīō fierī factus sum become, happen; fit (220) there occurs
firmus -a -um *adj.* strong, stout
fissilis -e *adj.* easily split
flagellum -ī *n.* whip, scourge
flamma -ae *f.* flame
flectō -ere flexī flexum bend
fleō flēre flēvī flētum weep, lament
flētus -ūs *m.* weeping
flōs flōris *m.* flower
fluctus -ūs *m.* wave

fluentum -ī *n.* stream
flūmen flūminis *n.* river
fluvius -ī *m.* river
fodiō -ere fōdī fossum dig, pierce
folium -ī *n.* leaf
(for) fārī fātus *dep.* speak, say
fore *fut. infin. of* **sum**
forēs forium *f. pl.* door (*pl.*
  because of the 2 doors of a
  double doorway)
fōrma -ae *f.* shape, form
formīdō formīdinis *f.* terror
fornix -icis *m.* arch
fors *abl.* **forte** (*in these 2 cases
  only*) *f.* chance; (nom. as adv.)
  perhaps (537)
forte *adv.* by chance
fortis -e *adj.* brave, strong
fortūna -ae *f.* fortune, luck
fortūnātus -a -um *adj.* happy,
  fortunate
forus -ī *m.* gangway
frāter frātris *m.* brother
fraus fraudis *f.* deceit
fraxineus -a -um *adj.* made of ash
  wood
fremō -ere fremuī fremitum make
  a loud and confused noise
frēnum -ī *n.* rein
frequēns frequentis *adj.* crowded;
  as adv. in crowds (486)
frequentō -āre -āvī occupy in
  crowds
frētus -a -um *adj.* + *abl.* relying on
frīgeō -ēre am cold
frīgidus -a -um *adj.* cold
frīgus -oris *n.* cold
frondeō -ēre grow leaves
frondēscō -ere grow leaves
frōns frondis *f.* leaf, frond
frōns frontis *f.* forehead, brow
frūgēs -um *f. pl.* grain, meal
frūstrā *adv.* uselessly
frūstror -ārī *dep.* disappoint,
  frustrate
fuerit *from* **sum**
fugiō -ere fūgī flee

fugō -āre -āvī -ātum chase, put to
  flight
fuī, fueram *perfect, pluperfect of*
  sum
fulcrum -ī *n.* support, headrest
fulgeō -ēre fulsī, *and* **fulgō -ere**
  (826) shine, gleam
fulmen -inis *n.* thunderbolt
fulvus -a -um *adj.* tawny, yellow
fūmeus -a -um *adj.* smoky
funditus *adv.* utterly, totally
fundō -āre -āvī -ātum fix, settle,
  stabilise
fundō -ere fūdī fūsum pour
fundor -ī fūsus come in crowds,
  swarm
fundus -ī *m.* lowest part, bottom
fungor -ī fūnctus *dep.* + *abl.*
  perform
fūnus fūneris *n.* death, a corpse,
  funeral
furō -ere rage, rave
furor -ōris *m.* madness
fūrtō *adv.* stealthily, in secret
fūrtum -ī *n.* theft; fraud, deception
fūsus -a -um *adj., perf. part. of*
  fundō sprawling, spreading
futūrus -a -um *fut. part. of* **sum**

gaudeō -ēre gāvīsus sum *semi-
  dep.* rejoice
gaudium -ī *n.* joy, rejoicing
gelidus -a -um *adj.* cold
geminus -a -um *adj.* twin, two-fold
gemitus -ūs *m.* lamentation,
  wailing, cry of pain
gemō -ere gemuī groan; creak
  (413)
gena -ae *f.* cheek; eyelid (686)
gener -ī *m.* son-in-law
generō -āre -āvī -ātum beget,
  create
geniālis -e *adj.* festive
genitor -ōris *m.* father
genitus *perf. part.* **gignō**
gēns gentis *f.* people, nation,
  family

genus generis *n.* race, family; descendant (500, 792)
gerō -ere gessī gestum bear, wear
gignō -ere genuī genitum beget
glaucus -a -um *adj.* grey-green
globus -ī *m.* globe, sphere
glomeror -ārī -ātus *dep.* assemble
glōria -ae *f.* glory
gradior gradī gressus *dep.* walk
gradus -ūs *m.* step, pace
grāmen -inis *n.* grass
grāmineus -a -um *adj.* grassy
grātia -ae *f.* delight
gravis -e *adj.* heavy, grievous; unpleasant (201); pregnant (516)
gravō -āre -āvī -ātum weigh down
gressus -a -um *perf. part.* **gradior**
gressus -ūs *m.* stride, step
grex gregis *m.* flock
gubernāclum -ī *n.* steering-oar
gubernātor -ōris *m.* helmsman, steersman
gurges gurgitis *m.* whirlpool, flood, sea (310)
guttur -is *n.* throat

habēna -ae *f.* rein
habeō -ēre habuī habitum have
habitō -āre -āvī live, dwell
hāc *adv.* this way
hāc ... tenus *adv.* this far
haereō -ēre haesī haesum cling, stick
hālitus -ūs *m.* breath, exhalation
harēna -ae *f.* sand, silt
hasta -ae *f.* spear
haud *adv.* not
hauriō -īre hausī haustum drink in, absorb
hebetō -āre make dull
herba -ae *f.* grass
hērōs *declines as Greek noun* hero *see note on* 103
heu *interjection* alas!
hiātus -ūs *m.* gape, yawn
hībernus -a -um *adj.* wintry, stormy

hīc *adv.* here, at this time (290)
hic haec hoc *pron.* this; the latter (397)
hinc *adv.* from here, hence
hiō -āre -āvī gape
homo hominis *m. or f.* human being, man
honōs honōris *m.* honour
hōra -ae *f.* hour
horrendus -a -um *adj.* dreadful
horreō -ēre horruī bristle, shiver
horrēscō -ere horruī shudder, tremble
horridus -a -um *adj.* shocking, fearful
horrisonus -a -um *adj.* fearful-sounding
hortātor -ōris *m.* instigator
hortor -ārī -ātus *dep.* encourage, urge
hospita -ae *f. adj.* foreign
hostis -is *m.* enemy
hūc *adv.* here, hither
humī *locative of* **humus** on the ground
humō -āre -āvī -ātum bury
humus -ī *f.* ground
hymenaeus -ī *m.* wedding-song, (*in pl.*) wedding

ī īte *imperative of* **eō**
iaceō -ēre -iacuī lie
iactāns -ntis *adj.* boastful
iactō -āre -āvī -ātum toss, buffet
iam *adv.* already, now
iam ... iam at one moment ... at another (647)
iam iam *adv.* at any moment now
iamprīdem *adv.* for a long time now
iānitor -ōris *m.* doorkeeper
iānua -ae *f.* gateway
ībam *etc: imperf. of* **eō**
ibi *adv.* there
īciō *or* **īcō -ere īcī ictum** strike
īdem eadem idem *pron.* the same, also (*see note on* 115)
iecur iecoris *n.* liver

ignārus -a -um *adj.* ignorant

igneus -a -um *adj.* fiery

ignis -is *m.* fire

īlex īlicis *f.* holm oak tree, ilex

ille illa illud *pron.* that; the former (395)

imāgō imāginis *f.* appearance, image, visible form, ghost

imitābilis -e *adj.* imitable

imitor -ārī -ātus *dep.* imitate

immānis -e *adj.* monstrous, huge, awe-inspiring

immemor -is *adj.* forgetful

immēnsus -a -um *adj.* unmeasured, endless

immergō -ere -mersī immersum immerse, plunge, sink (*trans.*)

immineō -ēre hang over, threaten

immittō -ere -mīsī -missum fling, hurl, send into + *dat* (312)

immortālis -e *adj.* immortal

imperium -ī *n.* rule, command

impius -a -um *adj.* wicked, treacherous

impōnō -ere -posuī -positum impose, put x (*acc.*) onto y (*dat.*)

impūne *adv.* unharmed

īmus -a -um *adj.* lowest

in *prep.* + *acc.* into, onto, towards, with a view to (395), until (569), in expectation of (798); + *abl.* in, on

inamābilis -e *adj.* unlovable

inānis -e *adj.* empty, futile

incānus -a -um *adj.* grey, grizzled

incendō -ere -cendī -cēnsum kindle, burn

incertus -a -um *adj.* uncertain, fitful

incestō -āre pollute, defile

incipiō -ere -cēpī -ceptum begin

inclūdō -ere -clūsī -clūsum shut in, imprison

inclutus -a -um *adj.* glorious

incohō -āre -āvī -ātum plan out, make roughly

incolō -ere -coluī -cultum occupy

incolumis -e *adj.* safe

increpō -āre -crepuī -crepitum scold

incubō -āre -cubuī + *dat.* lie on, keep for oneself, hoard

incultus -a -um *adj.* unkempt

inde *adv.* from there; then (201)

indēbitus -a -um *adj.* un-owed, not due

indignus -a -um *adj.* undeserved, shocking

indulgeō -ēre indulsī indulge, give in to

inextrīcābilis -e *adj.* insoluble

īnfāns īnfantis *m. or f.* infant

īnfēlīx īnfēlīcis *adj.* unlucky, unhappy

īnferior -ius *adj.* lower, inferior

īnfernus -a -um *adj.* infernal, of the world below

īnficiō -ere -fēcī -fectum dye, stain

īnfōrmis -e *adj.* shapeless, dreary

īnfundō -ere -fūdī -fūsum pour in

ingemō -ere -gemuī groan

ingēns ingentis *adj.* huge

ingrātus -a -um *adj.* ungrateful

ingredior -gredī -gressus *dep.* walk on

inhonestus -a -um *adj.* dishonourable, shocking

inhumātus -a -um *adj.* unburied

iniciō -ere -iēcī -iectum throw x (*acc.*) on y (*dat.*)

inimīcus -a -um *adj.* unfriendly, hostile

inīquus -a -um *adj.* unfair, unequal, unjust

iniussus -a -um *adj.* unbidden, without orders

inlūstris -e *adj.* glorious

innectō -ere -nexuī -nexum bind, entwine; contrive (609)

innō -āre -nāvī swim in, sail on + *acc.*

innumerus -a -um *adj.* numberless

innūptus -a -um *adj.* unmarried

inolēscō -ere become ingrained

inopīnus -a -um *adj.* unexpected

inops inopis *adj.* helpless
inremeābilis -e *adj.* that cannot be re-crossed
inrumpō -ere -rūpī -ruptum burst in
inruō -ere -ruī charge at, attack
īnsānus -a -um *adj.* insane, mad
īnscius -a -um *adj.* ignorant, unaware
īnsidiae -ārum *f. pl.* trap, treachery
īnsīdō -ere -sēdī -sessum settle
īnsignis -e *adj.* conspicuous
īnsistō -ere īnstitī + *acc.* set foot on
īnsomnium -ī *n.* dream
īnsōns īnsontis *adj.* innocent
īnspīrō -āre -āvī -ātum breathe (something) into (someone)
īnstar *neut. noun with only this form* equivalent (*see on* 865)
īnstaurō -āre -āvī -ātum renew, perform over again
īnstituō -ere īnstituī īnstitūtum establish, set up
īnstruō -ere -strūxī -strūctum draw up (an army)
īnsuētus -a -um *adj.* unaccustomed, unfamiliar
īnsultō -āre -āvī leap on
īnsum -esse -fuī I am in, I am part (of something)
intāctus -a -um *adj.* untouched
intentō -āre -āvī -ātum direct, brandish
inter *prep.* + *acc.* among, between
intereā *adv.* meanwhile
interfūsus -a -um *adj.* flowing between
intexō -ere -texuī -textum weave
intonō -āre -tonuī thunder
intrā *prep.* + *acc.* into, inside
intrō -āre -āvī enter
intus *adv.* side
invādō -ere -vāsī -vāsum plunge in, force one's way in, attack
invalidus -a -um *adj.* weak, feeble
invectus -a -um *perf. part.* **invehō** riding

invehō -ere -vēxī -vectum carry
inveniō – īre -vēnī -ventum find
invergō -ere pour x (*acc.*) onto y (*dat.*)
invictus -a -um *adj.* unconquered
invīsus sum (invideō) I am hated
invītus -a -um *adj.* unwilling, reluctant
invius -a -um *adj.* pathless, impassable
involvō -ere -volvī -volūtum wrap, roll up
ipse ipsa ipsum *pron.* -self *emphatic* ('I myself did it')
īra -ae *f.* anger
is ea id *pron.* the, this, that
iste ista istud *pron.* this of yours, that of yours
istinc *adv.* from there, from where you are
ita *adv.* thus
iter itineris *n.* road, journey
iterum *adv.* again, for a second time
ītō *imperative of* **eō** go!
itūrus -a -um *fut. part.* of eo
iubeō -ēre iussī iussum order
iūcundus -a -um *adj.* pleasant
iūdex iūdicis *m.* juryman
iūgerum -ī *n.* acre
iugum -ī *n.* ridge, hill, thwart/cross-bench (411), yoke (804)
iungō -ere iūnxī iūnctum join, clasp
iūrō -āre -āvī swear
iussum -ī *n.* order
iūstitia -ae *f.* justice
iuvat ... *impersonal verb* it pleases; **iuvat mē** (*acc.*) **facere** it pleases me to do ...
iuvencus -ī *m.* bullock
iuvenis -is *m.* young man
iuxtā *adv.* nearby; *prep* + *acc.* next to

lābēs -is *f.* defect, taint

lābor (1) **lābī lāpsus** *dep.* glide,
  fall
labor (2) **labōris** *m.* (*nom.* **labōs**
  277) difficulty, trouble
lacer -a -um *adj.* mutilated
lacrima -ae *f.* tear
lacrimō -āre -āvī weep
lacus -ūs *m.* lake, pool
laetor laetārī laetātus *dep.* rejoice,
  take pleasure
laetus -a -um *adj.* glad, happy
laevā *adv.* on the left
laevus -a -um *adj.* left-hand
lampas lampadis *acc.* **lampada** *f.*
  torch
laniō -āre -āvī -ātum cut up,
  butcher
lāpsus, *perf. part.* **lābor** (1)
largus -a -um wide, spacious,
  copious
lātē *adv.* over a wide area
lateō -ēre latuī hide (intrans), lurk,
  be concealed (406)
latex laticis *m.* water
lātrātus -ūs *m.* barking
lātrō -āre -āvī bark
lātus -a -um *adj.* wide; *adv.* late,
  over a wide area
latus lateris *n.* side
laurus -ūs *f.* laurel, bay
laus laudis *f.* praise, glory
lavō -āre lāvī lautum / lōtum
  wash
laxō -āre -āvī -ātum clear, open up
legō -ere lēgī lēctum choose, pick
  up, pick out (755)
lēniō -īre -īvī -ītum soothe
lēnis -e *adj.* gentle, soft
lentus -a -um *adj.* pliant, supple
lētum -ī *n.* death
levis -e *adj.* light, hovering
lēx lēgis *f.* law
lībāmen -inis *n.* offering
lībertās -ātis *f.* freedom
licet licēre licuit *impersonal,* +
  infin. or subj. it is permitted;
  with subjunctive, although
līlium -ī *n.* lily

līmen līminis *n.* door, threshold
līmus -ī *m.* mud
lingua -ae *f.* tongue
linquō -ere līquī leave
liqueō -ēre am liquid, am clear
liquidus -a -um *adj.* flowing,
  yielding, clear
lītus lītoris *n.* shore
lituus -ī *m.* trumpet
līvidus -a -um *adj.* dull grey,
  muddy
locus -ī *m.*; *pl.* **locī** *m. or* **loca** *n.*
  place
longaevus -a -um *adj.* long-lived
longus -a -um *adj.* **longē** *adv.* long;
  adv. far off, at a distance
loquor loquī locūtus *dep.* speak
lūceō -ēre lūxī shine
luctor -ārī -ātus *dep.* wrestle
lūctus -ūs *m.* grief
lūcus -ī *m.* grove, wood
lūdibrium -ī *n.* plaything, mockery
lūdus -ī *m.* game, sport
lūgeō -ēre mourn
lūmen lūminis *n.* light, day, *in pl.*
  eyes
lūna -ae *f.* moon
lūstrō -āre -āvī walk round (231,
  note), review
lūx lūcis *f.* light
luxus -ūs *m.* luxury

mactō -āre -āvī -ātum sacrifice
madidus -a -um *adj.* soaking
maestus -a -um *adj.* sad, gloomy
magis *adv.* more
magister magistrī *m.* master
magnanimus -a -um *adj.* great-
  hearted
magnus -a -um *adj.* great
māior māius *adj.* larger
malesuādus -a -um *adj.* tempting,
  suggesting evil
malignus -a -um *adj.* grudging
malus -a -um *adj.* bad; **mala** *n. pl.*
  bad things, misfortune
mandātum -ī *n.* instructions

mandō -āre -āvī -ātum commit, entrust

maneō -ēre mānsī mānsum remain, await

mānēs -ium *m. pl.* the spirits of the dead, ghosts

manus -ūs *f.* hand, band (of men), force (395), deed (684)

mare -is *n.* sea

marmor -is *n.* marble

marmoreus -a -um *adj.* made of marble; glittering (729)

māter mātris *f.* mother

māternus -a -um *adj.* (his) mother's (193)

maximus -a -um *adj., superlative of* **magnus** greatest

meātus -ūs *m.* movement

mē *see* **ego**

mēcum = **cum mē**

medicātus -a -um *adj.* drugged

medius -a -um *adj.* middle (of), in the middle

mel mellis *n.* honey

melior melius better (*comparative of* **bonus**)

membrum -ī *n.* limb

meminī -isse *imper.* **mementō** *defective verb* remember

memor -is *adj.* mindful

memorō -āre -āvī -ātum mention, speak

mēns mentis *f.* mind

mēnsa -ae *f.* table

mēnsis -is *m.* month

mentum -ī *n.* chin

mereor -ērī meritus *dep.* earn, deserve

mergō -ere mersī mersum plunge, sink (*trans.*), overwhelm

metallum -ī *n.* metal

metuō -ere metuī fear

metus -ūs *m.* fear

meus -a -um *adj.* my

mī, mihi *see* **ego**

mīlle *indeclinable adj.* one thousand

mina -ae *f.* threat

minimē *adv.* least

ministerium -ī *n.* service

ministrō -āre -āvī tend, serve

minor minus *adj.* smaller

minōrēs -um *pl.* later generations

minus *adv.* less

miror -ārī mīrātus *dep.* am amazed

mīrus -a -um *adj.* surprising, remarkable

misceō -ēre miscuī mixtum mix, confuse, combine

miser -a -um *adj.* wretched, sad

miserandus -a -um *adj.* pitiable

misereor -ērī miseritus *dep.* take pity

miseror -ārī -ātus *dep.* pity

mittō -ere mīsī missum send, throw, dismiss

modus -ī *m.* way, fashion

moenia moenium *n. pl.* walls, castle

mōlēs -is *f.* mass, size

mōlior -īrī mōlītus *dep.* do something with difficulty, toil along (477)

mollis -e *adj.* delicate, soft

moneō -ēre monuī monitum warn, advise

monimentum -ī *n.* reminder, memorial

monitus -ūs *m.* warning, advice

mōns montis *m.* mountain

mōnstrō -āre -āvī -ātum show, point out

mōnstrum -ī *n.* monster, oddity

mora -ae *f.* delay

morbus -ī *m.* illness, disease

moribundus -a -um *adj.* dying, mortal

moror morārī morātus *dep.* delay, hold up

mors mortis *f.* death

mortālis -e *adj.* mortal

mortiferus -a -um *adj.* death-bringing

mōs mōris *m.* custom, propriety

moveō -ēre mōvī mōtum move (physically or emotionally)

mūgiō -īre bellow, groan

multī -ae -a *adj.* many

multum *adv.* much

multus -a -um *adj.* much

mūnus mūneris *n.* gift, duty (630)

murmur -is *n.* humming

mūrus -ī *m.* wall

myrteus -a -um *adj.* made of myrtle trees

nam *conj.* for

namque *conj.* for

nārēs -ium *f. pl.* nostrils

nāscor nāscī nātus *dep.* I am born

nāta -ae *f.* daughter

nātus -ī *m.* son

nāvis -is *f.* ship

nāvita -ae *m.* (= **nauta**) sailor, boatman

-ne *interrogative particle attached to a word turns its sentence into a question*

nē *conj.* + *imperative introduces prohibition:* 'don't ...'

nē *conj.* + *subjunctive introduces*
(i) *purpose clause* ('in case ...')
(ii) *fear clause* ('lest ...') (*no others in this Book*); *a second clause is introduced not by* **et nē** *but by* **nēve** *or* **neu**

nec *conj* nor

nec nōn also, too

necesse *indeclinable adj.* necessary, unavoidable

nefandus -a -um *adj.* wicked, unspeakable

nefās *indeclinable adj.* unlawful, forbidden (391)

nemus nemoris *n.* wood, grove

nepōs nepōtis *m.* grandson, descendant

neque *conj.* nor, and not

nequeō nequīre nequīvī I am unable

nēquīquam *adv.* in vain, to no purpose

nesciō -īre nesciī I do not know

neu, nēve *conj. see* **nē**

nī = **nisi** *conj.* unless, if not

niger nigra nigrum *adj.* black

nigrāns nigrantis *adj.* black

nihil *indeclinable pronoun* nothing

nimbus -ī *m.* storm-cloud

nimium *adv.* too much

niteō -ēre nituī gleam, shine

nītor nītī nīsus / nixus lean on (+ *abl.*)

niveus -a -um *adj.* snow-white

nōbīs *see* **nōs**

noceō -ēre nocuī + *dat.* injure, damage

nocturnus -a -um *adj.* nocturnal, *as adv.* by night

nōdus -ī *m.* knot

nōmen nōminis *n.* name

nōn *adv.* not

nondum *adv.* not yet

nōrunt = **nōvērunt** *see* **nōscō**

nōs, nōs, nostrī / nostrum, nōbīs, nōbīs *pron.* we, us

nōscō -ere nōvī nōtum learn, recognise (809), **novi** (*perf.*) I know

noster nostra nostrum *adj.* our, *often* my

nōtus -a -um *adj.* well-known

novem *adj.* nine

noviēs *adv.* nine times

novissimus -a -um *adj.* last

novus -a -um *adj.* new, strange

nox noctis *f.* night

noxius -a -um *adj.* damaging, harmful

nūbilum -ī *n.* mist, cloud

nūllus -a -um *gen.* **nūllīus** *adj.* no, not any, not (405)

nūmen nūminis *n.* divinity, spirit; divine authority (368)

numerī -ōrum *m. pl.* rhythm

numerus -ī *m.* number

nunc *adv.* now

nūntius -ī *m.* messenger, message

nūper *adv.* recently

ō *interj.* O!

ob *prep.* + *acc.* on account of

obeō obīre obiī go over, go into (167), cover

obiciō -ere -iēcī -iectum throw x (*acc.*) at y (*dat.*)

oblīvia -ōrum *n. pl.* forgetfulness

obloquor -ī -locūtus *dep.* make to sound (646)

obmūtēscō -ere -mūtuī fall silent

oborior -īrī -ortus *dep.* well up, arise

obruō -ere obruī obrutum overwhelm

obscūrus -a -um *adj.* dark, unintelligible, hardly visible (268)

observō -āre -servāvī -servātum look carefully, study

obstō -āre obstitī + *dat.* resist, oppose

obuncus -a -um *adj.* hooked, curved

obvertō -ere -vertī -versum turn x (*acc.*) to face y (*dat.*)

obvius -a -um *adj.* meeting, in the way of (+ *dat.*)

occupō -āre -āvī -ātum seize

occurrō -ere occurrī + *dat.* meet

oculus -ī *m.* eye

odōrātus -a -um *adj.* scented

offa -ae *f.* morsel, ball of food

offerō offerre obtulī oblātum offer, present

oleō -ēre oluī smell

oleum -ī *n.* olive oil

olīva -ae *f.* olive-tree

olīvum -ī *n.* olive oil

olle = ille

omniparēns -entis *adj.* giving birth to everything

omnipotēns -entis *adj.* all-powerful

omnis -e *adj.* all

opācō -āre -āvī shade, darken

opācus -a -um *adj.* dark, gloomy

operiō -īre operuī opertum cover, hide

opīmus -a -um *adj.* rich (*but see on line 856*)

optimus -a -um *adj.* excellent (*superlative of* **bonus**)

optō -āre -āvī -ātum long for, desire, choose

opus est + *abl.* there is need of

opus operis *n.* work, task

ōra -ae *f.* shore

ōrbis -is *m.* circle, round

ōrdior -īrī ōrsus *dep.* begin

ōrdō ōrdinis *m.* line, proper order (723)

orgia -ōrum *n. pl.* secret rites

orīgō orīginis *f.* source, origin

ornus -ī *f.* mountain ash

ōrō -āre -āvī -ātum pray, beg

ōrsus *see* **ōrdior**

ortus -ūs *m.* rising

ōs ōris *n.* mouth, face

os ossis *n.* bone

ostendō -ere ostendī ostentum show

ostentō -āre -āvī -ātum display

ōstium -ī *n.* doorway, opening

ōtium -ī *n.* leisure, idleness

ovō -āre celebrate, triumph

pācō -āre -āvī -ātum pacify

paeān paeānis *m.* paean, hymn to Apollo

palaestra -ae *f.* wrestling-ground

palla -ae *f.* dress, cloak

palleō -ēre palluī am pale; *part.* **pallēns -entis**: pale, pallid

palma -ae *f.* palm (of hand)

palūs palūdis *f.* marsh

pampineus -a -um *adj.* made of vine-tendrils

pandō -ere pandī passum spread out, reveal, open

pār paris *adj., adv.* **pariter** similar, equal

parce! *imper.* hold!

parcō parcere pepercī + *dat.* spare

parēns parentis *m. or f.* parent

pariō parere peperī partum bear
(children), get, bring about
(435)

pariter equally, together

parō -āre -āvī -ātum prepare

pars partis *f.* part, some (6);
direction (440, 540)

partus -ūs *m.* birth, bearing

parum *adv.* too little, *often
equivalent to* not

parumper *adv.* for a short time

parvus -a -um *adj.* small, little

pāscō -ere pāvī feed, graze

passim *adv. eve*rywhere

passus *see* **patior**

passus -ūs *m.* step, pace

pateō -ēre patuī am open

pater patris *m.* father

patera -ae *f.* bowl, dish

patiēns -entis *adj.* tolerant (of ...)

patior patī passus *dep.* suffer

patria -ae *f.* native country,
fatherland

patrius -a -um *adj.* father's,
paternal

patruus -ī *m.* uncle (father's
brother)

paucī -ae -a *adj.* few

paulātim *adv.* gradually, little by
little

pauper -is *adj.* poor

pauperiēs -ēī *f.* poverty

pavitō -āre be terrified

pāx pācis *f.* peace

pecten pectinis *n.* plectrum

pectus pectoris *n.* breast, heart

pecus pecudis *f.* sheep, *pl.* beasts
in general (728)

pedes peditis *m.* footsoldier; *as
adv.* on foot

pelagus -ī *n.* sea

pellō -ere pepulī pulsum drive off

pendeō -ēre pependī hang, linger

pendō -ere pependī hang, weigh;
pay (20)

penetrālia -ium *n. pl.* a secret
shrine

penitus *adv.* deep inside, remotely

penna -ae *f.* wing

per *prep. with acc.* through, along,
by ('I swear by heaven'),
throughout

peragō -ere -ēgī -āctum work out,
deal with (105); continue (384)

percurrō -ere -currī -cursum go
over, recount, cover

percutiō -ere -cussī -cussum strike

peredō -ere -ēdī -ēsum eat away,
consume

perferō -ferre -tulī -lātum bear,
endure

perficiō -ere -fēcī -fectum
complete

pergō -ere perrēxī perrēctum
proceed, go

perīculum *or* **perīclum -ī** *n.*
danger

perimō -ere -ēmī -ēmptum
destroy

perlegō -ere -lēgī -lēctum read
through

perōdī -ōdisse -ōsus *defective verb*
loathe

personō -āre -sonuī fill with sound

pēs pedis *m.* foot

pestis -is *f.* plague, evil

petō -ere petīvī petītum seek,
make for

phalānx phalangis *f.* phalanx
(489)

piāculum -ī *n.* offering (to appease
an offended god); offence
(which calls for appeasement)

picea -ae *f.* pitch pine tree

pietās -ātis *f.* loyalty, faithfulness

pinguis -e *adj.* rich, fertile

piō -āre -āvī -ātum appease

pius -a -um *adj.* dutiful, good

placidus -a -um *adj.* peaceful

plangor -ōris *m.* sound of distress,
wailing

plaudō -ere plausī plausum
stamp, clap

plēnus -a -um *adj.* full

plūrimus -a -um *adj.* very much,
(*pl.*) very many

plūs plūris *adj.* more
poena -ae *f., often as pl.* penalty, punishment
poenās dē tē sūmō I inflict punishment on you
pondus -eris *n.* weight
pōnō -ere posuī positum place, establish (19); set aside (611)
pontus -ī *m.* sea
populāris -e *adj.* of the people, democratic
populō -āre -āvī -ātum ravage, strip
populus -ī *m.* people, population
porrigō -ere porrēxī porrēctum spread out
porrō *adv.* over there, yonder
porta -ae *f.* gate
portitor -ōris *m.* harbour-master, ferryman
portō -āre -āvī -ātum carry
portus -ūs *m.* port, harbour
poscō -ere poposcī demand
possum posse potuī am able
post *adv., and prep.* + *acc.* after
postquam *conj.* after, when
postumus -a -um *adj.* last, last-born
potēns potentis *adj.* powerful
poterant *see* **possum**
potes 2 *sing. pres.* **possum** you can
potior potīrī potītus *dep.* + *abl.* achieve, get possession of
pōtō -āre -āvī -ātum drink deeply
praeceps praecipitis *adj.* sheer, headlong; **in praeceps** straight down
praeceptum -ī *n.* instruction
praecipiō -ere -cēpī -ceptum anticipate
praecipitō -āre -āvī -ātum tumble
praecipuē *adv.* especially
praeda -ae *f.* booty, loot
praeficiō -ere -fēcī -fectum put x (*acc.*) in charge of y (*dat.*)
praemittō -ere -mīsī -missum send ahead

praenatō -āre -āvī float past, drift past
praepes praepetis *adj.* swift
praescius -a -um *adj.* having foreknowledge of
praesideō -ēre -sēdī + *dat.* preside over
praestāns praestantis *adj.* superior
praestat -āre praestitit it is better
praetendō -ere -tendī -tentum stretch over, in front of
praetereā *adv.* besides, in addition
praeterlābor -ī -lāpsus *dep.* flow past
praetexō -ere -texuī -textum fringe, form a border to
prātum -ī *n.* meadow
precēs -um *f. pl.* prayers
precor -ārī precātus *dep.* pray
premō -ere pressī pressum press, crush, check
prendō *or* **prehendō -ere prehendī prehēnsum** grasp
prēnsō -āre -āvī grasp
pretium -ī *n.* price
prīmum *adv.* first
prīmus -a -um *adj.* first
prīncipiō *adv.* to begin with
prīncipium -ī *n* beginning
prior prius *adj.* earlier, first
prīscus -a -um *adj.* ancient, old-fashioned
prīstinus -a -um *adj.* original, previous
prius *adv.* before, first
prius quam *conj.* before, until
prō *prep.* + *abl.* on behalf of
procerēs -um *m. pl.* leaders
procul *adv.* at a distance
prōcumbō -ere -cubuī -cubitum fall headlong
prōdeō prōdīre prōdiī go ahead
prōdigium -ī *n.* portent, miraculous event, sign
profānus – a -um *adj.* profane, unholy
prōferō -ferre -tulī -lātum carry forward

profundus -a -um *adj.* deep
prōgeniēs -ēī *f.* offspring
prohibeō -ēre prohibuī prohibitum forbid
prōiciō -ere -iēcī -iectum cast away
prōlēs -is *f.* offspring, family (648)
prōmittō -ere -mīsī -missum promise
propāgō -inis *f.* species, race
properē *adv.* quickly
propinquō -āre -āvī + *dat.* come near
propior propius *adj.* nearer
proprius -a -um *adj.* one's own
prōra -ae *f.* prow, the bows of a ship
prōsequor -ī -secūtus *dep.* follow, accompany
prōspiciō -ere -spexī -spectum catch sight of, espy
prōtinus *adv.* straight on
proximus -a -um *adj.* nearest, next
pūbēs -is *f.* race, stock, brood
puella -ae *f.* girl
puer -ī *m.* boy, child
pugna -ae *f.* fight, battle
pugnō -āre -āvī -ātum fight
pulcher pulchra pulchrum *adj.* beautiful, fair
pulsō -āre -āvī -ātum strike, beat
pulsus -ūs *m.* thumping, beat
puppis -is *f.* stern (of a ship); ship
purpureus -a -um *adj.* purple, crimson; radiant (641)
pūrus -a -um *adj.* pure
putō -āre -āvī -ātum think through, work out in mind
pyra -ae *f.* funeral pyre

quā *conj.* where (*rel.*); in some way (*indef.*) (882)
quadrīgae -ārum *f. pl.* four-horse chariot
quaerō -ere quaesīvī quaesītum seek
quaesītor -ōris *m.* judge, president

quālis -e *adj.* of what kind (205, 270 'just as', *see note*)
quam *adv.* (1) how, *as in* 'how much!' (2) than, (3) **quam multa** (309, 311) as many as
quamquam *conj.* although
quandō *adv., interrog. or rel.* when, since
quantum *adv.* so far as
quantus -a -um *adj.* (*interrog*) how much? (*rel.*) (as much) as (200)
quārtus -a -um *adj.* fourth
quassō -āre shake, brandish
quatiō -ere shake, make to writhe
quattuor *adj.* four
-que *conj.* and (*translate before the word to which it is attached*)
queō quīre quīvī be able
quercus -ūs *f.* oak
quī qua quod *indefinite pron. and adj.* any
quī quae quod (1) *relative pron.* who, which
quī quae quod (2) *interrogative pron. and adj.* what ...? **quās urbēs**: what cities?
quid? *adv.* why? (123, 389, 601)
quiēs quiētis *f.* rest, sleep
quiēscō -ere quiēvī quiētum calm down, rest
quīn *conj.* yes indeed (33), furthermore, in actual fact (115)
quīnquāgintā *indeclinable adj.* fifty
quis quid *indefinite pronoun* anyone, anything
quis? quid? *pron., sometimes adj.* (670) who? what?
quisquam quidquam *or* **quicquam** (not) anyone, anything
quisque quidque *pron.* each individual
quisquis quidquid *pron.* whoever, whatever
quīvī *see* **queō**
quō *adv.* to where

222

quod *pron.* and as for that (363)
quod sī but if
quondam *adv.* once, formerly, at any time (876)
quoque *conj.* also
quotannīs *adv.* every year

rabidus -a -um *adj.* wild, raving
rabiēs -ēī *f.* madness
radius -ī *m.* spoke, pointer (850)
rāmus -ī *m.* branch, spray
rapidus -a -um *adj.* hurrying, snatching
rapiō rapere rapuī raptum seize, plunder (8), hurry (*trans.*) (845)
ratis -is *f.* boat, ship
raucus -a -um *adj.* hoarse, noisy
rebellis -e *adj.* rebellious, renewing war
recēns recentis *adj.* fresh
recēnseō -ēre -cēnsuī review
recipiō -ere -cēpī -ceptum get back, recover
recolō -ere recoluī consider, go over
rēctus -a -um *adj.* straight
recubō -āre lie
reddō -ere reddidī redditum give back, restore, return; recall (768)
redeō redīre rediī reditum return, go back
redimō -ere redēmī redēmptum buy back, redeem
redūcō -ere -dūxī -ductum withdraw, bring back
reductus -a -um *adj.* secluded
referō referre rettulī relātum bring, bring back, take, put, put back
refīgō -ere -fīxī -fīxum unfasten, remove
refringō -ere -frēgī -frāctum break off
refugiō -ere -fūgī run away, go for refuge
refulgeō -ēre -fulsī shine out

refundō -ere -fūdī -fūsum pour back; *in pass.* overflow
rēgificus -a -um *adj.* royal
rēgīna -ae *f.* queen
regiō -ōnis *f.* region
rēgnō -āre -āvī -ātum reign, rule over
rēgnum -ī *n.* kingdom
regō -ere rēxī rēctum guide
relinquō -ere relīquī relictum leave
rēliquiae -ārum *f. pl.* remains
rēmigium -ī *n.* oars, rowing equipment
remūgiō -īre boom
rēmus -ī *m.* oar
renāscor -ī renātus *dep.* am born again
reor rērī ratus *dep.* think
reperiō -īre repperī repertum find
repōnō -ere -posuī -positum *or* **repostum** put away, place
reposcō -ere demand
requiēs *acc.* **requiem** *f.* rest
requīrō -ere -quīsīvī -quīsītum seek, search for
rēs rēī *f.* thing, matter; *in pl.* circumstances
rescindō -ere -scidī -scissum tear down
reses residis *adj.* sedentary
resīdō -ere resēdī settle down, subside
resolvō -ere -solvī -solūtum solve, unwind, relax (422)
respiciō -ere -spexī -spectum look round
respondeō -ēre respondī respōnsum answer, correspond
respōnsum -ī *n.* answer, response
restituō -ere -stituī -stitūtum restore
revellō -ere -vellī -vulsum wrench off
revertō -ere -vertī -versum turn back (*transitive*)
revīsō -ere -vīsī -vīsum revisit

revocō -āre -vocāvī -vocātum
recall, retrace (128)
revolvō -ere -volvī -volūtum turn
back
rēx rēgis *m.* king
rigō -āre -āvī -ātum wet, moisten
rīmor -ārī -ātus *dep.* explore,
ferret around
rīmōsus -a -um *adj.* having gaps,
leaky
rīpa -ae *f.* river-bank
rīte *adv.* duly, properly
rīvus -ī *m.* watercourse, stream
rōbur rōboris *n.* oak tree, wood of
the oak
rogus -ī *m.* funeral pyre
rōs rōris *m.* dew, water
roseus -a -um *adj.* rose-coloured
rōstrum -ī *n.* beak
rota -ae *f.* wheel
rumpō -ere rūpī ruptum break
ruō -ere ruī rush, hurry
rūpēs -is *f.* rock, cliff
rūrsus *adv.* back again

sacer sacra sacrum *adj.* sacred,
accursed (*see on* 573)
sacerdōs sacerdōtis *m. and f.*
priest, priestess
sacrō -āre -āvī -ātum dedicate
saeculum -ī *n.* age, century
saepe *adv., comp.* **saepius** often
saeta -ae *f.* bristle
saeviō -īre be angry
saevus -a -um *adj.* savage, brutal
sal salis *n.* sea
saltem *adv.* at least
saltus -ūs *m.* leap, jump
salūs salūtis *f.* safety, deliverance
sānctus -a -um *adj.* holy
sanguis sanguinis *m.* blood
satis *adv.* enough
satus *perf. part.* **serō** (2)
saxum –ī *n.* rock
scelerātus -a -um *adj.* wicked, evil
scelus sceleris *n.* crime
scīlicet *adv.* obviously

scindō -ere scidī scissum split,
cleave
scrūpeus -a -um *adj.* rocky and
jagged
sē iactāre boast
sē suī sibi sē (*acc. also* **sēsē**),
reflexive pron. himself, herself,
itself, themselves
sēclūdō -ere -clūsī -clūsum set
apart
secō -āre secuī sectum cut
sēcrētum -ī *n.* separate (place)
sēcrētus -a -um *adj.* set apart,
secluded
sēcum *pron.* with himself, herself,
themselves
secūris -is *f.* axe
sēcūrus -a -um *adj.* untroubled,
free from care
sed *conj.,* **sed enim** (28) but, but in
fact
sedeō -ēre sēdī sessum sit
sēdēs -is *f.* proper place, resting
place
semel *adv.* once
sēmen sēminis *n.* seed
sēminō -āre -āvī -ātum sow, beget
semper *adv.* always
senecta -ae *f.* old age
senectūs -ūtis *f.* old age
senior -is *adj.* aged
sēnsus -ūs *m.* sense, understanding
sentus -a -um *adj.* rough
sepeliō -īre sepelīvī sepultum
bury, overwhelm (424)
septem *adj.* seven
septemgeminus -a -um *adj.*
sevenfold
septēnī-ae -a *adj.* seven each
sepulcrum -ī *n.* tomb
sepultus *see* **sepeliō**
sequor sequī secūtus follow, seek
(457)
serēnus -a -um *adj.* clear
sermō sermōnis *m.* conversation,
speech
serō (1) **-ere seruī sertum** join up,
string together

serō (2) **-ere sēvī satum** sow, beget; **satus** + *abl.:* begotten by, descended from

sērus -a -um *adj.* late, too late

servō -āre -āvī -ātum save, tend, keep (in sight: 200)

sēsē *pron. alt. form of acc.* **sē**

seu *conj.* whether

sevērus -a -um *adj.* stern, grim

sī *conj.* if, if only (187)

sibi *see* **sē**

sīc *adv.* thus

siccus -a -um *adj.* dry

sīdō -ere sēdī sessum sit

sīdus sīderis *n.* star, constellation

signō -āre -āvī -ātum distinguish, mark

signum -ī *n.* indication, sign, standard (military) (825)

silēns silentis *adj.* silent

silentēs *m. pl.* the silent ones, the dead

sileō -ēre siluī am silent

silex silicis *m. or f.* flint

silva -ae *f.* wood, forest

sim, sīs, sit etc.: *pres. subj.* **sum**

similis -e *adj., superlative* **simillimus** similar

simplex simplicis *adj.* simple, pure

simul *adv.* at the same time, together

simulō -āre -āvī -ātum put on, pretend, mimic

sine *prep.* + *abl.* without

singulī -ae -a *adj.* each individual

sinister -tra -trum *adj.* left-hand, on the left

sinō -ere sīvī allow

sinus -ūs *m.* bend

sistō -ere set, place, stop (*trans.*), steady (858)

situs -ūs *m.* decay, neglect

socer -ī *m.* father-in-law

socius -ī *m.* ally, companion, friend

sōl -is *m.* sun

sōlācium -ī *n.* consolation, comfort

soleō -ēre solitus sum *semi-dep.* + *infin.* am accustomed to

solidus -a -um *adj.* solid, whole

solium -ī *n.* throne

sollemnis -e *adj.* annual, solemn

solum -ī *n.* ground

sōlus -a -um; *gen.* **sōlīus,** *dat.* **sōlī;** *adj.* alone, lonely

solvō -ere solvī solūtum pay, set free

somnium -ī *n.* dream

somnus -ī *m.* sleep

sonitus -ūs *m.* sound

sonō sonāre sonuī sound

sōns sontis *adj.* guilty

sopor -ōris *m.* deep sleep, coma

sopōrō -āre make (something) sleepy

sopōrus -a -um *adj.* drowsy

sordidus -a -um *adj.* grimy, dirty

soror -ōris *f.* sister

sors sortis *f.* lot, condition, (the response of an) oracle

spargō -ere sparsī sparsum scatter, sprinkle

spatium -ī *n.* space, distance

speciēs -ēī *f.* appearance

spectāculum -ī *n.* sight, spectacle, entertainment

spēlunca -ae *f.* cave

spērō -āre -āvī hope

spēs -speī *f.* hope

spīritus -ūs *m.* breath, spirit

spīrō -āre -āvī breathe

spolia -ōrum *n. pl.* spoils

spoliō -āre -āvī -ātum strip, despoil, plunder

sponte suā of his / her / its / their own accord

spūmō -āre -āvī foam

spūmōsus -a -um *adj.* foaming

squālor -ōris *m.* squalor, filth

stabulō -āre -āvī make one's stall

stabulum -ī *n.* lair, shelter

stāgnum -ī *n.* pool, water

statuō -ere statuī statūtum set up

stella -ae *f.* star

sterilis -e *adj.* barren

sternō -ere strāvī strātum lay low

stimulus -ī *m.* goad, spur

stirps stirpis *f.* stock
stō stāre stetī stand; am fixed (300)
strāgēs -is *f.* slaughter
strepitus -ūs *m.* loud noise, din
strepō -ere strepuī resound, buzz
strictus *perf. part.* **stringō**
strīdeō -ēre hiss, grate
strīdor -ōris *m.* a grating noise
stringo -ere strīnxī strictum draw (sword)
struō -ere strūxī strūctum build
studium -ī *n.* energy, concentration
sub *prep.* + *abl.* under, down in
sub *prep.* + *acc.* down to, just before (255), below (790)
subdūcō -ere -dūxī -ductum remove
subeō subīre subiī + *acc. or dat.* approach, go down to, come after (812)
subiciō -ere -iēcī -iectum put, thrust beneath, overthrow
subigō -ere -ēgī -āctum propel, compel
subitō *adv.* suddenly
subitus -a -um *adj.* sudden
sublīmis -e *adj.* raised up, upwards (720)
subtrahō -ere -trāxī -tractum withdraw (*trans.*)
subvectō -āre carry
succīnctus -a -um *adj.* dressed ready for action
succipiō -ere -cēpī -ceptum take up
sulcus -ī *m.* furrow
sum esse fuī am, exist
summoveō -ēre -mōvī -mōtum move away
summus -a -um *adj.* highest
sumō -ere sūmpsī sūmptum take up
suntō *3rd pl. imperative of* **sum** let them be
super *prep.* + *acc. and abl.* above, on top of, over; *also adv.* above

supera -ōrum *n. pl.* the realms above, heaven
superbus -a -um *adj.* proud, arrogant
superēmineō -ēre stand out above
superī -ōrum *or* **superum** *m .pl.* those above, the gods; those on earth (480, 568)
supernē *adv.* upwards, from above (658)
superō -āre -āvī -ātum surmount, surpass, climb
superus -a -um *adj.* upper
supplex supplicis *m., or adj.* suppliant, begging; as adj: humble
supplicium -ī *n.* punishment, torture
suppōnō -ere -posuī -positum lay x (*acc.*) beneath y (*dat.*)
suppostus *for* **suppositus**, *perf. part.* **suppōnō**
suprēmus -a -um *adj.* last
surgō -ere surrēxī surrēctum rise, arise, grow
suscipiō -ere -cēpī -ceptum undertake; respond (723)
suspectus -ūs *m.* view upward
suspendō -ere -pendī -pēnsum hang up, dedicate
suspēnsus -a -um hanging; in suspense (722)
suspiciō -ere suspexī suspectum look up at
sūtilis -e *adj.* stitched
suus -a -um *reflexive adj.* his own (her, its, their) ('belonging to the subject of the sentence')

tābēs -is *f.* wasting away, decay
taceō -ēre tacuī am silent
tacitus -a -um *adj.* silent
taeda -ae *f.* pine-wood, a torch made of pine-wood
tālis -e *adj.* such
tam *adv.* so (as in so great/small)
tamen *conj.* but, neverthless
tandem *adv.* at last

tantum ... quantum as much ... as
tantum *adv.* only; so much
tantus -a -um *adj.* so great, so much
tardō -āre slow down (transitive), clog
tardus -a -um *adj.* sluggish
taurus -ī *m.* bull
tē *see* **tū**
tēctum -ī *n.* roof, house
tēcum = **cum tē** with you
tegō -ere tēxī tēctum cover, hide (*trans*)
tellūs tellūris *f.* land
tēlum -ī *n.* weapon
temerō -āre -āvī -ātum violate
temnō -ere make light of, despise
templum -ī *n.* temple
tempora -um *n. pl.* the temples of the head
tempus temporis *n.* time
tenāx tenācis *adj.* gripping, holding
tendō -ere tetendī *trans:* stretch out; *intrans:* go, head (in a certain direction); **tendere iter** (240): to make one's way
tenebrae -ārum *f. pl.* darkness
tenebrōsus -a -um *adj.* gloomy
teneō -ēre tenuī hold, grip, keep
tenuis -e *adj.* thin, insubstantial
tenus *prep.* + *abl.* as far as
tepidus -a -um *adj.* warm
ter *adv.* three times
teres teretis *adj.* smooth
tergum -ī *n.* back, hide (= skin)
terra -ae *f.* land, earth
terrēnus -a -um *adj.* made of earth
terreō -ēre terruī territum terrify
terribilis -e *adj.* terrible
tertius -a -um *adj.* third
testor -ārī -ātus *dep.* bear witness
thalamus -ī *m.* chamber
tibi *see* **tū**
tigris -is *f.* tigress
timeō -ēre timuī fear
timidus -a -um *adj.* timid, fearful
timor -ōris *m.* fear

tollō -ere sustulī sublātum raise, lift
tondeō -ēre cut, crop
torqueō -ēre torsī tortum twist, roll along (551)
torreō -ēre torruī tostum scorch, burn
torus -ī *m.* couch
torvus -a -um *adj.* fierce, grim
tot *indeclinable adj.* so many
totidem *indeclinable adj.* the same number of
totiēns *adv.* so many times
tōtus -a -um *adj.* whole
trabs trabis *f.* log, beam
trahō -ere trāxī tractum drag; draw out, prolong (537)
trāiciō -ere trāiēcī trāiectum cross
trāmes -itis *m.* path
trānō -āre -āvī swim through, cross
trāns *prep.* + *acc.* across
trānsmittō -ere -mīsī -missum cross, go over
trānsportō -āre -āvī -ātum carry over
tremefaciō -ere -fēcī -factum make to tremble
tremō -ere tremuī tremble
tremor -ōris *m.* trembling
trepidō -āre -āvī be agitated, panic
trepidus -a -um *adj.* agitated, alarmed, trembling
trēs tria *adj.* three
tricorpor -is *adj.* three-bodied
trifaux trifaucis *adj.* three-mouthed
triplex triplicis *adj.* triple, threefold
trīstis -e *adj.* gloomy, miserable, grim
triumphō -āre -āvī -ātum triumph over
triumphus -ī *m.* triumph
truncus -a -um *adj.* trimmed, cut down
truncus -ī *m.* trunk (of tree)
tū tē tuī tibi tē *pron.* you singular

tuba -ae *f.* trumpet
tueor tuērī *dep.* gaze on, look at
tum *adv.* then, next
tumeō -ēre tumuī swell
tumidus -a -um *adj.* swelling
tumultus -ūs *m.* tumult,
    disturbance, emergency (857)
tumulus -ī *m.* mound, tomb
tunc *adv.* then
turba -ae *f.* crowd
turbidus -a -um *adj.* muddy,
    murky
turbō -āre -āvī -ātum muddle,
    confuse, trouble; *intrans. in*
    800: be in turmoil
turbō turbinis *m.* whirlwind
tūreus -a -um *adj.* made of
    frankincense
turpis -e *adj.* shameful, disgusting
turris -is *f.* tower
turrītus -a -um *adj.* equipped /
    decorated with towers
tūtus -a -um *adj.* safe, protected
tuus -a -um *adj.* your

ūber -is *n.* udder, mother's breast
ubi *conj.* when
ulcīscor -ī ultus *dep.* avenge
ūllus -a -um *adj.* (not) any
ulmus -ī *f.* elm-tree
ulterior -ius *adj.* further
ultimus -a -um *adj.* last, furthest
ultor -ōris *m.* avenger
ultrā *prep.* + *acc.* beyond; *adv.*
    further
ultrīx ultrīcis *fem. adj.* avenging,
    tormenting
ultrō *adv.* on one's own initiative,
    unprovoked
ultus *perf. part.* **ulcīscor**
ululō -āre -āvī howl
ulva -ae *f.* sedge, reeds
umbra -ae *f.* shadow, shade
umbrifer -a -um *adj.* shady
umbrō -āre -āvī -ātum shade
umerus -ī *m.* shoulder
umquam *adv.* ever
unā *adv.* together

uncus -a -um *adj.* curved
unda -ae *f.* water, wave
unde *adv.* whence, from which
undō -āre seethe
unguō -ere ūnxī ūnctum anoint
ūnus -a -um *adj.* one, a single,
    only, single-handed (846)
urbs urbis *f.* city
urgeō -ēre press, harass
urna -ae *f.* urn
usquam *adv.* anywhere
usque continuously
ut + *subjunctive introduces*
    Indirect Command (that ...),
    Indirect Question (how ...),
    Purpose Clause (in order that
    ...) *and Result Clause* (such that
    ...).
ut + *indicative* as, when
ut prīmum *conj.* as soon as
utcumque *conj.* however, in
    whatever way
uterque utraque utrumque *pron.*
    both
ūtor ūtī ūsus *dep.* + *abl.* use, enjoy

vacca -ae *f.* cow
vacuus -a -um *adj.* empty
vādō -ere vāsī go
vadum -ī *n.* (shallow) water
vāgīna -ae *f.* sheath
vāgītus -ūs *m.* wailing (of infants)
vagor -ārī -ātus *dep.* wander, roam
valeō -ēre be strong enough to, be
    able to
validus -a -um *adj.* strong
vallis -is *f.* valley
vānus -a -um *adj.* empty,
    meaningless
varius -a -um *adj.* varied,
    changing
vastus -a -um *adj.* desolate,
    endless, huge
vātēs -is *m. and f.* prophet(ess)
-ve *conj.* or (*translate before the
    word to which it is attached*)
vectō -āre carry, convey
vectus *perf. part.* **vehō**

Vocabulary

vehō -ere vēxī vectum carry
vel *conj.* or
vēlāmen vēlāminis *n.* covering
vellent *imperf. subj.* volō (2)
vellus velleris *n.* fleece
vēlum -ī *n.* sail
velut *adv.* just as
vēna -ae *f.* vein
vēndō -ere vēndidī vēnditum sell
venerābilis -e *adj.* holy
veniō -īre vēnī ventum come,
    arrive
ventōsus -a -um *adj.* windy
ventus -ī *m.* wind
verbera -um *n. pl.* blows
verbum -ī *n.* word
vereor -ērī veritus *dep.* fear
vērē *adv.* truly
vērō *adv.* indeed, in fact
verrō -ere sweep
versō -āre -āvī -ātum turn, toss
vertex verticis *m.* head
vertō -ere vertī versum turn (aim
    101)
vērus -a -um *adj.* true
vēscor vēscī *dep.* + *abl.* feast, feed
    on
vester vestra vestrum *adj.* your
    (*pl.*)
vestibulum -ī *n.* entrance, forecourt
vestīgium -ī *n.* footprint
vestīgō -āre -āvī -ātum track, trace
vestiō -īre -īvī -ītum clothe, dress
vestis -is *f.* dress, clothing
vetō -āre vetuī vetitum forbid
vetus veteris *adj.* old
via -ae *f.* way, road
vicis *gen.* (*no nominative*) exchange
vicissim *adv.* in turn
victor -ōris *m.* victor, (*as adj.*)
    victorious (168)
videō -ēre vīdī vīsum see
videor -ērī vīsus *dep.* seem
vigor -ōris *m.* vigour, strength
vīmen vīminis *n.* stem
vinclum / vinculum -ī *n.* chain,
    bonds

vincō -ere vīcī victum conquer,
    overcome
vīnum -ī *n.* wine
violentus -a -um *adj.* violent
vīpereus -a -um *adj.* snaky
vir virī *m., gen. pl.* virum (552)
    man
virectum -ī *n.* a green space
vireō -ēre grow green
vīrēs *see* vīs
virga -ae *f.* rod, shoot, branch
    (409)
virgō virginis *f.* virgin
virgultum -ī *n.* bush, shrub
viridis -e *adj.* green
virtūs virtūtis *f.* courage,
    excellence
vīs vim (*no gen. or dat.*) vī, *pl.*
    vīrēs vīrium vīribus strength
    (in both sing and pl)
vīscera -um *n. pl.* flesh, carcass;
    entrails (599)
viscum -ī *n.* mistletoe
vīsus -ūs *m.* sight
vīta -ae *f.* life, spirit (292)
vitta -ae *f.* woollen band
vīvus -a -um living
vix *adv.* scarcely, hardly, with
    difficulty
vocō -āre -āvī -ātum call, summon
volēns *pres. part.* volo (2)
    willingly, gladly
volitō -āre -āvī flutter, drift
volō (1) volāre -āvī fly; move
    rapidly (706); *pres. part.*
    volantēs 'birds' (239)
volō (2) velle voluī want, wish,
    mean (318)
volucer -cris -cre *adj.* winged,
    fleeting
voluntās -ātis *f.* will, wish
volūtō -āre -āvī turn over (in
    mind), consider
volvō -ere volvī volūtum roll; in
    pass. wallow, grovel
vorāgō vorāginis *f.* abyss, depth
vōs vōs vestrum vōbīs vōbīs *pron.*
    you (*pl.*)

229

vōtum -ī *n.* vow
vōx vōcis *f.* voice, word, sound
  (646)
vulgō *adv.* commonly, generally
vulnus vulneris *n.* wound

vult *from* **volō** (2): 'he / she
  wishes'
vultur -is *m.* vulture
vultus -ūs *m.* face, expression

Abbreviations

abl.: ablative
abl. abs.: ablative absolute
acc.: accusative
adj.: adjective
adv.: adverb
cf.: short for *confer*, i.e. 'compare'
dep.: deponent
f. and fem.: feminine
ff.: and following (lines)
fut.: future
Gk.: Greek
G&W: Gould and Whiteley
imper.: imperative
imperf.: imperfect
indic.: indicative
infin.: infinitive
interj.: interjection
intrans.: intransitive
intro.: introduction
lit.: literal, literally

m. and masc.: masculine
n. and neut.: neuter
obj.: object
OCD: *Oxford Classical Dictionary*
OLD: *Oxford Latin Dictionary*
part.: participle
pl.: plural
perf.: perfect
pluperf.: pluperfect
prep.: preposition
pres.: present
pron.: pronoun
rel.: relative
RG: *Res Gestae Divi Augusti*
sing.: singular
subj.: subjunctive, or subject
tr.: translate
trans.: transitive
voc.: vocative